GLOBAL CULTURE: CONSCIOUSNESS AND CONNECTIVITY

Global Connections

Series Editor: Robert Holton, Trinity College, Dublin

Global Connections builds on the multi-dimensional and continuously expanding interest in Globalization. The main objective of the series is to focus on 'connectedness' and provide readable case studies across a broad range of areas such as social and cultural life, economic, political and technological activities.

The series aims to move beyond abstract generalities and stereotypes: 'Global' is considered in the broadest sense of the word, embracing connections between different nations, regions and localities, including activities that are trans-national, and trans-local in scope; 'Connections' refers to movements of people, ideas, resources, and all forms of communication as well as the opportunities and constraints faced in making, engaging with, and sometimes resisting globalization.

The series is interdisciplinary in focus and publishes monographs and collections of essays by new and established scholars. It fills a niche in the market for books that make the study of globalization more concrete and accessible.

Also published in this series:

Violence and Gender in the Globalized World
The Intimate and the Extimate
Edited by Sanja Bahun and V.G. Julie Rajan
ISBN 978-1-4724-5374-7

Global Exposure in East Asia
A Comparative Study of Microglobalization
Ming-Chang Tsai
ISBN 978-1-4094-4146-5

Global Inequalities Beyond Occidentalism
Manuela Boatcă
ISBN 978-1-4094-4279-0

Global Knowledge Production in the Social Sciences
Made in Circulation
Edited by Wiebke Keim, Ercüment Çelik, Christian Ersche and Veronika Wöhrer
ISBN 978-1-4724-2617-8

Global Culture: Consciousness and Connectivity

Edited by

ROLAND ROBERTSON
*University of Aberdeen, UK, University of Pittsburgh, USA
and Tsinghua University, Beijing, China*

DIDEM BUHARI-GULMEZ
Istanbul Kemerburgaz University, Turkey

ASHGATE

© Roland Robertson, Didem Buhari-Gulmez and the contributors 2016

All rights reserved. No part of this publication may be reproduced, stored in a retrieval system or transmitted in any form or by any means, electronic, mechanical, photocopying, recording or otherwise without the prior permission of the publisher.

Roland Robertson and Didem Buhari-Gulmez have asserted their right under the Copyright, Designs and Patents Act, 1988, to be identified as the editors of this work.

Published by
Ashgate Publishing Limited
Wey Court East
Union Road
Farnham
Surrey, GU9 7PT
England

Ashgate Publishing Company
110 Cherry Street
Suite 3-1
Burlington, VT 05401-3818
USA

www.ashgate.com

British Library Cataloguing in Publication Data
A catalogue record for this book is available from the British Library

The Library of Congress has cataloged the printed edition as follows:
Robertson, Roland.
  Global culture : consciousness and connectivity / by Roland Robertson and Didem Buhari-Gulmez.
      pages cm. – (Global connections)
  Includes bibliographical references and index.
  ISBN 978-1-4724-2349-8 (hardback) – ISBN 978-1-4724-2350-4 (ebook) – ISBN 978-1-4724-2351-1 (epub) 1. Culture and globalization. 2. Civilization, Modern – 21st century. I. Buhari-Gulmez, Didem. II. Title.
  HM621.R6275 2016
  303.48'2–dc23

2015022818

ISBN: 9781472423498 (hbk)
ISBN: 9781472423504 (ebk – PDF)
ISBN: 9781472423511 (ebk – ePUB)

Printed in the United Kingdom by Henry Ling Limited,
at the Dorset Press, Dorchester, DT1 1HD

Contents

List of Figures and Tables		*vii*
Notes on Contributors		*ix*
Acknowledgements		*xiii*

Introduction   1
Roland Robertson

1   Global Culture and Consciousness   5
    Roland Robertson

2   Globalization and Global Consciousness: Levels of Connectivity   21
    Paul James and Manfred B. Steger

3   Connectivity and Consciousness: How Globalities are Constituted through Communication Flows   41
    Barrie Axford

4   Globalization's Cultural Consequences Revisited   55
    Robert J. Holton

5   Dynamics of World Culture: Global Rationalism and Problematizing Norms, Again   75
    George M. Thomas

6   Rationalizing Global Consciousness: Scientized Education as the Foundation of Organization, Citizenship, and Personhood   93
    Gili S. Drori

7   Jesuits, Connectivity, and the Uneven Development of Global Consciousness since the Sixteenth Century   109
    José Casanova

8   Glocalization and Global Sport   127
    Richard Giulianotti

9   Global Culture in Motion   143
    Peggy Levitt

10	China in the Process of Globalization: A Primarily Cultural Perspective *Wang Ning*	161
11	'America' in Global Culture *Frank J. Lechner*	179
12	Taking Japan Seriously Again: The Cultural Economy of Glocalization and Self-Orientalization *Koji Kobayashi*	193

Conclusion 211
Roland Robertson and Didem Buhari-Gulmez

Index *215*

List of Figures and Tables

Figures

6.1	Science and education as foundations for social development: A realist approach	94
6.2	The role of scientized education in constituting contemporary world society: An institutionalist approach	103
12.1	Nike and Asics' models of strategic creative alliances in 2010	199

Tables

2.1	Levels of the social in relation to levels of theoretical analysis	27

Notes on Contributors

Barrie Axford is Professor of Politics at Oxford Brookes University and Director of the Centre for Global Politics, Economy and Society. He is a member of the Executive Board of the Global Studies Association and serves on the international editorial boards of the journals: *Globalizations, Telematics and Informatics, The International Journal of Electronic Governance and Reinventions*, and the *Journal of Undergraduate Research*. His books include *The Global System: Politics, Economics and Culture* (Palgrave Macmillan 1996), *New Media and Politics* (Sage 2001), *Cultures and/of Globalization* (Cambridge Scholars Publishing 2011) and *Theories of Globalization* (Polity Press 2013). He is working on a book dealing with communication and world society.

Didem Buhari-Gulmez is a Lecturer in International Relations at Istanbul Kemerburgaz University. She was previously a postdoctoral visiting fellow at London School of Economics and Political Science, European Institute (Research on South Eastern Europe) sponsored by TUBITAK. She taught at Oxford Brookes University and Royal Holloway, University of London. She has published on World Society theory, Europeanization studies, and Turkish politics at various journals, including International Political Sociology, New Global Studies, Southeast European and Black Sea Studies, European Union Studies Association Review, and Journal of Contemporary European Studies.

José Casanova is Professor of Sociology and Senior Fellow at the Berkley Center for Religion, Peace, and World Affairs at Georgetown University, where he heads the Program on Religion, Globalization, and the Secular. Previously he served as Professor of Sociology at the New School for Social Research in New York from 1987 to 2007. He has published works on a broad range of subjects, including religion and globalization, migration and religious pluralism, transnational religions, and sociological theory. His best-known work, *Public Religions in the Modern World* (University of Chicago Press 1994) has become a modern classic and has been translated into seven languages, including Japanese, Arabic, and Turkish, and is forthcoming in Chinese, Indonesian, and Farsi.

Gili S. Drori is Associate Professor of Sociology and Anthropology at The Hebrew University of Jerusalem, Israel and previously served as lecturer at Stanford University's International Relations programme. Her publications speak to her research interests in globalization and glocalization; organizational change and rationalization; world society theory; science, innovation and higher education; technology divides; and, culture and policy regimes. Among them are: *Science in the Modern World Polity: Institutionalization and Globalization* (with John W. Meyer, Francisco O. Ramirez, and Evan Schofer; Stanford University Press 2003), *Globalization and Organization: World Society and Organizational Change* (edited with John W. Meyer and Hokyu Hwang;, Oxford University Press 2006), and *Global Themes and Local Variations in Organization and Management: Perspectives on Glocalization* (edited with Markus A. Höllerer and Peter Walgenbach; Routledge 2014).

Richard Giulianotti is Professor of Sociology in the School of Sport, Exercise and Health Sciences at Loughborough University, and also Professor II at Telemark University College, Norway. His main research interests are in the fields of sport, globalization, development and peace, sport mega-events, crime and deviance, cultural identities, and qualitative methods. He is author of the books *Football: A Sociology of the Global Game* (Polity 1999); *Sport: A Critical Sociology* (Polity 2005, revised edition 2015); *Ethics, Money and Sport* (with Adrian Walsh; Routledge 2007); and, *Globalization and Football* (with Roland Robertson; Sage 2009).

Robert J. Holton is Emeritus Professor of Sociology and Fellow, Trinity College, Dublin, and Adjunct Professor of Sociology in the Hawke Research Institute, University of South Australia. He has written extensively on many aspects of globalization, most recently *Globalization and the Nation-State* (Palgrave Macmillan 2011), *Global Finance* (Routledge 2012), and *Global Inequalities* (Palgrave Macmillan 2014). He has recently joined Bryan Turner as co-editor of the second edition of the *Routledge International Handbook of Globalization Studies*. He is currently working on a study of theories of the end of capitalism.

Paul James is Director of the Institute for Culture and Society, and Professor of Globalization and Cultural Diversity at the University of Western Sydney. He is Scientific Advisor to the Senate Department for Urban Development, Berlin, a Fellow of the Royal Society of the Arts, London, and Honorary Professor at King's College London. He is author or editor of 31 books, including most importantly *Globalism, Nationalism, Tribalism* (Sage Publications 2006). He is editor of a 16-volume landmark series mapping the field of globalization (Sage Publications). His latest book is *Urban Sustainability in Theory and Practice: Circles of Sustainability* (Routledge 2015).

Koji Kobayashi is a Lecturer in the Department of Tourism, Sport and Society at Lincoln University, New Zealand. His research interests include globalization, national identity, media, policy and management as they relate to sport and recreation. His work has appeared in journals such as *Sociology of Sport Journal*, *International Review for the Sociology of Sport*, and *Sport in Society*.

Frank J. Lechner is Professor of Sociology at Emory University (Atlanta). In addition to papers on religion, sports, and theory, his books include *World Culture: Origins and Consequences* (with John Boli; Blackwell 2004), *The Netherlands: Globalization and National Identity* (Routledge 2008), and *Globalization: The Making of World Society* (Wiley-Blackwell 2009). With John Boli he also edited *The Globalization Reader* (Wiley-Blackwell, 5th edition, 2015). His current work deals with aspects of American exceptionalism.

Peggy Levitt is Chair and Professor of Sociology at Wellesley College and the co-Director of the Transnational Studies Initiative at Harvard University. Her most recent book is *Artifacts and Allegiances: How Museums Put the Nation and the World on Display* (University of California Press 2015). In 2014, she received an Honorary Doctoral Degree from Maastricht University. Her previous books include *Religion on the Edge* (Oxford University Press 2012), *God Needs No Passport: Immigrants and the Changing American Religious Landscape* (New Press 2007), *The Transnational Studies Reader* (Routledge 2007), *The Changing Face of Home: The Transnational Lives of the Second Generation* (Russell Sage 2002), and *The Transnational Villagers* (UC Press 2001). A film based on her work, *Art Across Borders*, came out in 2009.

Roland Robertson is Distinguished Professor of Sociology Emeritus, University of Pittsburgh; Professor Emeritus of Sociology and Global Society, University of Aberdeen and Distinguished Guest Professor of Cultural Studies, Tsinghua University, Beijing. His authored or co-authored books include *The Sociological Interpretation of Religion* (Schocken Books 1970), *Meaning and Change* (Oxford/ New York University Press 1970), *International Systems and the Modernization of Societies* (with J.P. Nettle; Basic Books 1968), *Globalization and Football* (with Richard Giulianotti; Sage 2009), and *Globalization: Social Theory and Global Culture* (Sage 1992). His edited or co-edited books include *Global Modernities* (with Mike Featherstone and Scott Lash; Sage 1995), *Talcott Parson: Theorist of Modernity* (with Bryan S. Turner; Sage 1991), *European Cosmopolitanism in Question* (with Anne Sophie Krossa; Palgrave Macmillan 2012), *Church-State Relations* (with Thomas Robbins; Transaction Books 1987), *Globalization and Sport* (with Richard Giulianotti; Blackwell 2007), *Encyclopedia of Globalization* (with Jan Aart Scholte; Routledge 2007), *Identity and Authority* (with Burkart Holzner; Blackwell 1980), and *European Glocalization in Global Context* (Palgrave Macmillan 2014). His work has been translated into more than twenty languages and he has won numerous prizes and awards for his work. He has held visiting positions in a number of countries. His present work is centered upon globality and cosmology.

Manfred B. Steger is Professor of Political Science at the University of Hawai'i-Manoa and Professor of Global Studies at RMIT University in Melbourne, Australia. He has served as an academic consultant on globalization for the US

State Department and is the author or editor of over twenty books on globalization, global history, and the history of political ideas, including: *The Rise of the Global Imaginary: Political Ideologies from the French Revolution to the Global War on Terror* (Oxford University Press, 2008), and *Justice Globalism: Ideology, Crises, Policy* (Sage, 2013).

George M. Thomas is Professor of Politics and Global Studies at Arizona State University. He has published on globalization, world culture, non-state actors, and religion in world society, including; *Constructing World Culture: International Nongovernmental Organizations Since 1875* (co-editor with John Boli, Stanford University Press 1999); (with J.W. Meyer, J. Boli, and F.O. Ramirez) 'World society and the nation-state,' *American Journal of Sociology* 103 (July): 144–81, 1997; *Revivalism and Cultural Change* (University of Chicago Press 1989). His current projects include a study of contentions over religious rights in world society focusing on religion cases in international courts and a study of global accounting of catastrophes focusing on discourse of international organizations.

Wang Ning is Changjiang Distinguished Professor of English and Comparative Literature and Director of the Center for Comparative Literature and Cultural Studies at Tsinghua University and Zhiyuan Chair Professor of Humanities at Shanghai Jiao Tong University in China. Apart from his numerous books and articles in Chinese, he has published two English books: *Globalization and Cultural Translation* (Marshall Cavendish Academic 2004), and *Translated Modernities: Literary and Cultural Perspectives on Globalization and China* (Legas 2010). He is one of the associate editors of the *Routledge Encyclopedia of Globalization* (2006) and the editor in chief of its Chinese translation (2011). He has also published extensively in English and edited ten special issues for many international prestigious journals such as *European Review*, *Modern Language Quarterly*, *Comparative Literature Studies*, *Semiotica*, *Neohelicon*, *Perspectives: Studies in Translatology*, *Amerasia Journal*, *ARIEL*, *Narrative*, and *Telos*.

Acknowledgements

The editors wish to thank the editor of the series in which this book appears, Robert Holton, and to acknowledge the great assistance of Judith Velody and Seckin Baris Gulmez.

This book would never have come to life without the great help of Neil Jordan of Ashgate. Also, we extend our special thanks to TUBITAK for sponsoring Didem's research between 2014 and 2015.

Introduction

Roland Robertson

The issue of global culture has been greatly neglected. In fact, I would speculate that about 80 percent or even more of writings or pronouncements on globalization have defined it as centered upon the phenomenon of connectivity (or interconnectedness). Quite apart from the limitations of the latter approach, it is surely the case that the issue of culture at the global level is more than worth pursuing. This pursuit has become particularly evident and necessary in light of the ever-increasing rhetoric concerning such phenomena as space travel and exploration, talk of the possibility of life on other planets, and, generally, discourse concerning the cosmos as a whole. In other words, we increasingly tend to think of the beginning and end of life. The latter, of course, is not merely a matter of science or indeed of science fiction. It has been a leitmotif of religion in its eschatological vein for thousands of years. In any case it is becoming increasingly evident that the entire issue of science fiction is merging with the scientific study 'proper' of the planet which we inhabit. In fact, the spheres of cosmology, science fiction and, not least, religion increasingly overlap.

There are barriers other than that of the overemphasis upon connectivity in the discourse of global culture. Perhaps the most important of these has been and still is war across the globe, many wars of increasing intensity. Some would even argue that we are presently experiencing the early stages of a third and new kind of world war. Acknowledgment of the latter does not, however, by any means obliterate the necessity or possibility of speaking of global culture; not least because we increasingly recognize that wars are really about claims to be the agents, the definers of a particular circumstance—in this case the world as a whole, or even of the entire cosmos. Put another way, it has become increasingly obvious that it is ideational and symbolic factors that constitute, in the last instance, the most crucial factors in human life. Failure to fully confront this theorem runs strongly against the grain of traditional 'left-wing' thinking. Attending to this issue, is a highly salient theme of the majority of chapters that follow.

Another reason for the neglect of the theme of global culture is that, in spite of recent anthropological contributions to this topic, the idea persists that we should always think of culture in the sense of it being a binding agent—something which binds or holds a sociocultural unit together. This approach has, however, been increasingly thrown into doubt by a number of anthropological and sociological studies. Again, some of these will be addressed in later chapters.

Yet another inhibiter of the study of global culture has been the strong, but fast dying, talk of globalization as a mainly political-economic phenomenon. Such use of the concept of globalization still persists; particularly in the pages of newspapers and journals devoted to the economic condition of regions and, indeed, of the whole world. More specifically, the conception of globalization as being centered upon marketization, free trade, open markets and such matters is still the convention in prominent quarters of political and economic life. However, ever since the protests against the World Trade Organization (WTO) at the end of 1999, the claim that the very protests against what was seen at the time to constitute globalization gave rise to the overriding idea that there was such a phenomenon as what has come to be known as globalization from below. The latter was increasingly seen to involve a much more comprehensive process involving cultural and social—as well as political and economic—dimensions. Indeed, the demonstrations against the WTO in Seattle, USA in late 1999 was undoubtedly a watershed with respect to the manner in which we tend to speak of globalization; in spite of the persistent, narrow use of the term by economists, politicians and, unfortunately, a number of social scientists.

In the chapters in this volume the pivotal aspects of global culture and related themes are given sustained attention. It opens with contributions by Roland Robertson, Paul James and Manfred Steger, Barrie Axford and Robert Holton; each dealing with particular aspects of the relationship between connectivity and culture or consciousness. In fact, the relationship between the two latter concepts are very explicitly discussed in the chapters by Robertson, on the one hand, and James and Steger, on the other.

The chapters that immediately follow involve a particular approach to globalization by George Thomas and Gili Drori, this being centered upon scientization and the entire issue of rationalization at the global level. Both Thomas and Drori take their cues from neo-institutional and world-polity theory.

In the succeeding two chapters, the themes of global religion and global sport are discussed by Jose Casanova and Richard Giulianotti respectively. In addition to Robertson's early discussion of glocalization, the pivotal theme of Giulianotti's chapter is centered upon glocalization with regard to sport. Casanova's chapter deals with the historical matter of what he describes as connectivity and the uneven development of global consciousness with respect to the rise and expansion eastwards of the Jesuits, a particularly crucial historical circumstance.

Peggy Levitt, in her chapter, crosses and links together a number of aspects of global culture. Specifically, she addresses the topic of the relationship between migrating people and migrating culture, with particular attention to the place of cities in this relationship. Both migration and global urbanization have been crucial in the general process of globalization.

The final three chapters deal with particular regions or countries of the world as a whole. Wang Ning deals with the increasingly significant position of China in the world, in the process attending to the very significant matters of literary translation and glocalization. In his chapter on 'America' Frank Lechner insightfully considers the 'mythical' origins of the position of America in the world. He shows that the heretofore hegemonic position of America was long ago foretold by intellectuals writing about the USA before it became a dominant power. The book concludes with a chapter by Koji Kobayashi on the great rival of China, namely Japan, which is presently and very problematically reasserting itself in the face of the rise of China, and its relegation from the position of 'number one' in the world.

A summation is provided by the co-editors, Roland Robertson and Didem Buhari-Gulmez.

Chapter 1
Global Culture and Consciousness

Roland Robertson

In my previous attempts to come to terms with the idea of global culture I tended to restrict myself to what I now consider to be the more obvious aspects of the latter. A few examples are to be found in Nettl and Robertson (1968) and Robertson (1992, 2007c). However, I do not intend here to eschew my previous contributions. Rather, I build upon and to a large extent revise these. In other words, the present effort is more ambitious than previous ones and, more specifically, takes into account many recent developments, even though I think the significance of some of these have been exaggerated (Robertson, 2007a; Groebner, 2007). However, before proceeding, it should be said that even though culture as an academic theme has remarkably and rapidly risen in recent years, notably in the UK, the US and parts of Europe, *relatively* little has been published concerning culture across the world; although Germany was almost certainly the home of much of the extremely significant intellectual work on culture from the late eighteenth century onwards. The so-called strong program in cultural sociology (e.g. Alexander, Smith and Lo, 2010) has more or less completely neglected this theme. However, there are at least two outstanding exceptions to these generalizations concerning global (or world) culture—namely *World Culture* by Lechner and Boli (2005) and Boli and Thomas (1999). It should be noted that Lechner and Thomas are contributors to the present volume.

In the chapters of this volume that follow various authors explore, in one way or another, the relationship between global connectivity and global consciousness—a relationship that is by no means simple. In any case, I would like to add to my claim concerning the great emphasis on connectivity in studies of globalization, that a not inconsiderable number of authors compound their mistake by speaking of globalization as involving increasing global integration. A good example of this is the argument of Goldin and Mariathasan that globalization means 'the process of increasing integration and cross-border flows' (Goldin and Mariathasan, 2014, p. xiii). Moreover, they contend that this process has been 'the most powerful driver of human progress in the history of humanity' (Goldin and Mariathasan, 2014, p. viii). As will be seen, I have strong reservations about such contentions, particularly since they do not even mention, in their volume on the risks created by globalization, the crucial theme of *glocalization* (e.g. Robertson, 2014a, 2014b). Considering the latter has much to add to the 'normal' commentary on, or discourses about, globalization, this is, in fact, a glaring lacuna (Robertson 2015).

Concerning the relationship between connectivity and consciousness, an observation by Durkheim is of great assistance. Durkheim (1974, p. 24) argued that 'society has for its substratum the mass of associated individuals ... .The representations which form a network of social life arise from the relations between the individuals thus combined or the secondary groups that are between the individuals and the total society.' Durkheim (1974, pp. 24–5) goes on to say that 'there is nothing surprising in the fact that collective representations, produced by the action and reaction between individual minds that form the society, do not directly derive from the latter and consequently surpass them.' The point conveyed by this quotation is that neither consciousness nor culture derives directly from connectivity. Rather, consciousness and culture both have significant degrees of autonomy in relation to the latter. Moreover, culture facilitates, or enables, consciousness. Specifically, people cannot be conscious separately from their being cultural participants. In other words, culture makes consciousness possible (Appadurai, 2013, pp. 285–300).

It should here be emphasized, a little ironically, that it is probably in the realm of contemporary historical studies that the global turn has been most conspicuous (Robertson, 1996; 1998). This may well be due, at least in large part, to the absence of obsession with the primarily economic use of 'globalization,' as well as the fact that historians came to the study of the global somewhat later than social scientists. Moyn and Sartori (2013, p. 1) have articulated this issue cogently:

> Among the last decade's most notable developments in the historians' guild has been a turn toward 'global history.' The roots of global history are older, in different tendencies in international history to strain beyond its usual diplomatic agents or in world history to make into approved topics the transnational flows of populations, diseases, and goods. But the citizens of the post-Cold War world ... conceived of themselves as living in an age of 'globalization' and pushed this trend to impressive heights.

As far as historical studies are concerned, where it could be argued that the global turn has been most evident, particularly since the late 1990s and the early 2000s, and in spite of some historians alarm at the very idea of globalization, it is highly relevant to mention a little later in this chapter, somewhat selectively, a few examples of recent concern with globality among professional historians. In any case, the entire issue of the pedagogy of global studies has increased rapidly in recent years and has, in the process, manifested the phenomenon of glocality (Baker, 2014 and Baker and Le Tendre, 2005). Conversely, schooling has become a major product of global culture.

Quite apart from books on the subject of global history in the large, a considerable number of more specialist books by historians have shown that the world has been much more global than recent history has suggested *both* in the sense of extensive connectivity and (increasingly) *reflexive* global consciousness. Undoubtedly this is largely due to the fact that we are now very conscious of the global circumstance, via such phenomena as climate change; space exploration, travel and potential tourism; electronic communication of various kinds and related phenomena.

Closely related to these are various developments in science fiction and what might be called the apocalyptic, or millennial, imagination. Science fiction has, of course, become increasingly significant in culture(s) across the world. And even though many may consider this to be a form of Americanization, particularly via Hollywood film, the fact is that it has by no means been merely an American phenomenon (Conrad, 2015). This is excellently demonstrated by Jameson (2005) in his extensive writings about utopian science and other forms of science fiction. In his discourse on what he calls 'fear and loathing in globalization' Jameson cogently demonstrates the global significance of science fiction.

On the other hand, writing in particular reference to Russia, Banerjee (2012) amply demonstrates the great and continuing convergence of science, science fiction, psychology, philosophy, and other disciplines; and the relevance of this convergence to a vast range of conventional and near-global issues, issues including such matters as higher consciousness, neurological processes, space exploration and conceptions of immortality. A good example of Russia's global significance with respect to science fiction is the way in which the virtual completion of the Trans-Siberian Railroad came to feature so prominently in published scientific, illustrated magazines, as well as in science fiction generally (Banerjee, 2012, p. 33). To quote Banerjee, 'rushing past the windows of the train Siberia was the only place in the world to offer an unlimited view of the deep past preceding human history and Promethean promises of a technological future.' In fact, the Paris World Exposition of 1900 featured 'The World Railway.' Banerjee goes on to state that the train transports Russia itself 'into a mobile, ever-expanding East that eventually merges back with the West and encompasses the entire globe.'

This is probably the most appropriate place to emphasize the importance of the World Expositions that have taken place since they first began with the Great Exhibition held in London's Hyde Park in 1851. This is widely considered as the first modern world's fair. Rydell (1984) has provided an excellent audit of the world fairs held in the USA from the Centennial Exhibition held in Philadelphia in 1876 to the Expositions in San Francisco and San Diego in 1915 and 1916. Both of the latter were designed to commemorate the opening of the Panama Canal, that opening obviously being of world-historical significance. However, it should be emphasized that, during the twentieth century and the early part of the present one, such small fairs have become increasingly global and spread around the world. Needless to say, most world fairs and expositions have been particularly celebrative of the national culture of the countries concerned. On the other hand, they have also almost always paid much attention to the cultures of other countries. The latter is well exampled by the Milan Exposition of 2015.

Returning directly to historians turn to the global it might well be argued that Jardine and Brotton were among the very first to globalize what was previously considered to be a purely Western phenomenon: *Global Interests: Renaissance Art between East and West* (2000). Before that book was published the Renaissance had almost always been considered a European phenomenon. Wills considers the significance of 1688 in his *1688: A Global History* (2001). Armitage explores the global significance of the American declaration of independence in his book *The Declaration of Independence: A Global History* (2007). Another example is that of Desan, Hunt, and Nelson (2013) in their book *The French Revolution in Global Perspective*. Yet another illustration of the global approach to a particular historical problem is the recent book by Doyle (2015), entitled *The Cause of All Nations: An International History of the American Civil War* that explores in considerable detail the manner in which the civil war in America involved parties and interested participants from numerous parts of the world; at least—more accurately—in the Western parts thereof. Much more global, however, is the book by Beckert (2015), *Empire of Cotton*.

A particularly outstanding case is provided by Osterhammel's *The Transformation of the World: a Global History of the Nineteenth Century* (2014). A key feature of the latter is the author's commitment to overcoming what he indicates as being narrow Eurocentric conceptions of world history. Osterhammel argues that only two or three decades ago a history of the modern world could still blithely proceed on the assumption of 'Europe's special path.' To quote Osterhammel (2014, p. xxi) 'historians are trying to break with European (or "Western") smugness and to remove the sting of "special path" notions by means of generalization and relativization.' He goes on to argue that the nineteenth century must be reconsidered accordingly. His book is particularly significant in the present context because it deals simultaneously with the world as a whole *and* the post-enlightenment period in Europe. Even though he declares his intention to be the relativization of Europe he, nonetheless, is not of a subaltern or a post-colonial persuasion.

Perhaps the most significant and continuous contribution to the kind of history that I have been discussing is to be seen in the oeuvre of Linda Colley, who has consistently cast her numerous works in a global frame, ranging from her *Britons: Forging the Nation, 1707–1837* (1992) to her *The Ordeal of Elizabeth Marsh: A Woman in World History* (2007) and *Captives: Britain, Empire and the World, 1600–1850* (2010). Moreover she has explored the significance of the global-*cosmopolitan* turn among American historians in her short piece, 'Wide-Angled' (2013). Another case, of a rather different nature, is provided by Sachsenmaier (2011) in his book that is mainly devoted to the global histories of the USA, Germany, and China, *Global Perspectives on Global History: Theories and Approaches in a Connected World*. This is an important contribution, even though it emphasizes connectivity and relegates consciousness.

A somewhat different approach that incorporates global perspectives (but again, stressing connectivity) is provided by the volume edited by Edwards and Gaonkar (2012), *Globalizing American Studies*. In fact, even though the concept has no explicit presence in this book, the issue of glocalization is absolutely, if only implicitly, central; since the volume as a whole clearly illustrates the ways in which the study of the USA varies from place to place and, indeed, over time.

One of the major rationales for invoking these examples is that they raise the question as to why we have come to have national histories at all. Why should we think of the world as being constituted by nations, amalgamations of nations, or even regions within nations? Why, in other words, do we not *start* globally (or even cosmically)? This question may appear to be somewhat out of line with my own analytic depiction of what I have called *the global field* insofar as, in the latter, the nation, or the nation-state, is included as *part of* the global field itself (Robertson, 1992). However, my response to any such query would be that what we have come to call, over the last two decades or more, globalization has, in my view, been in part constituted by developments directly concerning changes in the form of the nation-state and *not* the obliteration or disappearance of the latter.

To a considerable extent the global point of entry has been adopted by the work of a number of anthropologists or combinations of historians and anthropologists (e.g. Tsing, 1993; Gluck and Tsing, 2009). In the latter the authors have assembled a collection of essays revolving around the issue of the relationship between words and worlds, thereby emphasizing the importance of the theme of glocalization, even though Gluck and Tsing have paid very little attention to the latter concept per se.

During the past 25 years or so there have been a number of 'turns' in the social and natural sciences, although there has been something of a convergence between these two. As far as the social sciences are concerned we have witnessed and been participants in such turns as the reflexive turn, the cultural turn, and the global turn. Clearly in the context of the present book it is the last named that is the more important, although I would argue that it subsumes the first two rather than is to be regarded separately. The global turn is rapidly being overtaken by what some have called the cosmic turn (Dickens and Ormrod, 2007; cf. Einstein, 2009). Indeed, this particular 'overtaking' constitutes a significant theme of the present chapter.

Of particular relevance to what I have called the cosmic turn is the way in which the perspectives of anthropology, 'classical modern' literature (Gay, 2007) theology, astrophysics and cosmology are being combined into one discursive bundle. Major examples of this include Dickens and Ormrod, 2007; Frank, 2011; Nagel, 2012; Ebury, 2014; Evans, 2014; Unger and Smolin, 2015; Nancy and Barrau, 2015. Briefly stated, this actual and growing potential synthesis is rendering the entire idea of planet earth—indeed of the cosmos, or universe(s)—highly problematic, *largely* in spite of recent concern with climate change and pivotal issues of sustainability, not to speak of the rise of, and reaction to, what has frequently been called the new atheism. As will be seen the latter is, in a certain way, part of the idea that God is back (e.g. Micklethwait and Wooldridge, 2009; Robertson, 2007b, 2009; Miller, Sergeant and Flory, 2013; Goossaert and Palmer, 2012, pp. 359–404; Juergensmeyer, 2006).

Clearly, the dramatic rise of so-called ISIS and its various branches, affiliates, allies, or even rivals, in Africa, the Middle East and other regions is highly relevant to this topic and is particularly significant in any conception of global culture. It is seen in various quarters as a threat to the entire world (Pankhurst, 2013). On the other hand, in spite of the claims of ISIS, Al-Qaeda, and other forms of jihadism, Islam is by no means and, in any meaningful sense, homogenous or unified. This is clearly demonstrated in Lawrence's argument concerning the *considerable variety* of conceptions of Allah (Lawrence, 2015). In any case, the Islamic threat—as it is seen in many parts of the world—clearly emerged, at least in large part, from the so-called Arab Spring (Matthiessen, 2013). Also there is clearly a close connection between 'the new electronic technology' and ISIS. In this regard it should be emphasized that ISIS and numerous branches of jihadism have benefitted greatly from—indeed have contributed to—the increasingly new forms of modern 'warfare.'

The entire topic of culture as rendered in global terms has leapt into particular and problematic prominence in recent years because of the enormous amount of concern with such issues as Internet culture (Porter, 1997), cyber-power (Jordan, 1999; Nayar, 2010) and the general issue of what is frequently called 'intelligence.' At the center of developments concerning the (problematic) connection between ISIS and the new electronic technology is the fashionable but inadequate theme of soft power (Nye, 2004). I consider the concept of soft power to be most deficient and exaggerated with respect to its importance. Simply stated, the idea of soft power has been employed as if such a phenomenon were relatively new, when in fact it is as 'old as the hills.' More precisely, and with much more conceptual clarity, Talcott Parsons long ago conceptualized the different major ways in which people 'get things done.' Most importantly, he made careful distinctions between money, power, influence, and the activation of moral commitments and, moreover, did this in reference to the global situation (Robertson, 1968).

The increasing attention on the part of nation states, and would-be nation states, to the value and significance of what in the past was simply called propaganda is one of the most intriguing features of inter-societal, international relations and world affairs generally and is a very striking feature of our times. To put this another way, it is now thought emphatically that indoctrination and, not least, counter-indoctrination are particularly crucial features of conflicts and tension in most parts of the world. This is particularly evident now with respect to matters of what were formally called *Realpolitik*, without any caveat; whereas now the very idea of *Realpolitik* has to be reformulated in light of the enormous and rapid growth of social media phenomena such as Twitter, Facebook and Instagram. Closely related is the fact that normal-traditional categories such as religion, culture, race, tradition and so on have become increasingly blurred (Roy, 2010); so paralleling the more obvious 'blurring' and proliferation of gender distinctions. These categories, particularly the last named, are presently pivotal in what appears to be a generalized, worldwide set of culture wars *within* societies. Specifically, many if not most countries are riven by disputes, indeed violent ones, between rival claims as to ideologies and styles of life preferences. Among the latter are such phenomena as abortion, marriage choice, sexuality, FGM, male circumcision, organ transplants and numerous other medical procedures.

The entire issue of the contemporary means of communication raises crucial issues about both global culture and consciousness, not to speak of connectivity. In fact, these 'new technologies' are possibly more important—or at least as important—as the entire issue of the relationship between the homogenization and heterogenization of global culture. In fact, these two features of the global circumstance now need to be coordinated.

The Internet and related forms of communication compel us to reconsider the idea of global culture. This has much to do with the 'hidden' nature of communication via the new social media and its relation to the significance in the modern world of erotic and sexual culture. The increasing prominence of erotic and sexual issues raises very important problems for the contemporary appraisal and analysis of the very idea of global culture and, indeed, global consciousness; not least because the conventional distinctions between the private and the public are clearly disappearing (Brown, 2010; Craig and Ludloff, 2011; Pasquale, 2015).

This is in certain respects a very elusive topic—elusive in the sense that much of this kind of communication occurs 'below the radar' (Bartlett, 2015). (It also 'interferes' with the conventional distinction between cultural and social phenomena). This is also quite frequently referred to as the dark side of the Internet; much of which is criminal, and many would say, immoral. However it would be entirely remiss to neglect this relatively unmentioned theme of global culture and the degree to which participants in the dark side of the Internet are *globally aware*. Stating that the 'dark side' is 'below the radar' is somewhat misleading. This is because there is a great deal of talk in mainline journals, magazines and other public media concerning what, so to speak, goes on 'below.' In other words, what is often considered to be very private and hidden is nowadays frequently referred to—if not in much specific detail—openly and publicly. One aspect of this is the fact that it is not at all unusual to find advertisements for adulterous relationships and infidelities in broadsheet, as opposed to tabloid, newspapers and magazines. One also finds this kind of phenomenon on mainline TV.

In a number of countries at the present time so-called revenge porn is increasingly common; this involving the alleged blackmail of people, more often than not women, by threatening to present, or actually presenting on the Internet, intimate—or indeed pornographic—material concerning the blackmailed subject. This is a prime example of the private being made public (e.g. Patterson, 2015). This parallels the distinction between being offline or online. In a larger and less controversial sense the entire idea of the globalization of the local—that parallels the publicizing of the private—is all too common and wide spread.

The issues of consciousness and connectivity come clearly into play in the following example. There has recently been the prosecution in 2015 of a 14-year-old teenager in northern England who was charged with instigating 'Jihadist' terrorism in Australia. It seems that this kind of case is not at all unusual and that extensive connectivity is rapidly increasing. Indeed, it would, until recently, have been very puzzling as to how people would have known, or been able to be in instantaneous contact with, like-minded people—or potentially so—all over the world. The question therefore arises whether consciousness of the world as a whole is a phenomenon of which participants in long-distance communication are fully aware. This is well encapsulated in the title of the book, *Close Up at a*

Distance (Kurgan, 2013). Of particular relevance here is what Tomlinson (2007) has called the culture of speed.

Such conceptions bring us to the relevance of the study of maps and cartography in general. Brotton (2012, p. 438) argues that 'maps offer a proposal about the world, rather than just a reflection of it, and every proposal emerges from a particular culture's prevailing assumptions and preoccupations.' The relationship between a map and such assumptions and preoccupations is never fixed, it is always reciprocal. Brotton argues that it is very difficult to establish how people internalize the manner in which a map represents spatial information concerning the world surrounding them. Brotton even invokes Harley and Woodward (1987) in order to make the point that evidence for the lack of map consciousness in primal societies is virtually non-existent. As Brotton (2012, p. 438) remarks 'A map can successfully innovate, but still apparently fail to affect people's perception of the world.'

Much of the above concerns such phenomena as Google Space, which is brought into our purview by Cresswell (2015, pp. 88–114) and, notably by Massey (1994, 2005), Massey's idea of a global sense of space is crucial in this regard. As Brotton (2012, p. 6) argues a 'world view gives rise to a world map; but the world map in turn defines its culture's view of the world. It is an exceptional act of symbiotic alchemy.'

As I have already queried, are people who communicate about sexual proclivities and practices from one continent to another aware of the global significance of their communication? This question has some relation to the question as to whether there is in fact what Rheingold called a virtual (worldwide) community. Indeed, for about 20 years the theme of Internet culture has been quite high on the agenda of scholars and students of modern communication, but with rapidly increasing publicity. As long ago as 1997 much of this interest was explored in *Internet Culture* (Porter, 1997). In fact, much of what presently is 'performed' electronically, particularly in respect of erotic and sexual matters, was a significant part of discussions even in the 1990s concerning the idea of the virtual community (Rheingold, 1993).

In the collection edited by Porter, various aspects of sexuality are seriously addressed. Lockard (1997) argues in the same book that if certain ideas prevalent in the late 1990s were to become true the '*nightmare of totalised communications, distinctions between online and offline* [would] *disappear and an all-embracing "virtual community"* [would] *replace outmoded offline reality*' (p. 224, emphasis added).

One of the most obvious ways in which consciousness precedes connectivity is to be found in the various myths concerning 'faraway' places, such as Eldorado, Shangri-La and Atlantis (see also Fiedler, 1968 and Tsing, 1993). In fact the entire idea of the *transcendent*, so much favored by followers of Jaspers (e.g. Bellah and Joas, 2012) could well be regarded as falling into this category. This is not to say that the present author fully subscribes to the axial age interpretation of Jaspers' work. The fact is that the idea of an axial age, that Jaspers himself did not claim to be original to him, was embedded in a much wider frame. Writing in his most well-known work, *The Origin and Goal of History* (Jaspers, 1949), shortly after the Second World War, Jaspers was particularly concerned with the future of the world; using the comparison of the East and the West (or Orient and Occident) as his starting point. He was greatly preoccupied with what he called the unity of history and the prospects for the unification of 'mankind.' Jaspers argued that 'The old method of comparison, through its newly acquired acuity, causes the unique to stand out all the more clearly. Engrossment in the specifically historical brings the enigma of the unique to more lucid consciousness' (Jaspers, 1949, p. 267). Jaspers' argument in this regard is well illustrated by relatively recent concerns with the concrete relations between the Occident and the Orient. This has in part been inspired by the great debate about the virtues, or lack thereof, of Said's *Orientalism* (1978; Robertson, 1990). A recent example of the importance of the interpenetration between East and West is Buruma and Margalit's (2004) *Occidentalism*. Even though it is not directly relevant to the idea of global culture Irwin's (2006) critique of Said's conception of orientalism is very valuable.

Specific examples could be provided in terms of the manner in which European peoples 'imagined' places and spaces far to the West. In fact, Shakespeare quite frequently referred to such (see Fiedler, 1968). The same kind of thinking applies to European views of a mythical east. In fact such myths are crucial in the comprehension and making of the world as a whole. Moreover, perception of 'the heavens' was a rather different manner of conceiving of one/us being placed in a much wider frame. Of course, at the same time as these places were imagined it was usually thought that they could be connected to the perceiver. However, the essential point remains.

Any contemporary discussion of global, or world, culture must clearly consider the vital but problematically linked issues of migration, diasporas, multiple consciousnesses (Appiah, 2015) and the near-worldwide rise of anti-immigrant movements. This bundle has a clear connection with the entire issue of multiculturalism and related themes. In fact, as Garton Ash (2012) has argued the term multiculturalism has become one of wholly uncertain meaning. He asks whether it refers to a social reality, a set of policies, a normative theory or an ideology. Garton Ash reports that when he served on a Council of Europe working group with members from a number of other European countries he found that 'multiculturalism' meant something different in every country; meanings that contradicted each other. In fact, what he calls multicultural literature 'with its tendency to pigeonhole people by culture, often fails to acknowledge the sheer diversity of this increasingly mixed-up world' (Garton Ash, 2012, p. 33). He goes on to argue that this mixed-up world must 'increasingly include the diversity to be found in a single human skin, mind, and heart' (Garton Ash, 2012, p. 33).

Clearly it is such phenomena as cheap air travel, the Internet, satellite TV and mobile phones that have brought homelands even closer than they were in comparison with cross-cultural and other intercultural connections at the beginning of the twentieth century. In other words, we now live in a world of increasing cultural, national, regional, local, religious, ethnic and other loyalties. In the process, the entire issue of different kinds and forms and degrees of citizenship has become highly and increasingly problematic. In this regard it might be said that virtually every contribution ends with a plea for greater clarity, a clarity that may in fact be unattainable. In fact, Garton Ash's article on this issue is a major (and certainly praiseworthy) example of this tendency.

In any case, such complexity opens spaces for a great variety of movements claiming to have 'the' solution; hence the rise of all kinds of 'radical' movements. A particular speculation that the present author has in this regard is that the apparent increase in mental illness in various parts of the world is largely due to the confusion created by these dilemmas. These dilemmas include, and give opportunities for, numerous claims as to what national identity consists in (Scheffer, 2011). In fact the search for national identities is, to say the least, extremely elusive. It is best to consider that search as a symptom rather than an end in itself. In other words, searches for national identity—that are found in every corner of the world—are in fact a major feature of global culture itself. The fact that we are presently confronted by increasingly walled communities, on the one hand, and heightened forms of communication and a relatively free-floating imagination, on the other, brings home the significance of world-wide and worldly contradictions and makes a single dominant or global imaginary virtually unattainable. In this sense, the old Hobbesian idea of the war of all against all becomes newly relevant. On the other hand, the very thematization of the latter makes it more likely—one says hopefully—that a 'solution' will appear. Indeed, as has been argued above, it has become increasingly obvious that 'wars' are principally about the 'fight' for cultural dominance or, better, cultural consensus. (In this respect it might well be argued that the entire world is becoming increasingly 'subjectified'— a contemporary version of solipsism?).

Conclusion

It is clear that much of the preceding has involved crossing the line between culture and other aspects of the human condition. This has been almost inevitable in the sense that it parallels or duplicates the present apparent condition of the world as a whole. In this sense the above has been an exploratory commentary on the present state of global culture, as well as the issue of global consciousness. In fact, consciousness largely arises from the confusion, or what one might call the relativization of everything (Campbell, 2005).

It has not been possible here to cover anything like all of the components or aspects of what can be called global culture. Among the most important of the lacunae are global spectacles and mega-events; globe-wide disputes concerning intellectual property; the growing if problematic fashion of copying and imitation (Wong, 2013); global food (Pilcher, 2012; Ray, 2012) and sport and sport stars such as the English Premiere League of football. An excellent example of the way in which such phenomena have become increasingly global is provided by the fact that there is a genre of visual art now called Internationalism (Phillips, 2012). There are other, even more obvious, examples in such realms as film, clothes fashion, music, and dance (Davis, 2015). The study of tango in global perspective by Davis is a truly outstanding contribution to the entire theme of global culture, particularly when regarded through the lens of glocalization. It should also be said that the distinction between world and international music (Inglis and Robertson, 2005) raises particular problems with respect to the analysis of global culture.

It can readily be seen that the subject of global culture in itself raises crucial questions of intellectual analyses of all kinds and, moreover, renders the demarcation of boundaries between different spheres of life extremely problematic and fluid.

References

Alexander, J.C., and P. Smith. 2010. 'The Strong Program: Origins, Achievements, and Prospects.' In *Handbook of Cultural* Sociology, edited by J.R. Hall, L. Grindstaff, and M.C. Lo, 1–24, London: Routledge.

Appadurai, A. 2013. *The Future as Cultural Fact: Essays on the Global Condition.* London: Verso.

Appiah, K.A. 2015. 'Race in the Modern World: The Problem of the Color Line.' *Foreign Affairs* 94(2): 1–8.

Baker, D. 2014. *The Schooled Society: The Educational Transformation of Global Culture.* Stanford, CA: Stanford University Press.

Baker, D.P., and G.K LeTendre. 2005. *National Differences, Global Similarities: World Culture and the Future of Schooling.* Stanford, CA: Stanford University Press.

Ballantyne, T., A. and Burton. 2012. 'Empires and the Reach of the Global.' In *A World Connecting 1870–1945*, edited by E.S. Rosenberg, 285–431. Cambridge, MA and London: The Belknap Press of Harvard University Press.

Banerjee, A. 2012. *We Modern People: Science Fiction and the Making of Russian Modernity.* Middletown, CT: Wesleyan University Press.

Barkawi, T. 2006. *Globalization and War.* Lanham, MD: Rowman and Littlefield.

Bartlett, James. 2015. *The Dark Net.* London: Windmill Books.

Beckert, S. 2015. *Empire of Cotton: A New History of Global Capitalism.* London: Allen Lane.

Bellah, R.N. and Joas, H. (eds). 2012. *The Axial Age and Its Consequences.* Cambridge, MA and London: The Belknap Press of Harvard University Press.

Beyer, P. (ed.). 2001. *Religion in the Process of Globalization.* Wurzburg: Ergon Verlag.

Boli, J. and Thomas, G.M. (eds) 1999. *Constructing World Culture: International Nongovernmental Organizations Since 1875.* Stanford: Stanford University Press.

Brown, M.F. 2003. *Who Owns Native Culture?* Cambridge MA and London UK: Harvard University Press.

Brown, W. 2010. *Walled States, Waning Sovereignty*. New York: Zone Books.

Buruma, I., and A. Margolit. 2004. *Occidentalism: The West in the Eyes of Its Enemies*. New York: Penguin Press.

Campbell, G.V.P. 2005. *Everything You Know Seems Wrong: Globalization and the Relativization of Tradition*. Lanham, MD: University Press of America.

Cockburn, P. 2014. *The Rise of Islamic State: ISIS and the New Revolution*. London: Verso.

Colley, L. 1992. *Britons: Forging the Nation, 1707–1837*. New Haven, CT: Yale University Press.

Colley, L. 2007. *The Ordeal of Elizabeth Marsh: A Woman in World History*. New York: Knopf.

Colley, L. 2010. *Captives: Britain, Empire and the World, 1600–1850*. New York: Random House.

Colley, L. 2013. 'Wide-Angled' [Review of Desan, Hunt and Nelson (2013)], *London Review of Books* 35(18): 18–19.

Conrad, P. 2015. *How the World was Won: The Americanization of Everywhere*. London: Thames and Hudson.

Cowen, T. 2002. *Creative Destruction: How Globalization Is Changing the World's Culture*. Princeton and Oxford: Princeton University Press.

Craig, T., and M.E. Ludloff. 2011. *Privacy and Big Data*. Sebastopol: O'Reilly.

Cresswell, T. 2015. *Place: An Introduction*, 2nd edition. Oxford: Wiley Blackwell.

Davis, K. 2015. *Dancing Tango: Passionate Encounters in a Globalizing World*. New York: New York University Press.

Desan, S.L., L. Hunt, and W.M. Nelson (eds). 2013. *The French Revolution in Global Perspective*. Ithaca and London: Cornell University Press.

Dickens, P., and J.S. Ormrod. 2007. *Cosmic Society: Towards Sociology of the Universe*. London: Routledge.

Doyle, D.H. 2015. *The Cause of All Nations: An International History of the American Civil War*. New York: Basic Books.

Dufoix, S. 2003. *Diasporas*. Berkeley: University of California Press.

Ebury, K. 2014. *Modernism and Cosmology: Absurd Lights*. London: Palgrave Macmillan.

Edwards, B.T., and D.P. Gaonkar (eds). 2010. *Globalizing American Studies*. Chicago and London: Chicago University Press.

Einstein, A. 2009. [1931]. *Einstein: On Cosmic Religion and Other Opinions and Aphorisms*. New York: Dover Publications.

Evans, G.R. 2014. *First Light: A History of Creation Myths from Gilgamesh to the God Particle*. London: I.B. Tauris.

Fiedler, L.A. 1968. *The Return of the Vanishing American*. New York: Stein and Day.

Frank, A. 2011. *About Time: Cosmology And Culture At The Twilight Of The Big Bang*. New York: Free Press.

Garton Ash, T.G. 2012. 'Freedom & Diversity: A Liberal Pentagram for Living Together,' *The New York Review of Books* LIX (18), pp. 33–6.

Gay, P. 2007. *Modernism: The Lure of Heresy from Baudelaire to Beckett and Beyond.* London: Heinemann.

Gluck, C., and A.L. Tsing (eds). 2009. *Words in Motion: Toward a Global Lexicon.* Durham and London: Duke University Press.

Goldin, I., and M. Mariathasan. 2014. *The Butterfly Defect: How Globalization Creates Systemic Risks and What to Do About It.* Princeton and Oxford: Princeton University Press.

Goossaert, V., and D.A. Palmer. 2011. *The Religious Question in Modern China.* Chicago and London: University of Chicago Press.

Groebner, V. 2007. *Who Are You? Identification, Deception, and Surveillance in Early Modern Europe.* New York: Zone Books.

Harley, J.B., and D. Woodward (eds). 1987. The History of Cartography, vol.1. Chicago: Chicago University Press.

Inglis, D., and R. Robertson. 2005. '"World Music" and the Globalization of Sound.' In *The Sociology of Art: Ways of Seeing*, edited by D. Inglis, and J. Hughson, 156–70. Basingstoke: Palgrave Press.

Irwin, R. 2006. *For Lust of Knowing: The Orientalists and their Enemies.* London: Allen Lane.

Jameson, F. 2005. *Archeologies of the Future: The Desire Called Utopia and Other Science Fictions.* London: Verso.

Jordan, T. 1999. *Cyberpower: The Culture and Politics of Cyberspace and the Internet.* London and New York: Routledge.

Juergensmeyer, M. 2006. *The Oxford Handbook of Global Religions.* Oxford and New York: Oxford University Press.

Kurgan, L. 2013. *Close Up At A Distance: Mapping, Technology, and Politics.* New York: Zone Books.

Laudan, R. 2013. *Cuisine and Empire: Cooking in World History.* Berkeley, CA: University of California Press.

Lawrence, B.B. 2015. *Who Is Allah?* Edinburgh: Edinburgh University Press.

Lechner, F., and J. Boli. 2005. *World Culture: Origins and Consequences.* Oxford: Blackwell.

Massey, D. 1994. *Space, Place and Gender.* Minneapolis: University of Minnesota Press.

Massey, D. 2005. *For Space.* London: Sage Publications.

Matthiessen, T. 2013. *Sectarian Gulf: Bahrain, Saudi Arabia, and Arab Spring That Wasn't.* Stanford: Stanford University Press.

Micklethwait, J., and A. Wooldridge. 2009. *God is Back: How the Global Rise of Faith is Changing the World.* London: Allen Lane.

Miller, D.E., K.H. Sargeant, and R. Flory (eds). 2013. *Spirit and Power: The Church and Global Impact of Pentecostalism.* New York: Oxford University Press.

Mills, J. 2015. *Privacy in the New Media Age.* Gainesville FL: University Press of Florida.

Morozov, E. 2011. *The Net Delusion; How Not to Liberate The World*. London: Allen Lane.

Moyn, S., and A. Sartori (eds). 2013. *Global Intellectual History*. New York: Columbia University Press.

Nagel, T. 2012. *Mind and Cosmos*. Oxford: Oxford University Press.

Nancy, J.L., and A. Barrau. 2015. *What's These Worlds Coming To?* New York: Fordham University Press.

Nettl, J.P., and R. Robertson. 1968. *International Systems and the Modernization of Societies*. New York: Basic Books.

Nye, J.S. Jr. 2004. *Soft Power: The Means to Success in World Politics*. New York: Public Affairs.

Osterhammel, J. 2014. *The Transformation of the World: A Global History of the Nineteenth Century*. Princeton and Oxford: Princeton University Press.

Pankhurst, R. 2013. *The Inevitable Caliphate? A History of the Struggle for Global Islamic Union, 1924 to the Present*. London: Hurst and Co.

Pasquale, F. 2015. *The Black Box Society: The Secret Algorithms That Control Money and Information*. Cambridge MA and London: Harvard University Press.

Patterson, C. 2015. 'I'll show you mine if you show me yours.' *The Sunday Times Magazine*. February 8. 12–17.

Phillips, S. 2012. *... isms: Understanding Modern Art*. London: Bloomsbury.

Pilcher, J.M. 2012. *Planet Taco: A Global History of Mexican Food*. Oxford: Oxford University Press.

Porter, D. (ed.). 1997. *Internet Culture*. New York and London: Routledge.

Ray, K., and T. Srinivas. 2012. *Curried Cultures: Globalization, Food and South Asia*. Berkeley: University of California Press.

Rees, M. 2015. 'A Life in the Day.' The Sunday Times Magazine, 4 January.

Rheingold, H. 1993. *The Virtual Community: Homesteading on the Electronic Frontier*. Reading, MA: Addison Wesley.

Robertson, R. 1968. 'Strategic Relations Between National Societies: A Sociological Analysis.' *Journal of Conflict Resolution* XII(2): 16–33.

Robertson, R. 1990. 'Japan and the USA: The Interpenetration of National Identities and the Debate about Orientalism.' In *Dominant Ideologies*, edited by N. Abercrombie, S. Hill, and B. S. Turner, 182–98. London: Unwin Hyman.

Robertson, R. 1992. *Globalization: Global Culture and Social Theory*. London: Sage Publications.

Robertson, R. 1995. 'Glocalization: Time-Space and Homogeneity-Heterogeneity.' In *Global Modernities*, edited by M. Featherstone, S. Lash, and R. Robertson, 24–44. London: Sage Publications.

Robertson, R. 1996. *The New Global History: A Sociological Assessment*. Sao Paulo: Instituto de Estudos Avancados.

Robertson, R. 1998. 'The New Global History: History in the Global Age.' *Cultural Values* 2(2): 368–84.

Robertson, R. 2002. 'Le Dimensioni Della Cultura Globale.' In *Culture e Conflitti Nella Globalazzazione*, edited by E. Batini, and R. Ragionieri, 17–30. Florence: Leo S. Olschki Editore.

Robertson, R. 2007a. 'Open Societies, Closed Minds? Exploring the Ubiquity of Suspicion and Voyeurism.' *Globalizations* 4(3): 399–416.

Robertson, R. 2007b. 'Global Millennialism: A Postmortem on Secularization.' In *Religion, Globalization and Culture*, edited by P. Beyer, and L. Beaman, 9–34. Leiden: Brill.

Robertson, R. 2007c. 'Globalization, Culture and.' *The Blackwell Encyclopedia of Sociology* Vol. 4, edited by George Ritzer, p. 1964–1970. Malden, MA: Blackwell.

Robertson, R. 2009. 'Globalization, Theocratization and Politicized Civil Religion.' In *The Oxford Handbook of Religion*, edited by P. E. Clarke, 451–477. Oxford: Oxford University Press.

Robertson, R. 2014a. 'Situating Glocalization: A Relatively Autobiographical Intervention.' In *Global Themes and Local Variations in Organization and Management: Perspectives on Glocalization*, edited by G. S. Drori, M. A. Hollerer, and P. Walgenbach, p. 25–36. London: Routledge.

Robertson, R. (ed.). 2014b. *European Glocalization in Global Context*. London: Palgrave Macmillan.

Robertson, R. 2015. 'Beyond The Discourse of Globalization.' In *Glocalism: Journal of Culture, Politics, and Innovation*. Published online by *Globus et Locus* at www.glocalismjournal.net.

Rosenberg, E.S. (ed.). 2012. *A World Connecting 1870–1945*. Cambridge, MA and London: The Belknap Press of Harvard University Press.

Rosenberg, E.S. 2012. 'Introduction.' In *A World Connecting 1870–1945*, edited by E. S. Rosenberg, 3–25. Cambridge, MA and London: The Belknap Press of Harvard University Press.

Roy, O. 2010. *Holy Ignorance: When Religion and Culture Part Ways*. New York: Columbia University Press.

Rydell, R.W. 1984. *All the World's a Fair: Visions of Empire at American International Expositions, 1876–1916*. Chicago: University of Chicago Press.

Sachsenmaier, D. 2011. *Global Perspectives on Global History: Theories and Approaches in a Connected World*. New York: Cambridge University Press.

Said, E. 1978. *Orientalism: Western Conceptions of the Orient*. New York: Pantheon Books.

Scheffer, P. 2011. *Immigrant Nations*. Cambridge: Polity Press.

Sun, A. 2013. *Confucianism as a World Religion: Contested Histories and Contemporary Reality*. Princeton, NJ and Oxford, UK: Princeton University Press.

Tomlinson, J. 2007. *The Culture of Speed: The Coming of Immediacy*. London: Sage.

Tsing, A. 1993. *In the Realm of the Diamond Queen: Marginality in an Out-of-the-Way Place*. Princeton, NJ. Princeton University Press.

Unger, R.M., and L. Smolin. 2015. *The Singular Universe and the Reality of Time: A Proposal in Natural Philosophy.* Cambridge: Cambridge University Press.

Wilson, E.K., and M. Steger. 2013. 'Religious Globalisms in the Post-Secular Age.' *Globalizations* 10(3): 481–495.

Wong, W.W.Y. 2013. *Van Gogh on Demand: China and the Readymade.* Chicago and London: University of Chicago Press.

Chapter 2
Globalization and Global Consciousness: Levels of Connectivity

Paul James and Manfred B. Steger

Across the contemporary world, the question of connectivity has emerged as the normal condition of being and acting as a 'person-in-the-world'. Being connected has assumed multiple meanings; most of them are positive. Who, but perhaps a few customary villagers, traditional monks, and modern eccentrics, are happy be relegated to a communications backwater? Parochialism, reclusiveness, and isolation are nouns that conflict with those desirable places where modern and postmodern relations dominate. In globalizing cities across the world, hyperconnected individuals might complain about the intense demands extracted from them by their numerous information and communication technologies, but none of them want to be disconnected. Today's condition of connectivity has both important and banal consequences. For a new generation, mediated connectivity is basic to their identity – with significant consequences for their patterns of consumption and attachments to new commodities and brands. Being an acolyte of social media such as Twitter of Facebook has become a precondition for the construction of such an identity. In Hong Kong, London, New York, Paris, and Brossard, people queue outside Apple stores, willing to wait hours and days for the commercial release of new versions of the iPhone or iPad. Extremely useful for marketing purposes, such street scenes are also depressing images of a changing world of connectivity fetishism.

Indeed, since the arrival of the World Wide Web and the spread of mobile communications, mediated connectivity has been quietly normalized as central to a consolidating 'global imaginary' (Steger, 2008). In conjunction with the concept (and practice) of the 'network' and 'networking', connectivity has become foundational to an era of intensifying globalization – both objectively and subjectively. While communications-based and networked forms of connectivity represent, objectively, only one aspect of globalization, subjectively these forms have assumed an unprecedented centrality. Both this *phenomenal* sense and practical consciousness of the importance of 'being connected' has borne back upon mainstream writing in fields as diverse as sociology and the digital humanities – and not always in helpful ways.

For example, the growing transdisciplinary field of 'Global Studies' (Steger, 2013) grew up in this world where connectivity enthrals. Despite the considerable analytical attention given to patterns of connectivity (Castells, 2010), the subjective dimensions of connectivity have received little critical scrutiny (van Dijck, 2013).

Rather connectivity tends to be treated as the way of the present, with its objective patterns to be mapped in ever-greater detail. Indeed, these mapping exercises follow predominantly empirical methodologies. Because much of the global studies and communications literature considers the extensiveness and intensiveness of mediated and networked connections to be direct empirical questions – you have it or you don't; it can be measured by degree or it doesn't exist; it is stretched over this distance or that – objective connectivity has become *the* process that is used to measure 'globalization' in general. Thus, it has become the overriding proxy that stands in for the much more complex set of objective and subjective globalizing relations (Taylor et al., 2011). One of the first global studies writers to engage in these kinds of simplification, John Tomlinson (1999) insists that globalization *is* 'complex connectivity'. These kinds of equations have led to considerable confusion in mainstream social theory, including in globalization theory. Hence, we offer the following section as a necessary prelude for establishing an alternative analytical foundation.

Prelude

An important part of laying an alternative analytical foundation involves developing a definition of globalization that recognizes both the objective and subjective dimensions of the manifold processes that bring us into *relation* with others across the globe. The concept of 'relation' is used here more broadly than 'connectivity'. A relation can be spatially close and proximate or involve substantial absence – including through death. It can be layered across more embodied to more abstracted connections *and* disconnections. Social *relations* range from the embodied relations of friends and family-connected Diasporas to more abstract systemic relations carried by different modes of practice, both objectively and subjectively. These modes of practice include production, exchange, communication, inquiry and organization.

When used in abstract terms, 'connectivity' tends to be linked in the literature to only two of those modes, communication and exchange, in particular through mediated communication systems and financial exchange systems. This is where the emphasis is put on the delivery processes provided by ICTs or information and communication technologies. At the same time, in empirical or experiential terms, the notion of 'connectivity' tends to be stretched across all modes of practice to mean all interactivity and interchange at a distance. This ambiguity is problematic for understanding globalization. The problem is compounded by a second recently introduced ambiguity. Both corporate descriptions and personal testimonies regarding the role of social media platforms such as Facebook or Twitter tend to emphasize the personal, even intimate, possibilities of connecting to others more effectively. However, social media platforms are *at the same time* objectively abstract and automated platforms using algorithms to codify data and channel consumptions choices (van Dijck, 2013).

It only takes a moment to realize that the objective lines of communication and exchange that carry that connection are as important as the subjective experience of global connectivity and the feelings associated with it – and that these are in tension with each other. But because both the sensory experience of connectivity and the structures of technological connection are so 'obvious', they tend to be reduced to the natural outcome of what is now simply referred to as 'the network'. The concept of 'network' has thus assumed a sophisticated but uncritical pre-eminence, with its theorists actively conflating all social relations into it (Castells, 2010; Latour, 2010). This conflation of dimensions is the main culprit for the persistence of much confusion on the subject.

Thus, an adequate definition of globalization needs to recognize that connectivity is only one possible outcome of increasing extension of social relations across global space and time – even if it is experienced differently from a subjective point of view. An increasing emphasis on localization or local autonomy from the global are an equally possible outcomes of intensifying globalization, and it is not only possible but actually very likely to observe both increased connectivity and increased localization simultaneously (Robertson, 1993). It is also possible to have a globalizing communications system of intensifying connectivity that leads to uneven patterns of isolation. In political terms, for example, the Cold War constituted a global system that led to decreasing or demarcated connectivity for some states. In personal terms, it is now being recognized that globalizing social media systems work both to connect some and to isolate others – intensively in both extremes (Quartiroli, 2011). Moreover, to compound the issues that a definition needs to encompass, it is possible to have a rather thick consciousness of globalization (for example, the classical Greek and Roman consciousness of a heliocentric globe) while at the same time the objective relations of globalization remain thin and undeveloped.

Responding to this range of possibilities, we have defined globalization as the extension and intensification of social relations across world-space and world-time. We refer to 'world-space' in terms of the historically variable ways that it has been practised (objectively) and socially understood (subjectively) across changing world-time. This definition thus recognizes the importance of both objective and subjective relations, both practice and consciousness. In these terms, connectivity is understood as just one process of globalization in activity and thought/consciousness. This means that however much the condition of connectivity has entered contemporary consciousness of today's world, it is has only done so as part of a process that is much more comprehensive than mere empirical connection. This chapter thus seeks to understand the contemporary sensitivity to the condition of connectivity.

The second important part of the analytical foundation that we will use to establish our argument involves specifying different forms of consciousness. These forms relate to the usual four-fold *modern* distinction between data, information, knowledge and wisdom, but as we use them they relate in different ways to different ontological formations. They are not just modern notions. The first form is *sensory experience*, the phenomenal sense that something exists in relation to, or has an impact on, a person. The concept of 'affect' attests to this kind of consciousness, as does 'sense data'. But 'sensory experience' is less technically conceived than those abstract expressions. It is consciousness as embodied experience – felt, but not necessarily reflected upon. The modern experience of connectivity envelopes sensory experience. It is potentially everywhere, even when communications lines fail. In part, this is what gives connectivity its power.

The second form is *practical consciousness*. This involves knowing how to do things, knowing how to 'go on'. As writers as different as Wittgenstein and Marx have elaborated, it is basic to human engagement. The practical consciousness of connectivity is constantly self-confirming. The globalization of systems of information and communication technologies (ICTs) has delivered unprecedented practical possibilities of connection, and a generation people have assimilated the communicative techniques of the World Wide Web, the Internet and various social media platforms as practical consciousness.

The third form is *reflective consciousness*, the modality in which people reflect upon the first two forms. It is the stuff of ordinary philosophy and day-to-day thinking about what has been done and what is to be done. With the dominance of modern subjectivity this form involves the socially mediated production of the ego as the phenomenal, impermanent self, which knows the world experientially as it subjectively appears to it. However, as neuroscientific experiments have demonstrated, the unitary sense of self is a subjective representation. Citing these studies, German philosopher Thomas Metzinger (2010) argues that the ego can be likened to a 'tunnel that bores into reality' and thus gives apparent 'substance' to the ego by limiting what can be seen, heard, smelled and felt.

The fourth form is *reflexive consciousness*, reflecting on the basis of reflection, and interrogating the nature of knowing in the context of the constitutive conditions of being. While some writers have variously made reflexivity the condition of contemporary subjectivity (Beck, Giddens and Lash, 1994), here it is treated as much more than situations where an actor recognizes processes of socialization with this recognition bearing back upon and changing such processes. The reflexive process of interrogating the conditions of existence is tenuous, recursive, and always partial. Indeed, this essay is an exercise in such reflexive interrogation.

Laying the third of the foundation stones for this essay involves putting 'connectivity' in its place *ideationally*. But this is no easy feat. Connectivity differs from old more ideologically contested concepts such as 'freedom' or 'equality'. Conventional ideological clusters such as liberalism present us with ideals such as 'freedom', 'liberty', and 'autonomy' as conditions for normative ideals to which we should aspire. However, for all their naturalization as life-long objectives, these ideals remain contested and debated. Liberalism's freedom is juxtaposed to the conservative claim about the importance of obligation and the authority of the state. Liberalism's core concept of 'liberty' is qualified in the social-democratic tradition by its emphasis on 'equality' (Bobbio, 1988; Freeden, 1996). And the current dominant desire for autonomy is in some political traditions still set against the constraints of reciprocity and mutuality.

By contrast, the theme of connectivity appears to float free of such constraining qualifications. As we noted at the outset, it is associated with a *global imaginary* (Steger, 2008) of open networked relations as a predominantly positive form of social relations: affinity, community, accordance, association, and inclusion. This point will be crucial in later discussion. Somehow – through a multilevel process worth investigating closely – the concept of 'connectivity' missed out on the process of political philosophical dialogue that produces 'essentially contested concepts' (Gallie, 1955). When the condition of connectivity is juxtaposed against other conditions, it tends to be posed in opposition to an uncomfortable set of antonyms that nobody aspires to anyway: disjuncture, separation, detachment, isolation, closure, and exclusion.

As we argue in this chapter, one way out of this reductive tendency is to analyse the theme of connectivity through an understanding of different levels of social meaning: ideas, ideologies, imaginaries and ontologies. These are only analytical distinctions, and the notion of 'levels' serves as a metaphor designed to avoid the problem of analytical conflation. Still both of these concepts are both useful and necessary for showing – among other purposes – how the theme of connectivity can be valorised and taken for granted at the same time. What follows is our elaboration upon a method that we have been developing over the last few years as part of our efforts to produce 'engaged theory' that would help us understand the many aspects involved in the contemporary rise of a global imaginary (Steger, 2008; Steger and James, 2013). We contend that the theme of connectivity should be understood in terms of each of these levels of social meaning.

Four Levels of Social Meaning

What distinguishes these four levels of lived meaning – ideas, ideologies, imaginaries, and ontologies? Analytically, each level is constituted at an ever-greater generality, durability, and depth than the prior level. For example, ideas can be passing thoughts, and ideologies tend to move in and out of social contestation, but imaginaries move at a deeper level and, in different ways, frame the commonsense or 'background understandings' (Taylor, 2004) of an age. What is contested about imaginaries tends to be their ideological expressions. Most deeply, ontologies, such as how we live temporally or spatially, constitute the relatively enduring ground of our being. Whether we recognize it or not reflexively, our lives are formed in terms of ontologies of time, space and embodiment, from the way in which we move through the locales that we live to the website presentations of those locales. Those ideas that stand the test of time do so because they become embedded in ideological clusters, social imaginaries and ontological formations – that is, the ways in which we understand and live the basic conditions of our existence. It is indicative that according to an analysis of the Oxford English corpus of two billion words, all of the ten most common nouns in the English language – time, person, year, way, day, thing, man, world, life, hand – relate to the ontological categories of temporality, spatiality, embodiment, and performativity. The first word that appears outside of this frame is 'work', and even it could be understood as part of the performance of production. Nouns like shoes and ships, cauliflower and kings, do not figure in the most-used list in the English language.

Objective and subjective processes of globalization have been changing all of these four layers – at times, even at revolutionary speed. However, the deeper the processes of change, the slower the tendency for a new pattern to take hold as dominant and encompassing. These different kinds of meaning can be defined (and linked to the arguments in this chapter about connectivity) as follows.

At the first level, *ideas* are thoughts, opinions, beliefs and concepts. A person can hold an idea individually and uniquely, but ideas tend to swirl around communicating segments of meaning. They gain credence and legitimacy only in relation to larger patterns of social meaning. 'Connectivity' is obviously a concept (as well as a condition). But even though it is not a particularly technical or specialist term, it is not one of those ideas that are immediate and ever-present in our thoughts. An absence of connection or active exclusion evokes deep emotions, but 'connectivity' is not a word that is commonly used in day-to-day discussion outside of ICT-speak. This relative absence gives a clue to its current weight. In conjunction with its subjective force and its place in deeper layers of social meaning – to be discussed in a moment – the concept carries an ideational weight that experts can use as an analytical term with powerful empirical and rhetorical effect.

At the second level, *ideologies* are patterned clusters of normatively imbued ideas and concepts, including particular representations of power relations. They are conceptual maps that help people navigate the complexity of their social universe. They carry claims to social truth as, for example, expressed in the conventional ideologies of the national imaginary: liberalism, conservatism, socialism, communism, and fascism. 'Connectivity' is deeply imbued with normative assumptions, but its peculiarity becomes more obvious when analysed at this level. Unlike normatively aspired conditions such as freedom or equality, connectivity has largely escaped the circles of contestation that accompany most ideological developments. This lack of contestation adds to its ideational weight, at least for the moment.

At the third level, *imaginaries* are patterned convocations of the social whole. These deep-seated modes of understanding provide largely pre-reflexive parameters within which people imagine their social existence – expressed, for example, in conceptions of 'the global', 'the national', 'the moral order of our time' (Taylor, 2004). They are the convocations that express our inter-relation to each other. Here is where connectivity, at last, finds a comfortable home. At least for scholars, it helps to name our dominant sense of inter-relation today: global connectivity.

And at the fourth level, *ontologies* are patterned ways of *being* in the world. They are lived and experienced across all levels of consciousness as the grounding or existential conditions of the social: time, space, embodiment, performance and knowing. For example, modern ontologies of linear time, territorial space, and individualized embodiment frame the way in which we walk about the modern city. It is only within a modern sense of time that the ideologies of progress or economic growth can make sense. Even if prior ontologies affect how we see things like sacred spaces and events, they tend to be reconstituted in terms of such dominant understandings. The theme of connectivity has a deep though contradictory relation to each of these categories that we will explore later.

Across remainder of the chapter, these four levels of social meaning provide the overarching structure for our discussion. In particular, we link them to dominant frames for understanding our contemporary world: globalism and modernism. These links have consequences for how we think and act in relation to issues of connectivity as one aspect of social integration. Although we primarily concentrate on questions of social meaning, this should not be taken to imply that meaning and practice are disconnected. Table 2.1 provides a simplified picture of our overall method.

Table 2.1   Levels of the social in relation to levels of theoretical analysis

Levels of the social	Doing	Acting	Relating	Being
Levels of analysis	I. Empirical	II. Conjunctural	III. Integrational	IV. Categorical
Objects of analysis I: Levels of social meaning	Ideas	Ideologies	Imaginaries	Ontologies
Objects of analysis II: Levels of social relations	Patterns of activity: E.g. • Institutions • Organizations • Fields • Disciplines • Regimes	Patterns of practice: E.g. • Production • Exchange • Communication • Organization • Enquiry	Patterns of social negotiation ('Social themes'): E.g. • Accumulation/ Distribution • Needs/Limits • Identity/Difference • Autonomy/Authority • Inclusion/Exclusion	Patterns of social being ('Ontological categories'): E.g. • Corporeality • Temporality • Spatiality • Performativity • Epistemology
Objects of analysis III: Levels of social formation	Domains of social life: E.g. • Ecology • Economics • Politics • Culture	Modes of social practice: E.g. • Techno-scientism • Capitalism • Bureaucratism • Mediatism	Modes of social integration: E.g. • Face-to-face relations • Agency-extended relations • Object-extended relations • Disembodied relations	Modes of social being ('Ontological formations'): E.g. • Customary • Traditional • Modern • Postmodern

Having defined ideas, ideologies, imaginaries and ontologies, the body of our discussion now turns to elaborating what how the meaning of a globally connected world can be understood through ideas, ideologies, imaginaries and ontologies.

Ideas

Like other major social phenomena, ideas about connectivity are associated with patterns of meaning related to and about forms of material practice. The relationship between those practices and meanings is extraordinarily complicated and mutually constitutive. Contemporary ideas about connectivity come to us framed by two counter-images within the dominant global imaginary. On the one hand there is space-ship earth, Gaia, and the image of planet earth as a single interconnected system. According to one dominant approach that draws on the interconnectivity theme, a butterfly flaps its wings in the Amazon Basic and a storm develops on the other side of the globe. Accordingly, the projection of planet earth is as a vulnerable globe suspended in space. On the other hand, and in contention with the first set, there is a counter-idea of the global so powerful that it has a single reference point – *the market*. There is no more powerful global metaphor today than 'the market'. Markets – capitalist markets to be precise – have been so naturalized as an active globalizing force that they are now treated in the singular, with different markets in different localities understood as nodes in a network of financial and commodity exchange. At one level, this is increasingly true – hence the power of the claim – but there are still many places in the world where capitalism is only an intrusive layer of what otherwise still functions as a traditional or customary market. Because of the power of the idea of a flat earth, the term 'market' no longer needs the adjective 'global' in front of it to carry the meaning of global connectivity. However, to understand the power of these ideas we need to move to the level of ideology analysis.

Ideologies

Ideologies are patterns of ideas. One or two statements of contention do not an ideology make. It takes lots of ideas and the voices of many people to make an ideology. These patterns are formed through such processes as the power of repetition, the status of the speaker or source of the idea, and the 'given' sense that some ideas are right or wrong. In the area of globalization, four clusters of ideas are conceptually thick enough to warrant the status of mature ideologies: market globalisms, justice globalisms, imperial globalisms, and religious globalisms. Connectivity has become central to them all, and thus relatively uncontested between the different ideological constellations.

Market globalisms constitute the dominant set of ideologies in the early twenty-first century. Market globalism is built around a number of interrelated central claims: that globalization is about the liberalization and worldwide interconnection of markets (neoliberalism); that it is powered by neutral techno-economic forces; that the process is inexorable; that the process is leaderless and anonymous; and that everyone will be better off in the long run (Steger, 2009).

Justice globalism, by comparison, can be defined by its emphasis on equity, rights, diversity, and a more demanding sense of sustainability. It suggests that the currently dominant processes of globalization are powered by corporate interests; that the process can take different pathways; that the democracy carried by global processes tends to be thin and procedural; and that 'globalization-from-above' or 'corporate globalization' is associated with increasing inequities within and between nation-states, greater environmental destruction and a marginalization of the poor. (Steger, Goodman and Wilson, 2013). In relation to the theme of connectivity, justice globalism is akin to market globalism, its main competitor. Both ideologies draw upon a generalizing, deep-seated imaginary of global connectedness. For a time, one line of justice globalism was associated with an anti-connectivity movement as part of its back-to-the-country sensibility, but this has changed fundamentally over the past few decades. *Just* inclusion in the opportunities of global networks and positive connectivity in networks of global exchange have become central to the concerns of almost everybody on the political Left.

The third constellation includes various permutations of *religious globalisms*, which are often codified by the forces of the political Right (Wilson and Steger, 2013). Its most spectacular strain today is jihadist Islamism. Based on the populist evocation of an exceptional spiritual and political crisis, jihadist Islamists bemoan the contemporary age of *jahiliyya* (ignorance and pagan idolatry) and call for a renewed universalism of a global *umma* or a reworked meaning of a globally connected Islamic community. In the Christian version the City of Man is sinful and requires a renewed orientation to the City of God expanded globally. The so-called '10/40 Window' describes the zone between the 10th and 40th latitudes where Pentecostal Christianity needs to connect to those lost souls of other religions in Africa, the Middle East and Asia. Different groups such as World Vision and the Lausanne Committee for World Evangelization developed profiles of unconnected peoples (Pocock, van Rheenen and McConnell, 2005).

A fourth variant, *imperial globalism*, has been weakening over the last few years as a result of the Obama administration's renewed multilateralism and the fracturing of the Washington Consensus in the wake of the Global Financial Crisis. Developing out of market globalism and still retaining some of its central features, imperial globalism still operates as a powerful background force. Its central claim is that despite the coming 'Asian Century', global peace depends upon the global economic connectivity and military care of an informal, US-led, Western empire. This position continues to be taken for granted within many governing groups and elite US circles. Half a century ago, ideological conservatives and some liberals would have been arguing for isolationism, but it is now largely taken for granted that acting in the world is necessary. The emerging critiques of US-intervention have no parallel in the ideological debates over isolationism in the interwar years. Indeed, a cavalcade of journalists and politicians rush in whenever hints of isolationism are expressed.

For all their complexity as ideologies, and despite the obvious tensions between them and the differences across different settings, these four globalisms are part of a complex, roughly woven, patterned ideational fabric that increasingly presumes *the global* to be a defining condition of the present. This is the case even as we remain entangled in the national. The people who accept their central claims of these ideological clusters – whether from the political Right or Left – internalize the apparent inevitability and relative virtue of global interconnectivity and mobility across global time and space. However one might seek to understand global history, and whatever reversals we might face in the future, the consciousness of intensifying social connectivity has come to define the nature of our times. Even though proponents of justice globalism strenuously insist that 'another world is possible', they hardly question that growing global interdependence remains a central part of most, if not all, alternative futures. Indeed, one unmistaken sign of a maturing ideological constellation is that it comes to be represented in discourse as 'post-ideological'.

Our key proposition here is that, as the core concepts of political ideologies are patterned and configured by elite codifiers, they become conceptually thick enough to form relatively coherent and persistent articulations of the underlying social imaginary. Just as the formation of nations is associated with the ideologies of the national imaginary, processes of globalization are associated with 'globalisms' that expressing the global imaginary. These global ideologies both influence and make sense of globalizing practices. Appreciation and projection of connectivity cut across all these ideological differences.

Imaginaries

The concept of 'globalization' reflects a generalized recognition that global processes inform social life, but it is much more than that. Just as globalization affects most of everyday life – from the way in which we borrow money and source basic commodities to the way we use digital modalities to keep in touch with friends and family via social networking sites like Facebook, Twitter, and MySpace – our consciousness of the global runs deep. In this sense, then, the various ideologies associated with globalization have come to coalesce around a new sense of a global social whole. A *global social imaginary* has formed with profound and generalizing impact. This imaginary, for example, 'compels' many city leaders to feel that their city needs be a 'global city'. It engenders the current competition between cities for comparative global status. Why else would cities take the various league tables and prizes so seriously?

In the last decades, a number of prominent social thinkers have grappled with the notion that an *imaginary* is more than an ideologically contested representation of social integration and differentiation (Lefort, 1986; Castoriadis, 1991; Appadurai, 1996; Taylor, 2004). Pierre Bourdieu's conception of the *habitus* is also relevant here, defined as 'systems of durable, transposable dispositions, structured structures predisposed to function as structuring structures' (1990, p. 53).

However, the concept of the *habitus* is too explicitly normatively driven and locality-specific to be the same as what we are trying to get at. The concept of the 'social imaginary' in our use has a stronger sense of the social whole or the general 'given' social order. What is important to take from Bourdieu is a sense of how patterns of practice and ideas can *be seen* to be *objectively* outside of the particular practices and ideas of persons, even as those patterns were generated subjectively by persons acting in and through the *habitus*.

Charles Taylor (2004) provides a complementary way forward to defining the social imaginary. For him it is the 'ways people imagine their social existence, how they fit together with others, how things go on between them and their fellows, the expectations that are normally met, and the deeper normative notions and images that underlie these expectations' (p. 23). These imaginations set the common-sense background of lived social experience. In Taylor's exposition, the *modern* social imaginary has been built by three dynamics. The first is the separating out of *the economy* as a distinct domain, treated as an objectified reality, something that we have criticized for being assumed to be the natural state of things. The second is the simultaneous emergence of *the public sphere* as the place of increasingly mediated interchange, (counter-posed) to the intimate or *private sphere* in which ordinary life is affirmed. The third is the sovereignty of *the people*, treated as a new collective agency even as it is made up of individuals who see self-affirmation in the other spheres. These are three historical developments, among others, that are relevant to what might be called a *modern* ontological formation (of which more later), but in our approach such dynamics are no more than factorial considerations.

Our definition of the social imaginary builds upon both writers towards an alternative approach, namely, that an imaginary constitutes a patterned *convocation* of the lived *social whole*. The notion of 'convocation' is important here. It names the 'calling together' – the gathering of an assemblage of meanings, ideas, sensibilities. It does not involved the self-conscious defence or the active decontesting activity associated with ideological projection. The concept of 'the social whole' points to the way in which certain apparently simple terms such as 'our society', 'we', 'the city', and 'the market' carry taken-for-granted and interconnected meanings. This concept allows us to define the imaginary as broader than the dominant sense of community. A social whole, in other words, is not necessarily co-extensive with a projection of community relations or the ways that *a* people imagine their social existence. Nor does it need to be named as such. It can encompass a time, for example, when there exists only an inchoate sense of global community. There is today paradoxically a pre-reflexive sense that at one level 'we' as individuals, peoples, urban communities and nations have a common global fate. Put in different terms, the medium and the message – the practice of connectivity on a global scale and the content of messages of global interconnection and naturalized power – have become increasingly bound up with each other.

As recently as a generation ago, notions of the social whole – including 'the market' – were stretched across relations between nation-states and would, therefore, have been seen as co-extensive with the nation-state. Hence, the widespread use of the now anachronistic term 'inter*national* relations'. The concept of the 'international' lingers on as a powerful reference, but we now gloss over the base terms of the concept: 'inter' and 'national'. A generation ago when sociologists and political scientists analysed 'society', they tended to assume the boundaries of the nation – in the relevant literature this is referred to as 'methodological nationalism' (James, 1996; Beck, 2003). In other words, the social whole reflected a national imaginary that tended to be equated with the community of the nation-state. Now we find either that such concepts as 'city' and 'society' have become terms of ambivalence because they have become stretched between two contesting yet interdependent imaginaries: the national and the global. This helps to explain the contemporary excitement about networked connected cities. With the emerging dominance of the global, cities have come back into contention as having both local vigour and globalizing connecting beyond their national settings. This is experienced as newness.

Novelty is perhaps most obviously expressed in the proliferation of the prefix 'neo' that has attached itself to nearly all major 'isms' of our time: neoliberalism, neoconservatism, neo-Marxism, neofascism, and so on (Steger, 2008). Despite continuities there *is* something new about political ideologies: a new global imaginary is on the rise. It erupts with increasing frequency within and onto the familiar framework of the national, spewing its fiery lava across all geographical scales. Stoked by, among other things, technological change and scientific innovation, this global imaginary destabilizes the grand political ideologies codified by social elites in an earlier period. Debates over questions of connectivity, sustainability, and the resilience of the urbanizing planet are at the centre of this firestorm. It is not that these terms are to be questioned, but rather that they are present during debates about basic existence.

In summary, then, we have suggested that ideologies of globalization are part of an extended family that translate a generalized global imaginary into competing political programs and agendas where questions of connectivity have escaped mainstream scrutiny. Political impact of this sensibility has been redoubled by the spectacular rise of communications technologies. This has profound consequences for how debates about social life are conducted. For example, it also has consequences for how people think about cities. The term 'global cities' partakes of this consolidating imaginary, based on the idea that global cities are those that channel the connecting flows of capital, commodities and communications.

But it goes further. When Jeb Brugman (2009), for example, proclaims the existence of an urban revolution that has already transformed the planet into a single *City* (with a capital 'C'), a single converging connected urban system. He has taken the urban connectivity of this global imaginary to extend everywhere. His analysis breaks down on almost every level. Obviously there is uneven connectivity and separation with continuing non-hinterland rural zones and many places on the planet that are not comprehensively incorporated into a so-called 'flat earth' (Friedman, 2005). Obviously, new and intense competition has developed between globalizing cities, competition which means that the notion of a single urban system cannot be conflated with a utopia of globalizing social interrelations. Globalization and urbanization have not become the same process, even if the orbits of cities have become increasingly globalized (Spencer, 2014). Still, the problems with Brugmann's analysis point to the emerging dominance of a global imaginary. This explains why for him and others the connected urban complex thus becomes the globe. What is accurate in his analysis is that the dual forces of urbanization and globalization are changing the planet. But to understand this compounding change we need a very different kind of methodology that can: a) recognize dominant patterns of change *and* continuity; b) distinguish different and contradictory layers of connection *and* disconnection; and c) explain why contemporary approaches to urban life all tend to emphasize the virtues of connectivity.

It is understandable given the force of the global imaginary that writers are now saying that the interconnected urban system *is* the world or that the world is flat, but how does that allow for the development of a more sustainable and complex social imaginary? As Brendan Gleeson puts it, 'The imaginaries that [should stand] the test of time are, logically, those that do not refuse history or nature – ideas such as human solidarity, our dependence on nature, the possibility of failure and the frailty of human endeavor' (2010, p. 9).

Ontological Formations

Going deeper than the global imaginary is the long-term and continuing ontological dominance of *modern* ways of life. Thus both the ideologies and objective realities of global interconnection are currently tied to the ideologies and objective realities of both the Left and the Right. The modern Left enunciates modern progressiveness, connectivity and justice. The modern Right proclaims the necessity of progress, connectivity and economic growth. The concept of 'modernization' thus thuds to earth with an ideological and imaginary weight that links progress, connectivity, development, and modernity as intertwined necessities.

Why is connectivity so readily seen as both necessary and virtuous? To understand this, moving to the final layer of our investigation of the dimensions of social meaning, we must grapple with ontological categories such as time and space. As begun to be discussed earlier, we use the concept of 'ontologies' here as a short-hand term referring to the most basic framing categories of social existence: temporality, spatiality, corporeality, epistemology and so on. These are categories of being-in-the-world. They are historically constituted in the structures of human interrelations. If questions of ontology are fundamentally about matters of being, then everything involving 'being human' is ontological. Still, we are using the concept more precisely to refer to categories of human existence such as 'space' and 'time' that on the one hand are always talked about, and, on the other, are rarely interrogated, analysed, or historically contextualized except by philosophers and social theorists.

In this context, let us note that we employ the concepts of the *customary*, the *traditional*, the *modern* and the *postmodern* as provisionally useful designations to refer to fundamentally different ontological formations (James, 2006). These are different *ways of life*, with the term 'ways of life' meaning something much deeper than lifestyle choices. *Customary* ways of life, including *tribalism*, are defined by the dominance of particular socially specific modalities of space, time, embodiment, knowing and performance that can be characterized by analogical, genealogical and mythological practices and subjectivities. This, for example, would include notions of genealogical placement and kinship, the importance of mythological time connecting past and present, and the centrality of relations of embodied reciprocity between persons who spend most of their time in each other's presence.

Traditional ways of life can be characterized as carrying forward prior ontological forms from customary relations, but reconstitutes them in terms of universalizing cosmologies and political-metaphorical relations. An example here is the institution of the Christian Church. It carries forward older customary meanings and rituals – times of feasting, orientations to the sacred, and so on. At the same time, it meets the modern world ambiguously. Christian denominations may have modernized their practices of organization and become enmeshed in a modern monetary economy, but the various lineages of the Church, and most manifestly its Pentecostal variations, remain deeply bound up with a traditional cosmology of meaning and ritual, including the traditional notion of dominion over nature. Traditionally, Christians were one in God. Now with the dominance of modern ontologies, Christians seek connection to God.

A brief discussion of the themes of time and space will help bring to the surface this largely taken-for-granted connection between ontological categories, globalization and the concept of connectivity. Let us start with the ontological category of *spatiality*. Focusing on spatiality is crucial, since globalization is obviously a spatial process and issues of sustainability are taken to refer to places from the local to the global. Localities are nothing if not spatial configurations. The academic observation that to globalize means to compress time and space bringing enhance connectivity has long been part of public discourse. However, to be more historically specific, *contemporary* globalization is predominantly lived through a *modern* conception of spatiality linked to an abstracted geometry of compressed territories and sovereignties.

Modern space tends to subsume rather than replace traditional cosmological senses of spatiality held together by God or some other generalized Supreme Being. In other words, different formations are layered in dominance rather experiencing a simple epochal shift from an older form of temporality. Modern spaces overlay older forms with networks of interchange and movement. This accords with our presentation of contemporary globalization as generating new hybrid modernities anchored in changing conceptions of time and space. For example, those ideological prophets who espouse a Jihadist or Pentecostal variant of religious globalism tend to be stretched between a modern territorial sense of space and a neo-traditional sense of a universalizing *umma* or Christendom, respectively. In their neo-traditional layer of understanding, the social whole exists in, prior to, and beyond, modern global space. It means that, *for those who believe*, the cities of Jerusalem, Rome or Mecca lie at the various centres of different connecting spaces that integrate other urban and rural places around the world in a singular cosmology.

At the same time, particularly in fast-moving urban settings, we also find instances of ambiguous modern spatialities sliding into postmodern sensibilities that relate to contemporary globalization. Take, for example, airline-advertising maps that are post-territorial (postmodern) to the extent that they show multiple abstract vectors of travel – lines that connect multiple city-nodes and travel across empty space. These are maps without reference to the conventional mapping expressions of land and sea, nation-state and continental boundaries. To such a backdrop and with no global outline, an advertisement for KLM airlines assures potential customers that, 'You could fly from anywhere in the world to any destination'. Our contention here is that one comfortably knows how to read those maps despite the limited points of orientation, and one also knows that they signify global connectivity before reading the fine print – 'anywhere in the world'. This is basis of the so-called 'network society'. As Bouteligier (2012) has argued, globalization both gives rise to networked urban organizations and exposes the weaknesses of such organizations. Networked connectivity may be one of the key considerations that global organizations treat as the basis of their organizational strength, but it also becomes their weakness as they fail to understand that effective political integration (as opposed to just connectivity) has to be based on more than a website projection and a few high-profile meetings in different cities around the world.

The modern category of *temporality* is also important to the contemporary global imaginary, even if the notion of 'time' does not seem to be contained in the concept of globalization. More than that, it is crucial to underpinning the modern idea of connectivity – relative instantaneity. Modern time is the demarcated, linear, and empty time of the calendar and clock. It is the time of change, progress and development. We all become connected on a single time-line of history. This ontological sense that time moves 'forward' one-second-per-second is a modern convention rather than being intrinsically natural. It is neither scientifically verifiable (except as tautology), nor continuous with older cosmological senses of time. Modern time is abstracted from nature. It is sustained by a particular mode of modern analytical enquiry – the Newtonian treatment of time as unitary, linear and uniform. This 'scientific' time reached one of its defining moments in 1974 when the second came to be measured in atomic vibrations, allowing the post-sensory, post-practically conscious concept of 'nanoseconds' – one-billionth of a second.

The manifold sense of moving forward, maintaining temporal precision and achieving communications instantaneity has been globalized as the regulative framework for electronic transactions in the global marketplace. It drives the billions of transactions on Wall Street just as much as it imposes a non-regressive discipline on the millions of bidders on eBay, at a local real estate auction or waiting at a red traffic light. This then becomes a crucial point: a modern sense of time, like the market, has been globalized and now overlays older ontologies of temporality without erasing them. It is the dominant time of contemporary social life, and it lives in contradiction with older forms of time.

Modernism carries forward prior forms of being including time and space, but tends fundamentally to reconstitute them. It remakes them in terms of technical-abstracted modes of being. Thus even religious time becomes understood and practiced not primarily in terms of cosmological integration but through linear time-lines that connects the ritualized details of the past and present, as well as events *made by us* with an eye toward a 'better' future. Indeed, one of the key dynamics of modernity is the continuous transformation of present time by cultural and political designs for the future. This dynamic, linked to the scientific idea of the arrow of time moving inexorably second-by-second, means that change and interconnectivity become seen as related in processes in the task of making the future. Being left behind or isolated and unconnected (all temporal-spatial metaphors) become 'obviously' bad conditions to be avoided. This dynamic makes it hard to sustain good development, which sometimes entails keeping things the same or slowing down the connectivity imperative.

A further point is that ideologies tend to draw upon an assumed connection between modern time/space and globalizing processes to project their truth claims. These claims link together such concepts as 'connectivity', 'progress', 'development', 'growth', 'efficiency', and 'just-in-time'. They are not just any words. They are temporal-spatial concepts that are used to promote mainstream social change. In this context, concerns about sustainability and vulnerability mingle with extraordinary claims about the renewing capacity of technologies. It is part a general consciousness of modernity that arose as a vision that human beings can create social life in a new image. Our argument here is not to criticize change or connectivity per se. It is to challenge the uninterrogated dominance of either 'change for change's sake' or 'connectivity for connectivity's sake' that is seen as essentially good, simply because it involves change.

With the emerging dominance of the global imaginary, 'the city' has become *the* hotspot of change and connectivity (Sassen, 2001). Urban life now signifies a *world* of changing connections and openings. While particular nation-states and federated polities continue to legislate for each city's day-to-day activities, the feeling is that the city is post-national, legitimately connected to a global network of possibilities. A global city is now its own centre within a globalizing network, just as it provides spaces for individual movement and connectivity. Modern spaces from cities to nation-states remain territorialized and marked by abstract lines on maps – with places drawn in by our own histories.

At the same time, however, modern embodiment has become an individualized project used to project a choosing connected self. This self can choose to live in this locality or not. As modern epistemology (the nature of knowing) becomes an act of analytically dismembering and re-synthesizing information, our faith in the information technologies thus tends to redoubles despite massive evidence that this faith got us into trouble in the first place. Hence the idea of the 'Smart City' abounds. Unfortunately it is unthinkingly tied in practice to a form of modernism that is associated with the dominance of capitalist production relations, commodity and finance exchange, and techno-science. None of these processes have a glowing record in relation to sustainability questions. However, in the context of such a *world* of possibilities this record matters less than what frames our ideas, ideologies and imaginaries. Just as there may be multiple intelligences, not just IQ, so there are multiple ways of being 'smart', not only by putting in massive and complicated IT systems of abstract connectivity.

Concluding Remarks

Where do we go from here? A number of writers from Jane Jacobs (1961) and Richard Sennett (1994) to David Harvey (2013) and Sharon Zukin (2010) have argued that contemporary cities – rather than becoming just spaces of abstract connectivity – need to be built in such a way as to encourage enriching forms of embodied friction between different peoples. They argue that social life needs to return to the streets as more than simulated or commodified authenticity. Locals and strangers should rub shoulders – sometimes perhaps uncomfortably – as they move through in locally defined *places*. While agreeing with this vision, our argument presented here goes further by calling for the deepening of reflexively understood 'ontological friction'. What we mean is a creative facilitation of positive and painful intersections of engagement, which allow for different ontological orientations to be present in the same place. As Fry (2012) has emphasized, this includes our relationships to fellow human beings as well as to nature. The establishment of modern town square and the creation of urban commons – Tahrir Square in Egypt, Taksim Square in Turkey, Tiananmen Square in Beijing, Shahbagh Square in Dhaka, or Washington Square in New York – represent a necessary yet minimal condition of positive connectivity. To be sure, we have seen how such urban commons provide the setting for both short-lived political revolutions and quiet, relaxing family afternoons in the park. But the politics of the town square tends to remain largely one-dimensional. In the context of complex globalization, the urban project must dive much deeper.

Designing creative ontological connectivity – rather than just abstracted connectivity – entails building localities in a way that explicitly and reflexively recognizes ontological difference across different social formations, such as between relations of customary tribalism, cosmological traditionalism, constructivist modernism and relativizing postmodernism. It entails allowing various ontological frictions to play themselves out across the society-nature continuum. Local public spaces should facilitate people 'rubbing shoulders', but good design and positive engagement should also explicitly take into account the different ontological meanings that 'rubbing shoulders' or 'confronting nature' have for different people. In short, it is not globalizing connectivity per se that is either the problem or the answer. Rather, it is we submit that modern conceptions of 'connectivity' have come to overwhelm all other ways and modes of living in local places.

Acknowledgements

We want to thank the Australian Research Council (ARC) for generously funding research related to this chapter with a 2012–14 Discovery Grant (DP120100159): 'Globalization and the Formation of Meaning: The Career of a Concept'.

References

Appadurai, A. 1996. *Modernity At Large: Cultural Dimensions of Globalization*. Minneapolis, University of Minnesota Press.
Beck, U. 2003. 'Toward a New Critical Theory with Cosmopolitan Intent'. *Constellations* 10(4): 453–68.
Beck, U., A. Giddens, and S. Lash. 1994. *Reflexive Modernization: Politics, Tradition and Aesthetics in the Modern Social Order*. Stanford: Stanford University Press.
Bobbio, N. 1988. *Liberalism & Democracy*. London: Verso.
Bourdieu, P. 1990. *The Logic of Practice*. Cambridge: Polity Press.
Bouteligier, S. 2012. *Cities, Networks, and Global Environmental Governance: Spaces of Innovation, Places of Leadership*. New York: Routledge.
Brugman, J. 2009. *Welcome to the Urban Revolution: How Cities are Changing the World*. University of St Lucia: Queensland Press.
Castells, M. 2010. *The Rise of the Network Society*, 2nd edn, Cambridge: Blackwell Publishing.
Castoriadis, C. 1991. *The Imaginary Constitution of Society*. Cambridge: Polity Press.
van Dijck, J. 2013. *The Culture of Connectivity: A Critical History of the Social Media*. Oxford: Oxford University Press.
Freeden, M. 1996. *Ideologies and Political Theory*. Oxford: Oxford University Press.
Friedman, T. 2005. *The World is Flat: A Brief history of the Twentieth Century*. New York: Farrar, Straus and Giroux.
Fry, T. 2012. *Becoming Human by Design*. London: Berg.
Gallie, W. 1955, 'Essentially Contested Concepts'. *Proceedings of the Aristotelian Society* 56(1): 167–198.
Gleeson, B. 2010. *Lifeboat Cities*. Sydney: University of New South Wales Press.
Harvey, D. 2013. *Rebel Cities: From the Right to the City to the Urban Revolution*. London: Verso.
Jacobs, J., M. 1961. *The Death and Life of Great American Cities*. New York: Random House.
James, P. 1996. *Nation Formation: Towards a Theory of Abstract Community*. London: Sage.
James, P. 2006. *Globalism, Nationalism, Tribalism: Bringing Theory back in*. London: Sage.

Latour, B. 2010. 'Networks, Societies, Spheres: Reflections of an Actor Network Theorist'. Keynote speech for the International Seminar on Network Theory: Network Multidimensionality in the Digital Age. http://www.bruno-latour.fr/sites/default/files/121-CASTELLS-GB.pdf.

Lefort, C. 1986. *The Political Forms of Modern Society*. Cambridge: Polity Press.

Metzinger, T. 2010. *The Ego Tunnel: The Science of the Mind and the Myth of the Self*. New York: Basic Books.

Pocock, M., G. van Rheenen, and D. McConnell. 2005. *The Changing Face of World Missions*. Grand Rapids: Baker Academic.

Quartiroli, I. 2011. *The Digitally Divided Self: Relinquishing Our Awareness of the Internet*. Milano: Silens.

Robertson, R. 1992. *Globalization: Social Theory and Global Culture*. London: Sage.

Sassen, S. 2001. *The Global City: New York, London, Tokyo*, 2nd edn, Princeton: Princeton University Press.

Sennett, R. 1994. *Flesh and Stone: The Body and the City in Western Civilization*. London: Faber and Faber.

Spencer, J.H. 2014. *Globalization and Urbanization: The Global Urban Ecosystem*. Lanham: Rowman & Littlefield.

Steger, M.B. 2008. *The Rise of the Global Imaginary: Political Ideologies from the French Revolution to the Global War on Terror*. Oxford: Oxford University Press.

Steger, M.B. 2009. *Globalisms: The Great Ideological Struggle of the Twenty-First Century*, 3rd edn, Lanham: Rowman and Littlefield.

Steger, M.B. 2013. 'It's About Globalization, After All: Four Framings of Global Studies'. *Globalizations* 10(6): 771–7.

Steger, M.B., and P. James. 2013. 'Levels of Subjective Globalization: Ideologies, Imaginaries, Ontologies'. *Perspectives on Global Development and Technology* 12(1–2): 17–40.

Steger, M.B., J. Goodman, and E.K. Wilson. 2013. *Justice Globalism: Ideology, Crises, Policy*. London: Sage.

Taylor, C. 2004. *Modern Social Imaginaries*. Durham, NC: Duke University Press.

Taylor, C. 2007. *A Secular Age*. Cambridge, MA: Harvard University Press.

Taylor, P.J., P. Fei Ni, B. Derudder, M. Hoyler, J. Huang, and F. Witlox (eds). 2011. *Global Urban Analysis: A Survey of Cities in Globalization*. London: Earthscan.

Tomlinson, J. 1999. *Globalization and Culture*. Cambridge: Polity Press.

Wilson, E., and M.B. Steger. 'Religious Globalisms in the Post-Secular Age'. *Globalizations* 10(3): 481–95.

Zukin, S. 2010. *Naked City: The Death and Life of Authentic Urban Places*. Oxford: Oxford University Press.

Chapter 3
Connectivity and Consciousness: How Globalities are Constituted through Communication Flows

Barrie Axford

Patterns of global connectivity through communication can tell us a great deal about the changing nature of social interaction and the very idea of sociality. They depict a world in process and of ties, both fleeting and long term, afforded and established through such intertwining. There is no *a priori* reason to assume that the processes spawn atomized individuals and selves cut adrift from collective consciousness, although much commentary assumes all manner of social pathology. In what follows I will look at ways in which the creation of diverse publics and communities of interest and affect across borders is possible through digital technologies and formats, taking shape in ways framed by them. This area of discussion is crucial for understanding how globalization proceeds and for how globalities are possible.

The concept of globality is often used to denote the emergence of a single socio-political space on a planetary scale. But this depiction can be problematic, implying singularity and systematic integration achieved through linear processes of globalization. In more nuanced definitions it musters as a possible outcome, or an immanent potential, and thus offers a less demanding take on what constitutes evidence for global systemness.

For many observers globalization implies connectivity and exchange, with connectivity as a necessary, though not sufficient, measure of globality. Globality subsists in both practices and consciousness (Shaw, 1999), but what are the referents? In one account globality resides in 'thick economic, political and cultural interconnections and global flows that make currently existing political borders and economic barriers irrelevant' and that is entirely plausible (Steger, 2005, p. 13). But as I have noted elsewhere, looking for 'thick' associations to approximate the ontologies of national and societal imaginaries may be too skewed towards territorialist and societalist assumptions about the natural spaces of civic association and emotional attachment to provide a purchase on emergent globalities (Axford, 2012, 2013; Shaw, 1999).

Nonetheless, a strong definition of globality as consciousness opines that it comprises a 'self-consciously common framework of human society worldwide' (Shaw, 1999, p. 62). This gloss is prefigured in the universalist claims of both religious and, in the case of cosmopolitanism, secular world views. Robertson and Inglis argue that the notion of globality is applicable where 'the world is taken as a whole, where all parts of the global are seen as increasingly interconnected and where individual experience is connected to worldwide forces and circumstances' (2008, p. 23; Robertson, 2011). Which nicely conjoins spatial, cognitive and affective elements of global experience, even where global, or world-wide, is not equivalent to planetary compass.

So, the concept of globality speaks of worlds and a sense of worlds beyond mere connection and simple spatial referents (Axford, 2012). Most pertinent to this chapter, it is a concept that admits cognitions, interactions and sentiments of actors as these are imbricated with the 'indifferent globalities' of information technology (Hird, 2010; Clark, 2005). But indifferent globalities – in this case technologies with global reach – are worrying because in some accounts they are held to subsist apart from, or to display a 'logic' not predicated on, human mediation.

Any careful treatment of how globalities are made must look to the engagements between social and conscious and biophysical and technological (Clark, 2005) to comprehend an 'indelibly interconnected biosphere' (Hird, 2010, p. 62). Only then can we make sense of what Bernard Latour calls the biospheric 'parliament of things' that is certainly comprised of human domains, consciousness and actions, but whose totality is not limited to them (2000, p. 144).

Here I want to entertain concepts – connectivity through communication and consciousness, as well as mediatization – that should inform any theory of emergent globalities. The allusion to technological varieties of globality highlights the need to go beyond charting connections to explore cognition and affect on the part of situated and mobile actors, whose very constitution is indelibly tied to communication and communication technologies; all without reducing the actor to a passive recipient of media output and in slave to its aesthetics and protocols. Such an approach does not privilege actors at the expense of structures, or vice-versa, because it reveals the mutual constitution that takes place through the routine entanglement of human agents with communication technologies, especially the soft technologies of the Internet.

Globalization theory already accommodates the idea of mutual constitution (see Krucken and Drori, 2009). Here I want to endorse that argument and the extent to which some emergent globalities are comprehensible only by reference to the ways in which digital, social worlds enable actors to move in and through spaces in ways that transform time and consciousness. This is not simply a matter of examining the increasingly invisible interfaces between humans and hard/soft information technologies; or it is not just that. Rather, it is recognition that cultural structures are not external to actors but built into social practices, thus constituting them. Even the seemingly 'indifferent globalities' immanent in digital technologies are not so indifferent after all, but infected and inflected by human agency. Running through this, to paraphrase Castells, is the thesis that social life now takes place in the frame of media, though without the determination implied by that claim and largely without the moral ambivalence that informs it (2000).

Analytical and Empirical Domains

I will rehearse my argument about the constitution of emergent globalities by looking at the constitution of digital worlds in three analytical and empirical domains and by way of different exemplars. All afford insights into world-making practices. The domains are:

1. the creation of *global microstructures*, as coined by systems theorist Karin Knorr-Cetina (2007). Global microstructures in areas such as terrorism, diaspora and financial markets present some problems for the analyst seeking the raw materials of globality, because they clearly demonstrate relational connectivity heedless of borders, but may not be enough to 'effectively organize complex systems' (2007, p. 68). At the same time, they capture the extent to which globalities are often cohered, not to say constituted, by information technologies as important capillaries of global connectedness.
2. Certain instances and features of the '*logic of connective action*' as coined by Lance Bennett in his reworking of Mancur Olson's seminal thesis on the rules governing political mobilization, activism and membership when playing out a logic of *collective* action (Bennett and Soderberg, 2012; Olson, 1965). In particular, Bennett's account of the organization-less qualities of Internet activism seen, for example, in the *Occupy* movement, *Los Indignados* and across North Africa and the Middle East in recent years, bears on the prospects for solidarity and community away from, or not predicated on, models of society and community as stable forms of organization.
3. The idea of '*networked individualism*'. Along with other writers in this genre, Barry Wellman and his co-authors argue that massive social change is not only occurring at the interpersonal level but at the organizational, inter-organizational and even the world-systems and global levels. He discerns a 'move from densely-knit and tightly-bounded groups to sparsely-knit and loosely-bounded networks' (2003, p. 3; Beck and Beck-Gernsheim, 2002). Networked individualism has Internet use in a positive feedback loop with the shift from 'solidary, local, hierarchical groups and towards fragmented, partial, heavily communicating social networks' (Wellman et al. 2003). Wellman's research also details the 'social affordances' available through Internet connection and these underscore the sense of boundaries being shifted.

As we shall see, the idea of networked individualism does not, or need not, imply what Žižek calls 'a mechanistic, false individualism' (1998, p. 6) because Internet gatherings may be at least a trope for collective consciousness when they provide a virtual congregation where individuals muster and yet still carry out everyday rituals of subjectivity. It will be pertinent to examine variations on this theme to see how global consciousness subsists in technological and cultural environments that privilege the expression of personal narratives and vernacular experiences, but are modal at the same time.

Before coming to these analytical and empirical domains, I want to look a little more closely at the key concepts that structure this chapter. I have rehearsed globality, but will now expand on the themes of global consciousness, communicative connectivity and mediatization, the better to comprehend a highly contested discourse about world-making practices.

Consciousness – Global Consciousness

Of course, globality cannot be taken as a synonym for global consciousness, leaving aside the normative implications that are bundled with the idea. But the concept of consciousness is integral to the idea of globality despite its elusiveness. Stripped down, consciousness refers to an individual's ability to know and perceive. Through consciousness individuals have knowledge of the external world and of themselves. Consciousness does not, of itself, imply affect, although the expression is often used transitively to suggest 'conscious of .... x' in a way that predicates meaning.

And this is clearly the case with the idea of global consciousness, where the burden of address is that actors – as individuals and collectively – are not only aware of global condition(s), of global constraints and so on, but respond to that knowledge emotionally, as well as thorough an evaluation of how best to subsist in such circumstances. In other words, they have adopted a global mentality.

With this in mind Martin Shaw defines the global as a 'common consciousness of human society on a world scale: an increasing awareness of the totality of human social relations as the largest constitutive framework of all relations' and that seems apposite (2003, p. 146). In related vein, Jonathan Friedman argues that an analytical focus on globality as a constitutive framework for consciousness and action entails 'a theoretical framework within which the institutional structures of the world are themselves generated and reproduced through global processes' (2000, p. 142). In both accounts globality and consciousness are reflexively linked, but is this primarily through a kind of empathy, whereby all humanity has a built-in predilection for social understanding and social cooperation? Or is there room for the possibility that global awareness produces not empathy or any sense of intimacy – perhaps triggered by recognition and acceptance of shared fates – but identities in conflict and woundingly agonistic politics? Furthermore, is consciousness the same thing as imagination?

Pertinently, Shani Orgad talks about the 'global imagination' afforded through a variety of media representations in texts, images and discourses that 'travel across cultural and national boundaries' and whose meaning and significance may be transformed when appropriated by people in other cultures (2012, p. 39). The key question here, and one increasingly exercising media theorists, is how media representations that circulate in global public space feed and influence individual and collective imaginations (Orgad 2012; Taylor, 2002)? I will return to this matter below.

These distinctions are useful because they point up the ways in which the term consciousness is used and the room for obfuscation that attends its use. At one remove we are talking about individual awareness and choice, along with the opportunities afforded for the construction and articulation of self-narratives. At another, consciousness refers to a state of affairs, a backdrop to everyday behaviour and an institutionalized constraint on, or impetus to, certain kinds of action. In the latter guise we can advert a basic tenet of world-polity theory that emphasizes the socio-cultural character of the global system (Meyer, 2007, p. 262). In this scenario the very existence of a world polity is premised on evidence of widespread and growing cultural consciousness of what John Meyer calls 'civic virtue' on a world scale. The latter springs from an awareness of interdependence or shared risk – and thus vulnerability – when faced with the potential for outbreaks of 'destructive inhumanity' seen in the twentieth century (Meyer, 2007, p. 233).

Awareness on this scale is unlikely to produce the same ontological 'thickness' or sense of community and identity ascribed to national varieties of culture. The adoption of cultural norms by different actors, different societies, is not the much-rehearsed story of how 'a people' can be formed out of a common, imagined past, *pace* Anderson (1983). Rather, the idea of world culture or world society suggests a more fragile or possibly 'thinner', but still compelling, source of legitimacy and motivation whereby, increasingly, people believe they live in one world under universally valid and applicable standards or norms. The global isomorphism written about by world-polity theorists is expressed through forms of institutionalized consciousness.

Communicative Connectivity

Much of the academic literature on connectivity as well as a good deal of research on globalization, focuses on communicative connectivity. This focus embraces communication between agents who are co-present in the same physical space and various types of mediated communication that permit interaction not reliant on co-presence. Unlike systems-theoretic models (Luhmann, 1990) communication is the bridge between subjects and thus subvents a model of consciousness, while communicative dialogue is key to the growth of an increasingly modal cultural consciousness of global interdependence and of personal and collective embeddedness in world society.

But to give any such proposition analytical purchase we have to demonstrate that communication 'carries content'; that is, can provide for both inter-discursivity and shared meanings (Thomas, 2009, p. 116). Empirically, the focus must be on the ways in which digital communication technologies enable us to surmise and relocate distant contexts and relate to people, things and events that are remote from, even alien to, our everyday lives (Orgad, 2012). As Shani Orgad notes, this focus also pushes us to consider the prospects for 'mediated intimacy' or some trope for it, perhaps in the voguish language of 'friends' or 'likes', and it privileges the construction of *self*-narratives. This is not as damaging to the search for expressions of *modal* consciousness as it might seem, because when examining the imaginaries afforded by the Internet, we can see the scope for making (and changing) both individual and collective narratives. We can also trace the entanglements of indifferent technologies with subjectivities in a process of mutual constitution.

Mediatization

To do so requires attention to the ontology of thoroughly mediatized societies and cultures. Mediatization is the extent to which communication technologies play an increasing part in the framing and constitution of individual narratives and collective experiences. John Tomlinson writes of those 'impatient and immoderate' media that facilitate immediacy, even intimacy, by offering instant and increasingly bespoke delivery (2007, p. 231). Without giving way to technological determinism or media-centrism (Ampuja, 2012) it could be said that such technologies frame how we engage with them and each other by promoting and embodying the value of speed, immediacy and bespoke consumption as cultural aesthetics.

Of course the Internet, and especially the Web, is only one facet of the systematic *telemediatization* of culture. It is, however, an increasingly important facet when assessing the impact of connectivity on the personalization of communication and when weighing the density and impact of trans-border connections on social practices. Paul Virilio's corrosive take on this pattern of social-technical change has it that machines, including the hardware and cultural software of media technologies, increasingly constitute our environments (1991). Even in less brooding interpretations, engagements between human and machine cross the seeming boundaries of technical and social to comprise a world 'always in process', indeterminate (Leyshon and Thrift,1997, p. 126).

Understood thus the concept carries weighty baggage and encourages transformative thinking, some of it quite pessimistic. Previously, I noted Žižek's ambivalence over Internet culture as 'this neo-Jungian idea that we live in an age of mechanistic, false individualism' (1998). Yet he too discerns a possible mutation whereby by cyber-connection predicates the emergence of a 'collective mind', and 'thinking humanity' is freed from the confines of an organic body. Typically, his view can be read as either critique or approbation. For Hardt and Negri the production of things is increasingly overtaken by the production of information; and the production of information is dispersed and bespoke (2000, p. 51).

Recent media theory sometimes links the idea of collective consciousness to the rise of the Internet as a factor in the creation of global society. Indeed this may be what Žižek is prescribing. Consciousness, as discussed above, and the mutual constitution of human agency and non-human technologies holds the analytical key to any such prescription, primarily because the advent of Web-2 technologies and formats facilitates the 'return of the human' to networked information and communication technology. The return is afforded through blogs, vlogs, social network sites, app development, photo-sharing, video-sharing remixes, mash-ups; all evidence of content generation, circulation and making and distributing new applications (Dean, 2013). Let me turn to how this plays out in consideration of our three selected analytical and empirical domains.

Analytical and Empirical Domains

Global Microstructures: Connectivity and Consciousness in Financial Trading and Terrorist Networks

Attempts to demonstrate that communication 'carries content' in the sense I described earlier find valuable corroborative evidence in the sociology of financial markets and the recent academic engagement with financial sociology more generally (Knorr-Cetina and Preda, 2005). This work utilizes largely ethnographic research techniques to examine the sociological character of global information technologies. In 2002, Knorr-Cetina and Bruegger coined the serviceable concept of *global microstructures* to construe the duality of Internet technology systems as 'sequentially and culturally specific social actions performed repeatedly at a global distance' (Knorr-Cetina and Bruegger, 2002, p. 921). They were at pains to stress that the cross-national / global fields of transaction so described are at most proto networks – more like horizontal associations or intersubjective association and 'rich' and 'textured' communities – not systems of governance and rational structures of bureaucracy. Global microstructures are also institutionally light and, because they are digitally constituted, able to achieve global penetration quickly and cheaply. In short they constitute 'fields of practice' and should not be mistaken for complex institutional structures. (Knorr-Cetina, 2004, p. 214).

Financial micro-global structures are obviously elements in the re-spatialization of economic life and they are also based on 'temporalization', the continuous, iterative, 24-hour cycle of time zones that, in this sector at least, has replaced the linear rationality of modern institutional structures. At the same time financial markets still show 'a level of intersubjectivity that derives from the character of these markets as reflexively observed by participants in temporal continuity, synchronicity and immediacy' (Knorr-Cetina, 2005, p. 217). This is a telling observation, one that underscores the notion of 'carrying content'. For traders in financial markets all kinds of quotidian social forms, including conversation, remain important media for global transactions. In other words the routines practiced by market traders go far beyond connection and the exchange of information.

The ethnographic practices observed by Knorr-Cetina and her co-researchers reveal highly textured social systems and an environment reliant for its dynamism and success on creating and sustaining intersubjective, reciprocal relationships between traders. In financial markets trust is crucial for the functioning of the market and this comprises inter-personal as well as institutional reciprocity. Here we have a classic instance of what could be seen as technical and post-social interactions actually retaining features of routine and cohering sociality. Consciousness, even collective consciousness pervades, and local and global, social and technical, human and non-human agency cease to be antinomies, but are mutually constituted. Of course what we could be seeing is little more than imitative behaviour, 'thick' only in the instrumental sense that it is necessary to avoid the destruction or decay of the circuits of global finance. The melding of personal, and often instrumental or strategic, narratives with institutional mission and logic demarcate a global field that, in turn, relies on a form of collective consciousness to subsist.

When discussing terrorist networks, Knorr-Cetina identifies a quite different kind of emergent globality and global ecology, but one no less reliant upon consciousness. Like networks of financial traders and brokers, contemporary terrorist activity demonstrates virtualization of organization. Virtualization has four characteristics. First is the development of relationships with a wide range of potential partners, each having a particular competency that complements the others. Second, virtual organizing utilizes the mobility and responsiveness of information and communication technologies to overcome distance. Third, timing is a key aspect of relationships, with actors using responsiveness and availability to decide between strategic courses of action. Finally there must be trust between actors separated in space. Here too the alleged post-social implications of virtualization and mediatization – a loss of affect and disengagement from immediate experience – does not seem to apply even to agile networks of terrorists who are very dispersed and yet display a rude collective spirituality which looks like a variant of collective consciousness.

Mediatized cultures rely increasingly on 'visual images, stylistic connotations and symbolic associations' to comprise a world more and more in process (Gruneau and Wilson, 1993, p. 137). The current gloss on this eminently plausible account of mediatized global cultural economy turns on the role of scopic media in spanning and compressing the world. Scopic media are mainly screen-based technologies of observation and projection that 'render distant and invisible phenomena situationally present, unfold remote spaces and information worlds, and shift the boundaries between situation/system and the environment' (Knorr-Cetina, 2002, p. 83). Knorr-Cetina's more radical and contentious take on such developments is that scopic media transform social interaction into synthetic interaction, replacing face-to-face relations by face-to-screen relations and other forms of social coordination by scopic forms of coordination. Critically, the world becomes more visual and informational rather than material or natural.

The Logic of Connective Action

A variant of this theme is apparent in the part played by Internet technologies and platforms in political mobilization (Bennett and Soderberg, 2012). For the most part the empirical focus has been on network formation, sustainability and decay as afforded through social networking sites (SNSs) such as Twitter. These investigations challenge much received wisdom about the basis for collective action and collective identity formation, shedding new light on the links between online networks, social contagion and collective dynamics. The empirical detail of this growing body of work both underwrites and qualifies claims that platforms like FaceBook, Twitter and Reddit are helping to fashion, and themselves become, vehicles for global collective consciousness (see, for example, Axford, 2011). Once again, the key point is that sustained protests that are using digital media engage in activities far beyond simple despatch and receipt of messages. Rather they engage participants in a form of intersubjectivity and a sense of collective endeavour. Lance Bennett's work on alternative models of collective action suggests a possibly modal shift from group-based to network-based association as a new model of social movements; one that demonstrates the logic of *connective* action.

Received wisdom on the logic of sustainable and effective *collective* action assumes that it is essential to have formal organizations that coordinate action, mobilize resources and forge collective identities. But the logic of *connective* action suggests that participation becomes self-motivating as personally expressive content is shared with, and recognized by, others who, in turn, repeat these networked sharing activities. When interpersonal networks are enabled by technology platforms that coordinate and scale the networks, the resulting actions look like collective action, but without formal organization or the need for social identification. These action frames are successful because they offer easy-to-personalize identity frames (for example, 'we are the 99%') where anyone is invited to tell their own story within the frame. They also differ from collective action frames because they do not require identification shifts but let individuals express their own persona. Social media enable these frames and stories to be shared – where shared can mean no more than made visible – easily and, of course, extensively.

While the range of possible large-scale actions is not exhausted by such developments, the appearance of what Bennett calls 'self-organizing networks' – of which Occupy Wall Street is a prime example – is discommoding to the familiar logic of collective action that is reliant on strong organizational coordination and often requires firm ideological identification on the part of activists. Between the two poles is the 'organizationally enabled network' and, for example, it is this in-between variety that characterizes action-networks extant in the G20 protests in recent years. Organizationally enabled networks only loosely coordinate action. Action frames may be instigated by organizations but, crucially, they include personal frames. In G20 protests many people not affiliated with traditional organizations and NGOs felt able to submit their personal stories under inclusive and ideologically neutral, or unthreatening, themes, such as 'put people first'.

When messages circulate to diverse networks two kinds of action frames are available: personal (send your own message) and collective (sign up to *our* message, as in 'Eat the bankers'). In digitally networked actions the *meme* is the basic unit of communication. Memes – 'genes on the cultural side' – are shared through imitation and adapted to personal emotional expression. In turn these are passed on to others who imitate, adopt and share. Twitter and FaceBook are exemplary carriers of this kind of meme.

Bennett notes that there are two kinds of memes: inclusive personal memes and exclusive collective memes. The former, memes containing personal action frames, travel farther and are less culturally loaded because they are inflections of personal narratives, while the stories told can still become coherent and expressive of collective consciousness as people share similar experiences. Exclusive collective memes, that is, memes containing collective action frames, also travel as memes, but they are more likely to run up against barriers at the intersections of social networks defined by established political organizations, ideologies, class, gender, race, ethnicity and national identities.

Networked Individualism

Collective consciousness expressed thus and carried through Internet platforms may look like the random meeting of singular wills, or as Myra Hird says, 'a cacophony of different spirits and personalities' (2010, p. 58). Yet media theorists sometimes link the notion of Internet-mediated collective consciousness with the creation of a truly global society. My first two analytical and empirical domains suggest that if the claim has any validity it must reside in the extent to which messages carry meaning in networks of communication that often privilege self-narratives as a way of mapping and sharing experience. If true, this is a considerable insight into the possibilities for establishing a trope for society beyond the territorial state, pushing analysts to pay greater attention to the processes of ongoing communication as these mimic and reproduce, but crucially also transcend, the usual borders around cognition, affect and identity (Bechmann and Stehr, 2002).

My final domain essays more of this line of thinking, mainly in relation to the prospects for a global society trope in the guise of an increasingly modal networked individualism. Barry Wellman's research details the 'social affordances' available through Internet connection and the new political and social ecologies constituted through connection. The key affordances are *always being connected* or having the capacity so to be; the *personalization of communication*, such that 'the ensuing interactions are more tailored to individual preferences and needs, furthering a more individualized way of interacting and a way of mobilizing as fluid networks of partial commitment' and *globalized connectivity*, where this allows transnational linkages of different kinds. Again, this does not imply passivity on the part of the actor. As Roy Williams notes, 'affordances are not "in" the environment, but "in" your interaction with it' (2012, p. 3).

Wellman offers some compelling insights into how global affordances actually work in his accounts of Twitter as a social networking phenomenon and a trope for received ideas about community and identity (2011). He argues that the notion of 'community' has often been caught in a tension between concrete social relationships deemed as authentic and imagined sets of people perceived to be similar. The success of the Internet has refocused our attention on this tension. Pre-Twitter, the Internet enabled people who know each other to use social media – from e-mail to Facebook – to interact without meeting physically. 'Into this mix came Twitter, an asymmetric micro-blogging service: If you follow me, I do not have to follow you' (Gruzd et al., 2011, p. 1298). Connections on Twitter are not reliant on in-person contact, and many users have many more followers than they actually know. Yet, he argues, there is a possibility that Twitter can form the basis of interlinked personal communities and even foster and sustain a sense of community.

This benign and up-beat take on the social consequences of social-networking receives endorsement from various sources, some anecdotal and highly speculative, others based on rigorous research. Writing in the online publication *Bitcoin Trader* of February 5 2012, an anonymous correspondent opines 'in the last year or so, platforms like Facebook, Twitter, and Reddit have begun to demonstrate that they are incredible tools for enabling the global collective consciousness'. He/she goes on, 'Don't let stories of social media "addiction" shame you into stepping away from your computer. There's nothing wrong with fulfilling a desire to be part of something bigger than yourself'. In more authoritative vein on more-or-less the same issues, researchers for the UCL Global Social Media Project offer a gloss on Wellman's thesis of networked individualism and on the tendency to treat the idea as predicating the death of family bonds, a sense of ethnicity and of civility. Their work shows that in many parts of the world this is not happening. Collective signifiers such as family or ethnicity remain hugely important. Virtual attachments should not be seen as residual and, when viewed in the light of lives lived, in part, through media, they need not erode more visceral ties.

Conclusion

Lest we see all this as affording only abstract publics and an ersatz form of publicness or sociality, witness the occasions when virtual connection and virtual affect are indelibly linked to the ability of people (world citizens?) to appropriate meaning and 'gather' at – some phenomenal public space, as well as to mark out the terrain of previously un-thought of virtual communal spaces on the Internet. In my view such happenings have to be construed as instances of global consciousness and indicative of emergent globalities, even where they rehearse the familiar tensions between local and global. The 'synthetic situations' (Knorr-Cetina, 2009) described in this chapter are avatars of global complexity, the expression of connectivity and consciousness.

References

Ampuja, M. 2012. 'Globalization Theory, Media-Centrism and Neo-Liberalism: A Critique of Recent Intellectual Trends'. *Critical Sociology* 38(2): 281–301.

Anderson, B. 1983. *Imagined Communities*. London: Verso.
Axford, B. 2012. 'Mere Connection: Do Communication Flows Compensate for the Lack of World Society?'. in *Neue Grenzen des Sozialen Zwischen Globalisierung, Erkenntnis und Ästhetik*, edited by G. Peter and K. Reuss-Markus, pages. Springer VS-Springer Fachmedien Wiesbaden (VS-Verlag).
Axford, B. 2013. *Theories of Globalization*. Cambridge: Polity.
Bechmann, G., and N. Stehr. 2002. 'The Legacy of Niklas Luhmann'. *Society* 39 (Jan./Feb.): 67–75.
Beck, U., and E. Beck-Gernsheim. 2002. *Individualization: Institutionalized Individualism and its Social and Political Consequences*. London: Sage.
Beck, U., and N. Sznaider. 2006. 'Unpacking Cosmopolitanism for the Social Sciences: A Research Agenda'. *British Journal of Sociology* 57(1): 1–23.
Bennett, L., and A. Soderberg. 2012. *The Logic of Connective Action: Digital Media and the Personalization of Contentious Politics*. Cambridge: Cambridge University Press.
Castells, M. 2000. *The Rise of the Network Society: The Information Age: Economy, Society and Culture Vol. I*. 2nd edition. Cambridge, MA; Oxford, UK: Blackwell.
Clark, N. 2005. 'Ex-orbitant Globality'. *Theory, Culture & Society* 22(5): 165–85.
Dean, J. 2013. 'The Real Internet'. *International Journal of Zizek Studies* 4(1): 1–19.
Friedman, J. 2000. *Modernities, Class and the Contradictions of Globalization*. Walnut Creek: Altamira Press.
Gruneau, R., and D. Witson. 1993. *Hockey Night in Canada*. Toronto, Ontario: Garamond Press.
Gruzd, A., B. Wellman, and Y. Takhteyev. 2011. 'Imagining Twitter as an Imagined Community'. *American Behavioral Scientist* 55(10): 1294–318.
Hardt, M., and A. Negri. 2000. *Empire*. Cambridge MA: Harvard University Press.
Hird, M.J. 2010. 'Indifferent Globality: Gaia, Symbiosis and 'Other Worldliness'. *Theory, Culture and Society* 27(2–3): 54–72.
Knorr-Cetina, K. 2007. 'Microglobalization'. In *Frontiers of Globalization Research: Theoretical and Methodological approaches*, edited by I. Rossi, 65–93. New York: Springer.
Knorr-Cetina, K., and Bruegger, U. 2002. Traders' Engagement with Markets: A Postsocial Relationship. *Theory Culture Society*, 19(5–6): 161–85.
Knorr-Cetina, K. 2009. 'The Synthetic Situation: Interactionism for a Global World. *Symbolic Interactionism* 32(1): 61–87.
Krücken, G., and G.S. Drori (eds). 2009. *World Society: The Writings of John W. Meyer*. Oxford: Oxford University Press.
Latour, B. 2000. *We Have Never Been Modern*. Cambridge, MA: Harvard University Press.
Leyshon, A., and N. Thrift. 1997. *Money/Space: geographies of monetary transformation*. London and New York: Routledge.

Luhmann, N. 1990. *Die Wissenschaft der Gesellschaft*, Frankfurt: Suhrkamp (English translation of chapter 10: 'The Modernity of Science', *New German Critique* 61 (1994): 9–23.

Meyer, J.W. 2007. 'Globalization: Theory and Trends'. *International Journal of Comparative Sociology* 48 (4–5): 261–73.

Olson, M. Jr. 1965. *The Logic of Collective Action: Public Goods and the Theory of Groups*. Cambridge: Harvard University Press.

Orgad, S. 2012. *Media Representation and the Global Imagination*. Cambridge: Polity.

Robertson, R. 2011. 'Global Connectivity and Global Consciousness'. *American Behavioral Scientist* 55(10): 1336–45.

Robertson, R., and D. Inglis. 2008. 'The Elementary Forms of Globality: Durkheim and the Emergence and Nature of Global Life'. *Journal of Classical Sociology* 8(1): 5–25.

Shaw, M. 1999. *Theory of the Global State*. Cambridge: Cambridge University Press.

Shaw, M. 2003. 'The global transformation of the social sciences'. In *Global Civil Society Yearbook 2003*, edited by H. Anheier, M. Glasius, and M. Kaldor, 35–44. Oxford: Oxford University Press.

Thomas, G. 2009. 'World Polity, World Culture, World Society'. *International Political Sociology* 3(1): 115–19.

Tomlinson, J. 2007. *The Culture of Speed: the Coming of Immediacy*. London: Sage.

Virilio, P. 1991. *Lost Dimension*. New York: Semiotext(e).

Wellman, B., A. Quan-Hasse, W. Chen, H. Hampton, I. Dias de Isla, and R. Williams. 2012. 'Affordances and the New Political Ecologies'. Unpublished paper, Department of Mathematics, University of Portsmouth.

Žižek, S. 1998. 'Hysteria and Cyberspace: Interview with U. Gutmair and C. Flor'. *Telepolis*, 7 October. www.heise.de/tp/artikel/2/2492/1.html.

Chapter 4
Globalization's Cultural Consequences Revisited

Robert J. Holton

The cultural dimensions of globalization continue to pose challenging and complex questions for social analysts. One general feature of recent debates has been increasing recognition that globalization involves multiple processes of cross-border connectivity, interdependency and cognition, rather than a unitary logic arising from economic or technological evolution. Following pioneering work by Robertson (1992), globalization has come to be seen in terms of a complex inter-section of economic, political, cultural, and technological processes, rather than the operation of a single master-process such as dominance of the capitalist world-system (Holton, 2005, 2011; Urry, 2000). At the same time there are resistances and limits to globalization (Hirst and Thompson, 1996; Scott, 1997; Rieger and Leibfried, 2003; Calhoun, 2007; Holton, 2011), as well as complex inter-sections between the global and the local, seen by Robertson (1992, 1995), Swyngedouw (1997), and Holton (2011) through the idea of glocalization.

Giddens famously saw globalization as a 'runaway world' (1999), in which global culture embodies the restless mobility of global capitalism and forms of individual reflexivity stimulated through new communications and media technology. It remains very doubtful, however, whether we can speak of a single global culture or global village. Diversities of cultural identity and practice seem too entrenched to be ignored. Borders, whether political or cultural, may be permeable by trade or electronic communication, but they have not disappeared (Rumford, 2006, 2008). Cosmopolitan openness is a significant feature of the contemporary picture (Holton, 2009), but so is nationalism and localism. Not all contemporary identities and connectivities are global in scope or aspiration, notwithstanding the triumphalist rhetoric of globe-talk and media commentary.

So what place does culture occupy in this world of complex and somewhat contradictory trends? Around 15 years ago, I was asked to contribute a paper on the 'cultural consequences of globalization' to the *Annals of the American Academy of the Political and Social Sciences* (Holton, 2000). My argument then was that the complex challenges of understanding the cultural dimensions of globalization could be best understood in terms of the co-existence and inter-action of three distinct processes: homogenization, polarization, and hybridization. None of these represented a dominant trend, nor was there any sign of a tendency towards one rather than another. Fifteen years later I now revisit this argument to determine the extent to which it still holds up. What if anything has changed in this time, and why?

Some Initial Conceptual Issues

It is useful at the outset to clarify some pressing conceptual issues. First, it is important to provide a clear sense of the way the term globalization is used here. Amongst most economists, many political activists, and social observers, globalization is taken as a primarily economic phenomena associated with market deregulation, free trade, foreign direct investment and corporate power. The effects of this economistic approach on broader social life are reflected in economic discourse (Rodrik, 2011; Milanovic, 2011), business and journalism (Matthews, 2006), and significant strands within political economy (Palan, Murphy and Chavagneux, 2010; Piketty 2014), and world system theory (Wallerstein, 1974, 1990). It is also manifest in anti-globalization protests of various kinds. In all of this globalization means economic globalization. Culture is either ignored, or regarded as a reflex of the economy.

This diverse body of work has yielded insights into relations between economy and culture. These include the idea of liberalism as the ideology of the capitalist world-system (Wallerstein, 1990), and notions of global consumerism as a form of cultural domination produced by global capitalism – epitomized as Coca-Colonization (prominent among political activists) or McDonaldization (see Ritzer, 1993, 2007) – are also widespread. Yet there is growing concern about the simplistic assumptions of economic determinism often found (or at least implied) in this literature (Sznaider and Winter, 2003; Centeno and Cohen, 2010). The economy as such does not determine everything else. Accordingly analysts have increasingly adopted a multi-dimensional or multi-disciplinary approach in which capital and markets, governments and social movements, and cultural identities and institutions interact. This does not in any way dispose of the centrality of power asymmetries in the global order associated with capitalism and the most powerful nation-states. But it has opened up a looser more flexible way of treating cultural connectivities, inter-dependencies and modes of cognition.

This broad approach is well represented in the influential work of Beck (1992, 2002, 2003), and Castells (1996, 2001, 2007, 2012). Globalization is treated by both in terms of the interplay of capitalist economic processes, forms of political action including social movements, and cultural relationships in both institutional and personal settings. Beck has a stronger feel for environmental issues linked with his theories of risk society and the second age of modernity. Castells' analysis, by contrast, is centred more on changes in information technology and contrasting forms of networked social action, including the political challenges posed by contemporary 'networks of outrage and hope' (2012).

Second, there is the vexed question of what is meant by culture. This remains one of the most confused and complicated concepts in the sociological repertoire (Williams, 1976; Eagleton 2000). Is culture, some kind of residual category of social analysis, dealing with social processes that are somehow beyond the realms of the economy (markets, finance, production and consumption), and the polity (government, policy-making and broader governance). Culture might then pertain to leisure, the arts, matters of identity and consciousness – including both high culture and popular culture. If this strategy were satisfactory then tracing globalizations' cultural consequences would be a matter of analysing how global capitalism or the international system of nation-states and elite political governance networks influence this distinct and separate cultural domain. While the legacy of economic determinism inherited from Marxism and radical political economy has not by any means vanished in analyses of global culture, there are now a range of alternatives ranging from post-structuralism, and post-modernism, post-colonialism (Said, 1978, 1993; Bhabha, 1994; Mignolo, 1999; Appadurai, 1990, 1996), feminism (Spivak, 2003), and environmentalism (Beck, 1992), to cultural Marxism (Jameson, 1991, 2007) and cultural political economy (Jessop, 2010). Meanwhile beyond this lies the work of a number of scholars influenced in various ways by Weberian and Parsonian perspectives. These include Mann and Robertson. Whereas Mann (1986), and Mann and Riley (2007) focus more on macro-sociology of power and institutions, Robertson (1992) and Giulianotti and Robertson (2009) offer more insight into micro-macro linkages as they affect identity and cognition, action and performance.

Third, it is important to emphasize that the activities we may designate as instances of globalization and culture refer to social processes that are intimately linked with each other, and which operate both as causes and consequences. This raises a number of difficulties. One is that it is arbitrary to distinguish globalization and culture as if they were separate from each other. Another is that it becomes difficult to ascribe cause and effect. For example if globalization has cultural causes rather than being the simple product of economic processes, then it can be misleading to consider cultural consequences as if their causes lay entirely outside the cultural domain.

More important is the need to disaggregate the notion of globalization into a distinct sub-set of social processes. Thus 'globalization' as such doesn't cause anything. Rather aspects of social life and institutions placed under the umbrella heading of 'globalization' may have causal consequences. For example it is not globalization per se that may or may not cause global inequality and social protest, but more particular phenomena, such as free trade, deregulation of markets, foreign direct investment, and so forth. Similarly, it is not globalization as such that causes cultural trends such as expanding Internet use, greater global environmental concern, or the proliferation of identity politics, but more particular phenomena such as increased awareness of the world as a single place, marketing strategies of corporations, and resistance to global elite politics.

Homogenization, Polarization and Hybridization

The three ways of understanding globalization's cultural consequences that I posited in 2000, are still recognizable features of current analysis. Discussions of homogenization, polarization, and hybridization have widened and deepened in the last 15 years in a number of interesting ways. But there are equally newer themes and emphases that have emerged as well as older emphases that have become more prominent.

One theme of growing importance in the analysis of global connectivities, is that of media and culture in the global order, embracing issues of communications technology and digitally mediated social media. This has both 'top down' and 'bottom up' elements. The former engages with debates about corporate power over news, forms of entertainment and representations of global processes (Artz and Kamalipour, 2003; Mirrlees, 2013). The latter links more closely with questions of personal identity formation, and with new social movements and protest networks critical of capitalism (Juris, 2005; Castells, 2012). Other themes that have grown in significance since the attack on the Twin Towers in 2001, are ideas of a global civilizational war between radical Islam and alternative forms of secular political and cultural organization (Booth and Dunne, 2002), and notions of wars around terror (Kellner, 2003, 2007) as a defining feature of contemporary life These have deepened analyses of polarization as a major trend in global culture, and raised the possibility that polarization may be emerging as the dominant global trend.

In what follows I shall look first at the three broad trends noted above to investigate how successfully they have stood up to scrutiny, and what has been added to understandings of global culture over the last 15 years. Discussion then moves to alternative ways of analysing the cultural consequences of globalization that move beyond the homogenization, polarization, and hybridization framework.

Homogenization

The concept of homogenization in culture is closely linked with that of cultural convergence, where all countries, regions, and locations subject to processes of globalization are seen as entering similar developmental pathways to common institutions, identities and ways of life. Such assumptions lay behind the much criticized arguments of post-war modernization theory. Yet this perspective thought of the world largely in terms of a system of nation-states rather than a global order in which cross-border economic, political, and cultural connectivities were central features alongside nation-states. By the late twentieth and early twenty-first century's ideas of convergence had been re-cast in a more global direction. This involved the further intensification of capitalist globalization, the clearer emergence of global elites, and the Internet revolution.

There are three broad versions of the homogenization thesis. These can be labelled as (a) global consumer capitalism (often seen as Americanization), (b) a world culture centred on political norms, and (c) Internet culture. The emphasis in much thinking in the 1980s and 1990s was on the first of these, namely global cultural convergence through the mechanisms of consumer capitalism. The focus here was on a standardized brand image projected through mass advertising, deploying more or less standardized products and services across borders, whether it be McDonalds fast foods, Apple computers, or Hollywood movies. Products were seen as standardized and so were the shopping malls and hotels which shoppers and tourists frequented, whether in Singapore, St Louis, or Sao Paulo. And underlying all this were dreams and fantasies of affluence, personal success and erotic gratification.

In much work of this kind homogenization has been seen as synonymous with Americanization (Schiller, 1976; McChesney, 1999). This term has a long history (Stead, 2001), and connects with geo-politics as much as global consumerism (Berghahn, 2010). Over the course of the 1990's, the idea that cultural globalization equals Americanization came under serious challenge as too restrictive and simplistic (Appadurai, 1990; Warner, 1994; Fantasia, 1995; Tomlinson, 1999) This was partly because consumer capitalism was very far from being dominated by US corporations, and partly because of increasing doubt that whatever the origins of corporations and marketing strategies, the mere consumption of certain commodities by people across the world, did not necessitate full assimilation into the American sensibilities or the American way of life (Friedman, 1994; Dash, 2005).

In any case, global cultural flows are multi-lateral in character, including forms of cultural imperialism that seemed to be extinguishing local cultural diversity. Even if the idea of Americanization is replaced by the broader notion of Westernization, this is still vulnerable to the same kinds of criticism since multi-lateral cultural flows take an increasing non-Western form. Cultural power may emanate from Paris or the Vatican, but it may equally emerge from Mecca or Bombay as from Manhattan or Sunset Boulevard, Bollywood as much as Hollywood.

At a general level, the homogenization thesis is capable of extension into the Internet age and a virtual world of consumption and personal gratification, through a new generation of products and brands such as I-Phones and Android devices. These however lead well beyond the global consumer capitalism thesis, as I will show when looking at the third thesis labelled Internet culture. For the moment, my concern is more with the limits to the idea of global cultural homogenization via consumer capitalism. These were becoming more apparent in the 1990's, with growing awareness first that capitalist marketing strategies were shifting towards differentiated rather than standardized markets, and second that globalization in a broader sense did not simply generate convergence and conformity. It was in this context that Robertson (1992, 1995) developed the idea of glocalization, whereby global processes were often seen as inter-acting with local ones, rather than eroding localism and particularism. In a different but parallel manner, the post-colonial interest in cultural hybridity arose from a sense of the fluidity, diversity and non-generalizability of global cultural forms (Hallward, 2001) rather than their incorporation in a standardized Western or American model. These critical currents have provided a very robust critique of the first variant of the cultural homogenization thesis. But they do not necessarily or directly challenge other variants which emerged in the last two decades of the twentieth century.

The second world culture variant, developed by Meyer, Boli, Thomas and their associates (Meyer, Boli, Thomas and Ramirez, 1997; Boli and Thomas, 1999), building on earlier work by Meyer (1980), takes a more political and normative direction. They argue that the world polity was not dominated by the dictates of the capitalist world system, but rather by a world culture expressed in norms about how institutions and social actors should operate, and how problems should be addressed. This institutionalized world culture represents an evolving repertoire of principles and models. The empirical basis of this argument is drawn from convergent features of educational institutions across the world, from similar models that new states adopt in institution building, and norms such as human rights and world citizenship evident in international non-state organizations and movements. The time-frame of this stretches from the late nineteenth to the early twenty-first century.

In my earlier paper (2000), this approach was not considered. It does however expand the scope of the homogenization thesis. For one thing it docs seem quite close to prevailing senses of the 'world community' that arise in policy discussions about how to resolve geo-political crises like the rise of Islamic State, or humanitarian crises like the Ebola crisis. But it also extends beyond the elite world of global governance elites into the sphere of non-government organizations seeking to reform or transform the world order.

Yet there remain problems with this approach, not least with its homogenizing thrust. Critics doubt whether world culture exists in this highly integrated manner, and are also sceptical that new states simply converge on the same models of state-building and development. National interest remains a major focus in inter-state relations, while even emergent norms such as human rights and environmental sustainability come under significant challenge. More sympathetic evaluations may agree to a significant degree about an emergent cosmopolitan sensibility, but the world culture argument leaves it very unclear what place is left for the national and local, or for cultural diversity in the new order. It is therefore rather thin on mass identities and forms of community – issues that are very salient to assessing the scope of global political convergence (Axford, 2013).

A third version of the homogenization argument centres on new information and communications technology. Much of it is concerned with the cultural consequences of the Internet. In the 1990s, a significant strand of analysis argued that the rise of the Internet would create an informed global citizenry who would be more tolerant, peace-loving, and cosmopolitan rather than national in their identities (Cairncross, 1997; Stratton 1997). This amounted to a kind of de-territorialization of identity associated with mediated connectivity (Held, 2004). It also had radical implications, so it was claimed for greater democratization, with decentralized communications media now in the hands of the people.

Three crucial issues, however remain in doubt. First, there is no necessary relationship between Internet use and greater democracy, since it may act as a mode of control as much as a means of democratic mobilization (Best and Wade, 2009). Second, the assumption of a greater cosmopolitan tolerance arising from Internet use has proven untenable since a wide range of content circulates through social media and web traffic including violent racist and sexist material through mundane interpersonal connectivity to tolerant inter-cultural encounters. Third, arguments about the cultural consequences of the Internet do not necessarily generate homogenization. Rather they enable conflict, division and dissent, not all of which is contained within the normal cut and thrust of democratic deliberation.

The work of Manuel Castells is very significant here. He explores both the use of information technology as an integral element in the corporate flexibility of contemporary capitalism (2001), and the significance of social media networks for the 'counter-power' of movements protesting against undemocratic global power structures (2012). His most recent study *Networks of Outrage and Hope* (2012) is based on the protest movements of 2011 in North Africa, Spain, and the USA, which were born, diffused and sustained on the Internet. Instead of announcing homogenization in pursuit of cosmopolitan tolerance, they channel emotional outage and hope for a better world into contestation. He claims this amounts to class struggle, but not on the anti-capitalist model of the past (see the critique of Fuchs, 2014).

Another dimension to the cultural implications of the Internet is growing conflict between notions of privacy and freedom for democratic communications between citizens, on the one hand, and the surveillance mechanisms of states and corporations, on the other. Conflicts between freedom and surveillance have grown massively in cultural importance since my earlier paper, written in 2000. This is not the place to consider such issues further, except to say that the Internet age is very far from seeing new media function as an innocent forum for tolerant inter-communication between citizens. This ideal of what we might call a virtual cultural homogenization has simply not eventuated.

Taken overall, therefore, there are significant limits to the homogenization thesis in its various manifestations. More than this, it may be said that weaknesses already apparent fifteen years ago have sharpened over time. Cultural arrangements and institutions have not converged on a single global pattern. One reason for this is the increased salience of polarization across the early twenty-first century.

Polarization

The events of 9/11 and successive phases of the 'war on terror' up to present conflicts associated with Islamic State represent an intensification of polarizing trends apparent in the last third of the twentieth century. Many of these have historic roots in processes of Empire, colonization, and slavery (Holton, 2014). Rather than a global world polarized over social class and class struggle, it seems that cultural and civilizational schisms have a deeper and more profound presence. Analysts as diverse as Edward Said (1978, 1994), Benjamin Barber (1995), and Samuel Huntington (1996), have articulated very different versions of the polarization thesis, and these have gained increasing purchase as a result of the fusion of geo-political and geo-cultural struggles associated with the Middle East and the globalization of terror across all borders (Kellner, 2007).

Said's work is well known. The focus is on cultural dichotomies that have construct the Western and non-Western worlds in a manner that polarizes cultural life. Western cultural imperialism, in particular, operates through discursive modes of power and domination. Whereas the Orient has been represented by colonialists, explorers, academics and novelists over 200 years as stagnant and unchanging, erotic and authoritarian, the West is portrayed as dynamic and innovatory, rational, democratic, and tolerant. The dichotomy persists in contemporary stereotypes of Islamists like al Qaeda and Islamic State as inherently violent terrorists opposed to democracy and dialogue.

Said has extended his approach over time to note parallel dichotomies in non-Western cultural world views. Much Islamic or African thinking constructs notions of Occidentalism as immoral, individualistic and pathological compared with non-Western cultural practices viewed as more respectful of moral order and more supportive of community. His point with all such dichotomies – Occidentalist as well as Orientalist – is not that they are necessarily accurate but that they are widely believed and acted upon.

Said has nonetheless been criticized for neglect of the political economy of global cultural arrangements. He also downplays internal contrasts within Western views, including the cultural phenomenon of Westerners who in a sense become Easternized through intercultural contact. While personally committed to cultural multiplicity, difference and syncretism (1993), Said does little to trace its historical evolution, its strengths and weaknesses. So like all versions of the polarization thesis, his own reading offers little analysis of the opportunities and limitations on cross-cultural communication and cosmopolitan sensibility.

Barber (1995), approaches global polarization from a different direction. Rather than looking at patterns of discursive power founded on cultural dichotomy, he contrasts two cultural configurations, labelled McWorld and Jihad. While McWorld refers to a combination of fast food (McDonalds), fast music (MTV) and fast computers (Apple Mac), Jihad (meaning holy war or struggle in Arabic) stands for traditionalism, cultural authoritarianism and tribalism. The former is a powerful metaphor for global consumerism of goods and services, which we have encountered in analysing homogenization theory. But unlike that theory, McWorld does not stand alone. Rather it is challenged by Jihad which promises of moral liberation from mammon through communitarian political mobilization in pursuit of justice. Since neither McWorld nor Jihad are necessarily committed to democracy, Barber fears the political and cultural consequences of this divide. Critics have baulked somewhat at Barber's dismissal of any historic connection between capitalism and democracy, noting that he says little about the significance of property-ownership for civil society, which itself under girds democracy (Fidler, 1996).

An important implication of Barber's version of polarization theory is that Western economic globalization does not carry all before it. Rather it faces limits, especially in the cultural domain which seems harder to globalize than economic and political relationships and institutions. Barber is not however convinced that polarization of this kind will continue into the long term. Since the current location of much jihad is in the under-developed world, that is the future markets of McWorld, it may be that McWorld will win.

The question I posed 15 years ago is what drives resistance to McWorld? Is it a kind of anti-globalism that lies behind the fragmentation of the world into warring tribes, as suggested in much of Barber's argument? And is this simply a product of religious resistance as found in radical Islamic movements, or a wider a more disparate set of movements aiming at forms of social justice in the face of global inequality and human exploitation by authoritarian governments and dominant groups. In the latter case we are led back to Castells' (2012) discussion of networks of outrage and hope. In the former case, arguments about jihad link with powerful notions of war between civilizations associated with Samuel Huntington (1996).

From the viewpoint of the 1990s, Huntington saw an epoch of geo-political Cold War being replaced by a new epoch of cultural wars, which might lead to 'global civilizational war'. The civilizational cleavage he identified was that between the West and an emergent Islamic-Confucian axis. This is manifest in conflicts over matters such as human rights or the choice of venue for the Olympic Games. Westerners tend to line up on one-side of the divide, according to Huntington, and non-Westerners on the other.

The general idea of global cultural cleavage has considerable resonance because of resurgent radical Islam over the last 15 years. The destruction of the Twin Towers, and the cross-border activities of al Qaeda and Islamic State in the Middle East, Europe, North America, West Africa, and Indonesia seem to support this thesis. But there are serious problems with it too.

First and foremost a conceptual framework based on the idea of more of less unified civilizations defined largely by religion is difficult to sustain (Sen, 2006). Huntington's putative civilizations lack internal unity. Nor is it clear that most cultural conflict is grounded primarily in religion. The ethnic basis of conflicts, for example, which form many contemporary conflicts may have religious aspects, but also involve inequalities of power, often connected with minority status and racial discrimination. Fox (2002) argues that civilizational schism of the kind discussed by Huntington represents a small proportion of contemporary cultural conflict. Most of the ethnic conflicts prominent today lacks a clear civilizational element.

These empirical findings arise from the diverse sources of cultural conflict within as well as well as between what might be regarded as civilizations. Islam is not a monolithic cultural entity, but contains its own schism between Shia and Sunni which generates major cleavages of its own. Confucianism is also far more pragmatic than the resurgent radical Islam that Huntington sees as related parts of a single civilizational axis. Conflicts within the Sinic/Confucian world involve a mix of ethnic and political elements which do not fit neatly into macro-level propositions about a civilizational axis with Islam. Meanwhile what is conventionally described as 'the West' is itself very far from being a unified cultural entity (Rumford, 2008; Delanty, 2013). Fragmentation is evident in tensions between Europe and the USA over issues of neo-liberalism, social democracy, and cultural policy.

Cultural conflicts remain endemic within the global arena, but they do not amount to a civilizational polarization between West and non-West. This is not simply because there are no separate and uniform competing civilizations. It is also because of cross-cutting relationships and institutions linking West and the Islamic and Confucian world are increasingly found in business, and in joint attempts to control sub-political movements committed to terror. These do not extend as far as notions of strong elite convergence, as noted above. But they do amount to forms of co-operation which cut across notions of cultural war.

If globalization renders the idea of distinct but competing civilizations incoherent, what alternative kinds of analysis are possible? One option is to think in terms of the 'post-westernization of the world' (Rumford, 2008). This notion tries to make sense of several parallel but inter-secting processes. One is the globalization of the non-West, in terms of flows of capital, labour, and cultural practises. In this sense the non-West is increasingly integrated within the historic geographical West through investment flows, immigration, and cultural inter-action. Globalization, in this view, is no longer simply a Western project, or a synonym for western domination. A second process at work is the division or fragmentation of the West, and most notably a sense that Europe no longer accepts that the US is the West's 'leading nation'. This is reflected in geo-political conflicts over going to war in the Middle East. It is also seen in opposition to neo-liberal visions of world order, a strand of thinking intensifies as a result of the global financial crisis and the de-legitimization of free market capitalism.

This complex picture of a world of cross-cutting linkages and multiple levels of conflict, reflects the multiple forms that modernity may take (Eisenstadt, 2002; Delanty, 2013). Rather than a single unified Western model based around geo-political dominance and neo-liberalism, with Western 'moderns' fighting non-Western 'traditionalists', we have a very different post-Western melange that is hard to characterize in terms of polarization. It remains a world of serious conflict and schism, but not one marked by a single civilizational divide. Such sociological accounts of post-Westernization, strongly suggest that Huntington's polarization theory over-generalizes from an argument East–West conflict into an untenable presumption of civilizational schism.

In the discussion so far I have pointed to weaknesses in both convergence and polarization theory. Both tell powerful stories about globalization and culture, but neither is able to come to terms with profound complexities in the contemporary dynamics of the various processes at work in the global order. I now turn to examine a third approach – theories of hybridity and glocalization – which has promised to address the problem of complexity in a more adequate manner.

Hybridization/Glocalization

Since both convergence theory and the polarization thesis have serious limitations, where else should we look to make sense of the very complex and diverse cultural consequences of globalization? Fifteen years ago I took the third major option to be that of hybridization. In the present essay I now combine theories of hybridization more explicitly with theories of glocalization. These two theories are analytically distinct but overlap in their concern to make sense of global cultural complexity and diversity.

Hybridization involves inter-cultural mixing and syncretization. Hybridization is an approach that seeks to explain how it is that we find phenomena like 'Thai boxing by Moroccan girls in Amsterdam, Asian rap in London, Irish bagels, Chinese tacos, and Mardi Gras Indians in the United States' (Nederveen Pieterse, 1995, p. 53). It also applies to phenomena like national competitions to nominate an entry for the Eurovision song contest, whereas Hannerz (1990) points out the Swedish entry was a calypso performed by a Swede entitled 'Four Buggs and a Coca-Cola'! There is no overriding sense of global cultural convergence, or of cultural products contained within national barriers.

Rather than a world in which a single global culture is emerging as different and distinct cultures converge, hybridization theory holds to a vision of inter-cultural exchange and recombination in a diverse set of hybrid cultural repertoires and institutions. Rather than a world in which there is polarization between different cultural institutions and practises, whether on a national or civilizational basis, hybridization theory moves into a more fluid domain, consistent with concepts of liquid modernity (Bauman, 2000). The cultural diversity and complexity involved in hybridization arises because nations and regions are culturally permeable, such that many cultural processes are neither Western nor Eastern, African, Asian or European, cosmopolitan or local.

Theories of hybridization as global cultural melange (Garcia-Canclini, 1989; Bhabha, 1990, 1994; Lowe, 1991; Appadurai, 1996,) have much in common with theories of creolization (Hannerz, 1987; Friedman, 1990), and glocalization (Robertson, 1992), all of which emerged around the late 1980s and early to mid-1990s as theories of globalization took a more cultural turn. And beyond the academic world, notions of hybridization and cultural melange are key elements in literary work by writers like Naipaul (1961), and Rushdie (1988, 1995).

Notions of hybridity have made a significant contribution to understandings of relationships between globalization and culture, moving analysis beyond convergence and polarization. They have been particularly influential in understanding diasporic populations created through Imperial expansion, slavery and immigration, as in Gilroy's (1993) study of The Black Atlantic. Ideas of hybridity have also been applied to global phenomena such as world music, and to a wide range of examples of what are taken as cultural mixing and mingling including cultural representations in novels and poetry (see for example Kiortti and Nyman, 2007).

There are however pitfalls in this approach. Many focus in one way or another on the cultural politics of hybridity. Whereas in some initial formulations, hybridity was associated with the subversion of essentializing thinking about nation, race and ethnicity (Bhabha, 1990), others have downplayed subversive effects. Friedman (1997), for example, argues that notions of hybridity give an impression of cosmopolitanism which is belied by the intensification of ethnocentrism within diaspora. Spivak (2003) also warns against the celebration of 'cultural difference' in ways which obscure racist and neo-colonial legacies. Hutnyk (1997), meanwhile, identifies commercialized uniformity as an underlying theme in the seemingly culturally diverse domain of world music. While some critics of hybridity, re-assert alternative themes of cultural imperialism, and processes of hegemony, this objection was already anticipated by Garcia-Canclini (1995), and Nederveen Pieterse (1995), both of whom see power relations inscribed within hybridity. The net effect of all this is to leave discourses of hybridity in a rather indeterminate and ambivalent position on key questions about relations between globalization, culture and politics.

Another way of approaching issues of global cultural complexity, not fully considered in my earlier paper, is through the notion of glocalization as developed by Robertson (1992, 1995). Developed originally to come to terms with aspects of Japanese religious syncretism, Robertson developed the idea of glocalization in a more general direction to come to terms with complexities throughout the global order, not simply within cultural relationships.

The concept of glocalization, the inter-penetration or fusion of global and local elements in social relations, challenges both theories of homogenization and those of polarization. Globalization does not overcome and homogenize all that it encounters. Rather it faces limits when encountering particular national and local circumstances. These may be economic, political or cultural. Global cross-border processes rather than swallowing these up, find it necessary to come to terms with or adapt to them. This instead of a fundamental polarization between the global and the local, it is often the case that resistance or opposition to globalization is replaced by an interpenetration of global and local elements; hence glocalization. This doesn't undermine conflict, but it does produce a set of more syncretic social phenomena, which are neither global nor local. A number of examples may be cited. They include business practices, such as the shift in business strategies from standardized global commodities to niche marketing, or the combination of local knowledge with global strength in corporate structures. Other examples include cultural phenomena like jazz, world music or salsa which combine elements imported into new settings with local or indigenous practices (Roberts, 1992; Gilroy, 1993; Waxer, 2001; Connell and Gibson, 2004). Within social movements too we see glocal dimensions as in the rallying cry to 'Think Global and Act Local'. Even the most militant anti-globalization activists have made extensive use of global communications technology to transform circulation of news as well as generate further support.

Where then does glocalization differ from hybridization? This is not an easy question to sort out, largely because the two have considerable overlap in focussing on cultural borrowing, inter-penetration and syncretism. Nonetheless there are ways in which they differ, and these point to the more persuasive credentials of glocalization theory. The main difference is that glocalization offers a more conceptually anchored approach to processes of inter-cultural engagement, interpenetration, and possible fusion. Ideas of hybridization certainly challenged essentialist thinking about culture, race, and nation, and in some versions at least linked issues of cultural syncretism with political protest from below. But beyond that hybridization's somewhat free-floating theoretical thrust is a weakness, as is its lack of empirical range across global processes. Globalization theory, in the hands of Robertson is more securely grounded in a broader account of the global field and the human condition under conditions of globalization. While relatively well known, it deserves another rehearsal in the context of the questions raised in this chapter.

Thus the global field brings together familiar political-economic institutions such as national societies and the world system of societies, with the broader cultural phenomena of human kind and individual selves. The inter-acting forms of life within this global field produce challenges of what Robertson calls relativization. For example, notions of national sovereignty arising within national societies are confronted in global society with other national sovereignties, which while they may lead to conflict have also generated regulatory bodies such as the United Nations. Such institutions are not trans-national in the sense that they stand wholly above nations, but may usefully be seen as glocal at least at a macro-level, combining global and local elements. But what of the world of selves?

More explicit micro-level cultural themes emerge through engagements between local or national identities and senses of humankind as a distinct cognitive and expressive reference-point. Relativization and glocalization here arise out of encounters between local and global entities. Where the two are reconciled, we may speak of glocal identities. Examples of this include identities that combine a cosmopolitan or humanist sense of being part of a single human race with allegiances to nation and place (Holton, 2009).

The point here is not that global homogenization or global/local polarization are ruled out because glocal compromises or fusions always win out. They do not. Global forces, for example, may create senses of the local, as in global tourist marketing strategies targeted at particular places. The point is rather that social inter-action faces continuing challenges of relativization and a continuing array of glocal institutions and identities. In this way glocalization theory incorporates many of the insights of hybridization theory drawn primarily from studies of postcolonialism and global diaspora, within a far broader conceptual and empirical framework. This has extended through business and management (Abdullah, 1996; Drori, Höllerer, and Walgenbach, 2014), identity and language (Bastardas-Boada, 2012; Soldatova and Geer, 2013; Sung, 2014) to the development of football as a world game (Molina, 2007; Giulianotti and Robertson, 2006).

A key part of this broadening is a more convincing account of macro-micro-macro linkages between the world of institutions and the world of identities. In contrast with Castells' (1996) replay of Frankfurt school dichotomies between system and life-world, embodied in his contrast between the 'space of flows' and the 'space of place', Robertson offers a way of grounding less dichotomous and polarized accounts of system/life-world inter-actions.

At the same time, such strengths do not dispose of some difficulties with the glocalization approach. We lack any clear sense of the various modalities of glocalization. Also missing is any sense of the limitations of the theory, such as why it is that global homogenization or polarization between global and local may remain irreducible to each other. What is clear, nonetheless, is that theories of glocalization have helped to transform debates about the cultural consequences of globalization, going further than earlier theorists of hybridization managed to do.

It may be that glocalization is not so much a general theory of global culture as one of several trends within the global field. Underlying Robertson's development of the concept is that it emerges from a social ontology in which individual selves and macro-level institutions are caught in a dilemma between their location in a particular time and space (the local), and their location as part of a single interconnected world order (the global). The dilemma is how to come to terms with this dual location. This ontology does not have the necessary corollary that there is only one singular response to this dilemma, namely glocalization. It is equally possible that nationally-focussed particularism and global trans-nationalization may eventuate. The global arena is indeed characterized by three such empirical trends.

What a glocalization perspective adds to analysis of global complexity, is not then a substantive argument that glocalization will prevail over the other two. It is rather a methodological approach which encourages an awareness of complex and often contradictory inter-actions between global and local processes and identities. This is preferable to methodological nationalism which underplays trans-national trends drawing on evidence of resurgent nationalism. It is also preferable to methodological globalism, which over-plays the significance of trans-national trends, and continues to deny that the nation-state is remarkably robust.

Conclusion

It has been said that most general theories fail most of the time. This observation certainly applies to questions as to the cultural consequences of globalization. Neither homogenization/polarization, nor hybridization/glocalization emerge as sufficient by themselves as general ways of understanding the very complex terrain of global culture. This conclusion from my earlier paper (Holton, 2000), remains valid some 15 years later.

There is nonetheless a very significant degree of indeterminacy and uncertainty in this picture. Just as globalization is not, in some simple sense irreversible (James, 2001; Holton, 2011), it is not inconceivable that the relationship between the three major cultural trends discussed above may change, and one trend may become dominant – at least for a period – over the others. Globalization, especially in its economic and political manifestations, creates enormous resistance. This may further amplify the resurgence of nationalism, national identity, and calls to reassert national sovereignty. While it may be countered that technology and communication mean that the infrastructure of many institutions and social movements will continue to permeate borders, it is possible that new constellations of global economic and geo-political power may emerge with the rise of China. This in turn may make for a renewed form of polarization between East Asia and the West, and in the longer term, forms of cultural Sinification akin to earlier episodes of Americanization. Yet it is doubtful whether any form of convergence and homogenization will ever take strong or enduring forms, as a succession of historic attempts at global Empires, as Spain and Great Britain discovered.

Glocal complexity constantly reasserts itself in spite of the intentions and policies of powerful global interests. The current Indianization of world cricket provides a cultural example drawn from the world of sport. Lords of London no longer dominates the game on behalf of Britain and countries of white settlement even while cricket promotes certain older traditions alongside innovations in staging global cricket contests (Rumford and Wagg, 2010). What matters then is the series of syncretic forms that global cultural products take and how these are understood by those involved. Global complexities in this respect invite irony as much as earnest analytical deconstruction, as with Ashis Nandy's (2000, p. 1) comment that 'Cricket is an Indian game, accidentally discovered by the English'.

There is then an irreducible element of glocalization inherent in a cross-border world. This speaks not only to Robertson's social ontology of glocalization as a manifestation of the human condition, but also to the long historical sociology of cultural borrowing from others – whether acknowledged, ironic or unwitting (Curtin, 1984). In this sense glocalization may be logically different from the other two trends. While homogenization and polarization seek to abolish or control, glocalization is a way of bringing together and living with global difference. But it is a way of doing so without recourse to strong normative commitments to cosmopolitan social philosophy.

References

Abdullah, A. 1996. *Going Glocal: Cultural Dimensions in Malaysian Management*. Kuala Lumpur: Malaysian Institute of Management.

Appadurai, A. 1990. 'Disjuncture and Difference in the Global Cultural Economy'. In *Global Culture*, edited by M. Featherstone, 295–310. London: Sage.

Appadurai, A. 1996. *Modernity at Large: Cultural Dimensions of Globalization*. Minneapolis: Minneapolis University Press.

Artz, L., and Y. Kamalipour (eds). 2007. *The Media Globe: Trends in International Mass Media*. Lanham: Rowman and Littlefield.

Axford, B. 2013. *Theories of Globalization*. Cambridge: Polity.

Barber, B. 1995. *Jihad versus McWorld*. New York: Ballantine Books.

Bastardas-Boada, A. 2012. *Language and Identity Policies in the Glocal Age*. Barcelona: Institut d'Estudis Autonòmics.

Bauman, Z. 2000. *Liquid Modernity*. Cambridge: Polity Press.

Beck, U. 1992. *Risk Society: Towards a Sociology of Modernity*. London: Sage.

Beck, U. 2000. 'The Cosmopolitan Perspective: Society in the Second Age of Modernity'. *British Journal of Sociology* 15(1): 79–105.

Beck, U. 2003. *Power in the Global Age*. Cambridge: Polity Press.

Berghahn, V. 2010. 'The Debate on Americanization among Economic and Cultural Historians'. *Cold War History* 10(1): 107–30.
Best, M., and K. Wade. 2009. 'The Internet and Democracy: Global Catalyst or Democratic Dud'. *Bulletin of Science, Technology and Society* 29(4): 255–71.
Bhabha, H. 1990. 'The Third Space: Interview with Homi Bhabha'. In *Identity, Community, Culture, Difference*, edited by J. Rutherford, 207–21. London: Lawrence and Wishart.
Bhabha, H. 1994. *The Location of Culture*. London: Routledge.
Boli, J., and G. Thomas (eds). 1999. *Constructing World Culture: International Nongovernmental Organizations since 1875*. Stanford: Stanford University Press.
Booth, K., and T. Dunne (eds). 2002. *Worlds in Collision: Terror and the Future of Global Order.* Basingstoke and New York: Palgrave Macmillan.
Cairncross, F. 1997. *The Death of Distance: How the Communications Revolution Will Change Our Lives*. Boston: Harvard Business School Press.
Calhoun, C. 2007. *Nations Matter: Culture, History, and the Cosmopolitan Dream.* Abingdon: Routledge.
Castells, M. 1996. *The Rise of Network Society*. Oxford: Blackwell.
Castells, M. 2001. *The Internet Galaxy: Reflections on the Internet, Business, and Society*. Oxford: Oxford University Press.
Castells, M. 2012. *Networks of Outrage and Hope: Social Movements in the Internet Age*. Cambridge: Polity.
Castells, M., M. Fernandez-Ardevol, J. Qiu, and A. Sey. 2007. *Mobile Communication and Society a Global Perspective*. Cambridge MA: MIT Press.
Centeno, M., and J. Cohen. 2010. *Global Capitalism: A Sociological Perspective*. Cambridge: Polity.
Connell, J., and C. Gibson. 2004. 'World Music: Deterritorializing Place and Identity'. *Progress in Human Geography* 28(3): 342–61.
Curtin, P. 1984. *Cross-Cultural Trade in World History.* New York: Cambridge University Press.
Dash, K. 2005. 'McDonalds in India'. *The Garvin School of International Management*, Thunderbird Case Series no: A07-05-00151.
Delanty, G. 2013. *Formations of European Modernity: A Historical and Political Sociology of Europe.* Basingstoke: Palgrave Macmillan.
Drori, G., M. Höllerer, and P. Walgenbach (eds). 2014. *Global Themes and Local Variations in Organization and Management: Perspectives in Glocalization.* Abingdon: Routledge.
Eagleton, T. 2000. *The Idea of Culture*. Oxford: Blackwell.
Eisenstadt, S. 2002. 'Multiple Modernities'. In *Multiple Modernities*, edited by S. Eisenstadt, 1–29. New Brunswick: Transaction.
Fantasia, R. 1995. 'Fast Food in France'. *Theory and Society* 24(1): 201–43.
Fidler, D. 1996. 'Reflections on the McRevolution: A Review of Jihad versus McWorld'. *Indiana Journal of Global Legal Studies* 3(2): 501–17.

Fox, J. 2002. 'Ethnic Minorities and the Clash of Civilizations: A Quantitative Analysis of Huntington's Thesis'. *British Journal of Political Science* 32(1): 415–32.
Friedman, J. 1990. 'Being in the World: Globalization and Localization'. In *Global Culture*, edited by M. Featherstone, 311–28. London: Sage.
Friedman, J. 1994. *Cultural Identity and Global Process*. London: Sage.
Friedman, J. 1997. 'Global Crises, the Struggle for Cultural Identity, and Intellectual Pork-Barrelling: Cosmopolitans, Nationals, and Locals in an Age of Dehegemonisation'. In *Debating Cultural Hybridity*, edited by P. Werbner and T. Madood, 70–89. London: Zed Press.
Fuchs, C. 2014. 'Book review of Manuel Castells' 'Networks of Outrage and Hope''. *Media, Culture and Society* 36(1): 122–7.
Garcia-Canclini, N. 1995. *Hybrid Cultures: Strategies for Entering and Leaving Modernity*. Minneapolis: University of Minnesota Press.
Giddens, A. 1999. *Runaway World*. London: Profile.
Gilroy, P. 1993. *Black Atlantic: Modernity and Double-Consciousness*. London: Verso.
Giulianotti, R., and R. Robertson. 2006. 'Glocalization, Globalization, and Migration: The Case of Scottish Football Supporters in North America'. *International Sociology* 21(2): 171–98.
Hallward, P. 2001. *Absolutely Post-Colonial: Writing Between the Singular and the Specific*. Manchester: Manchester University Press.
Hannerz, U. 1987. 'The World in Creolisation'. *Africa* 57(4): 546–59.
Hannerz, U. 1990. 'Cosmopolitans and Locals in World Culture'. In *Global Culture*, edited by M. Featherstone, 237–52. London: Sage.
Held, D. 2004. *Global Covenant: The Social-Democratic Alternative to the Washington Consensus*. Cambridge: Polity.
Hirst, P., and G. Thompson. 1996. *Globalization in Question*. Cambridge: Polity.
Holton, R. 2000. 'Globalization's Cultural Consequences'. *Annals of the American Academy of the Political and Social Sciences* 570 (July): 140–52.
Holton, R. 2009. *Cosmopolitanisms*. Basingstoke: Palgrave Macmillan.
Holton, R. 2011. *Globalization and the Nation-State*, 2nd revised edn. Basingstoke: Palgrave Macmillan.
Holton, R. 2014. *Global Inequalities*. Basingstoke: Palgrave Macmillan.
Huntington, S. 1996. *The Clash of Civilizations and the Remaking of World Order*. New York: Simon and Schuster.
Hutnyk, J. 1997. 'Adorno at Womad: South Asian Crossover Music and the limits of Hybridity Talk'. In *Debating Cultural Hybridity*, edited by P. Werbner and T. Madood, 107–38. London: Zed Press.
Kellner, D. 2003. *From 9/11 to Terror War: the Dangers of the Bush Legacy*. Lanham: Rowman and Littlefield.
Kellner, D. 2007. 'Globalization, Terrorism, and Democracy: 9/11 and its Aftermath'. In *Frontiers of Globalization Research*, edited by I. Rossi, 243–68. New York: Springer.

Kiortti, J., and J. Nyman (eds). 2007 *Reconstructing Hybridity: Post-Colonial Studies in Transition*. Amsterdam: Rioppi.

James, H. 2001. *The End of Globalization: Lessons from the Great Depression*. Cambridge MA: Harvard University Press.

Jameson, F. 1991. *Post-Modernism: The Cultural Logic of Late Capitalism*. Durham, NC: Duke University Press.

Jameson, F. 2007. *Jameson on Jameson* (ed. Ian Buchanan). Durham: Duke University Press.

Jessop, B. 2010. 'Cultural Political Economy and Critical Policy Studies'. *Critical Policy Studies* 3(3–4): 336–56.

Juris, J. 2005. 'The New Digital Media and Activist Networking Within Anti-Corporate Globalization Movements'. *Annals of the American Academy of Political and Social Sciences* 597(1): 189–208.

McChesney, R. 1999. *Rich Media, Poor Democracy: Communication Politics in Dubious Times*. Urbana: University of Illinois Press.

Mann, M. 1986. *The Sources of Social Power, vol 1*. Cambridge: Cambridge University Press.

Mann, M., and D. Riley. 2007. 'Explaining Macro-Regional Trends in Global Income Inequalities, 1950–2000'. *Socio-Economic Review* 5(1): 81–115.

Mathews, J. 2006. 'Dragon Multinationals: New Players in 21st Century Globalization'. *Asia Pacific Journal of Management* 23(1): 5–27.

Meyer, J.W. 1980. 'The World Polity and the Authority of the Nation-State'. In *Studies of the World-System*, edited by A. Bergesen, 109–37. New York: Academic Press.

Meyer, J.W., J. Boli, G. Thomas, and F. Ramirez. 1997. 'World Society and the Nation State'. *American Journal of Sociology* 103(1): 144–81.

Mignolo, W. 1999. *Local Histories/Global Designs: Coloniality, Subaltern Knowledges, and Border Thinking*. Princeton: Princeton University Press.

Milanovic, B. 2011. *The Haves and the Have-Nots: A Brief and Idiosyncratic History of Global Inequality*. New York: Basic Books.

Mirlees, T. 2013. *Global Entertainment Media: Between Cultural Imperialism and Cultural Globalization*. New York: Routledge.

Molina, F. 2007. 'Socialization, 'Glocal' Identity, and Sport: Football between Global and Local'. *European Journal for Sport and Society* 4(1): 169–76.

Naipaul, V.S. 1961. *A House for Mr Biswas*. London: Andre Deutsch.

Nandy, A. 2000. *The Tao of Cricket: On Games of Destiny and the Destiny of Games*. New Delhi: Oxford University Press.

Nederveen Pieterse, J. 1995. 'Globalization as Hybridization'. In *Global Modernities*, edited by M. Featherstone, S. Lash, and R. Robertson, 45–68. London: Sage.

Palan, R., R. Murphy, and C. Chavagneux. 2009. *Tax Havens. How Globalization Really Works*. Ithaca: Cornell University Press.

Piketty, T. 2014. *Capital in the Twenty-First Century*. Cambridge MA: Harvard University Press.

Poster, M. 2001. *What's the Matter with the Internet*. Minneapolis: University of Minnesota Press.
Rieger, E., and S. Leibfried. 2003. *Limits to Globalization*. Cambridge: Polity.
Ritzer, G. 1993. *The McDonaldization of Society*. Thousand Oaks, CA: Pine Forge Press.
Ritzer, G. 2007. *The Globalization of Nothing*. London: Sage.
Roberts, M. 1992. '"World Music" and the Global Cultural Economy'. *Diaspora* 2(2): 229–42.
Robertson, R. 1992. *Globalization: Social Theory and Global Culture*. London: Sage.
Robertson, R. 1995. 'Glocalization: Time-Space and Homogeneity-Heterogeneity'. In *Global Modernities*, edited by M. Featherstone, S. Lash, and R. Robertson, 25–44. London: Sage.
Rodrik, D. 2011. *The Globalization Paradox: Why Global Markets, States, and Democracy Can't Co-exist*. Oxford: Oxford University Press.
Rumford, C. 2006. 'Theorizing Borders'. *European Journal of Social Theory* 9(2): 155–70.
Rumford, C. 2008. *Cosmopolitan Spaces: Europe, Globalization, Theory*. Abingdon: Routledge.
Rumford, C., and S. Wagg (eds). 2010. *Cricket and Globalization*. Newcastle: Cambridge Scholars Press.
Rushdie, S. 1988. *The Satanic Verses*. London: Viking.
Rushdie, S. 1995. *The Moor's Last Sigh*. London: Jonathan Cape.
Said, E. 1978. *Orientalism*. New York: Penguin.
Said, E. 1993. *Cultural Imperialism*. London: Chatto and Windus.
Schiller, H. 1976. *Communication and Cultural Domination*. New York: International Arts and Sciences.
Scott, A. (ed.). 1997. *The Limits of Globalization*. London: Routledge.
Sen, A. 2006. *Identity and Violence: The Illusion of Destiny*. London: Penguin.
Soldatova, G., and M. Geer. 2013. '"Glocal" Identity, Cultural Intelligence, and Language Fluency'. *Procedia – Social and Behavioural Sciences* 86(1): 469–75.
Spivak, G. 2003. *A Critique of Post-Colonial Reason*. Cambridge: Harvard University Press.
Stead, W. 1902. *The Americanization of the World: Or, the Trend of the Twentieth Century*. London: Review of Reviews.
Stratton, J. 1997. 'Cyberspace and the Globalization of Culture'. In *Internet Culture*, edited by D. Porter, 253–75. New York: Routledge.
Sung, C. 2014. 'Global, Local or Glocal. Identities of L2 Language Learners in English as a Lingua Franca Communication'. *Language, Culture, and Curriculum* 27(1): 43–57.
Swyngedouw, E. 1997. 'Neither Global nor Local: "Glocalization" and the Politics of Scale'. In *Spaces of Globalization: Reasserting the Power of the Local*, edited by K.R. Cox, 137–66. New York: Guilford Press.

Sznaider, N., and R. Winter (eds). 2003. *Global America: The Cultural Consequences of Globalization*. Liverpool: Liverpool University Press.

Tomlinson, J. 1999. *Globalization and Culture*. Chicago: University of Chicago Press.

Urry, J. 2000. *Sociology Beyond Societies*. London: Routledge.

Wallerstein, I. 1974. *The Modern World System: Capitalist Agriculture and the Origins of the European World Economy in the Sixteenth Century*. New York: Academic Press.

Wallerstein, I. 1990. 'Culture as the Ideological Battleground of the Modern World System'. In *Global Culture*, edited by M. Featherstone, 31–56. London: Sage.

Warner, M. 1994. 'Japanese Culture, Western Management: Taylorism and Human Resources in Japan'. *Organization Studies* 15(4): 509–33.

Waxer, L. 2001. 'Llegó la Salsa: the Rise of Salsa in Columbia and Venezuela'. in *Situating Salsa: Global Markets and Local Meanings in Latin Popular Music*, edited by Lise Waxer, 219–46. New York: Routledge.

Williams, R. 1976. *Keywords: A Vocabulary of Culture and Society*. London: Fontana.

Chapter 5

Dynamics of World Culture: Global Rationalism and Problematizing Norms, Again

George M. Thomas

A common interpretation of globalization is that technology-fueled networks and interdependencies generate disjointed, differentiated global fields. Actors are said to respond rationally by constructing normative incentive structures to coordinate and control each other and to manage uncertainty and risk. Such analyses omit culture except as local values and practices; yet, these analyses implicitly assume that actors apprehend the international. If, for example, states create and participate in international organizations to manage rationally interests and externalities within the capitalist world economy and the interstate system, they must be apprehending these systems as a whole, claiming and contesting sovereignties, identities, and purposes within a world polity. When, for example, individuals connect through social media with others across the globe, they not only are more connected, they also are conscious of their social horizon transcending national boundaries that now mark internal lines within a global whole. Connectivity and organizing, actors and actions, in other words, involve a consciousness of the global as a whole (Robertson, 1992)—what is here conceptualized as a world culture of instrumental rationalism (or global rationalism, Boli and Thomas, 1999) that cuts across or overarches networks and organizational fields (see Buhari-Gulmez, 2010). It thus is important to expand our understanding of global cultural processes.

In the present work, I pursue this directive by analyzing world culture through two interrelated lines of argument. First, I critically analyze the scholarship on the diffusion of international norms, using this as a basis for critically assessing the literatures on global disjuncture, difference, and functional differentiation, arguing that 'norms' are embedded within institutionalized cultural structures. Second, I delineate some conditions for global diffusion including the importance of sites of contention and domestication in global-local dynamics.

This study points to the global reality depicted in discourse of international governmental organizations (IGOs), international non-governmental organizations (INGOs), and states: the realities and pragmatic actions discursively represented and prescribed are interpretable in terms of an overarching global consciousness here understood to be characterized by an instrumental rationalism. This approach questions methodological rationalism and methodological individualism prevalent in scholarship. Concluding reflections suggest that focusing on global culture connects with critical theory's agenda of problematizing modern sovereign identities and subjectivities.

International Norm Diffusion

The extensive scholarship in political sociology and international relations (IR) theory on international norm diffusion focuses on why states create and accept norms. Scholarship conceptualizes a norm as an isolated imperative that is created by states as interest-driven rational actors. Analyses focus on why states adopt and comply with a norm, which is viewed as the norm spreading or 'cascading' from one to another. An international norm is presumed to be purposive and functional and thus the research turns on finding the needs, interests, and rationales of states. This view presupposes a methodological individualism and a methodological rationalism and is consistent with seeing the world as a network of interdependent states. This paradigm has produced many insights into state actions, but it also is limiting with notable shortcomings. What is loosely termed constructivism in IR theory has as a corrective brought in cultural aspects that involve the motivations of moral entrepreneurs and the role of identities in state adoption of norms (e.g., Finnemore and Sikkink, 1998; Barnett and Finnemore, 2004). Several problems with the ensuing back-and-forth debates are important to note: empirical patterns do not support the functional, instrumental understandings of norms; the role of non-state actors and moral entrepreneurs belies common conceptualizations of rational actors such as principal-agent models; and the concept of 'a norm' is imprecise and obscures its embeddedness.

Norms are embedded in institutionalized cultural structures, an ontology or order of things, and are associated with equally embedded categoric actor identities. A cultural perspective shifts our attention from autonomous actors, organizations, and singular norms to institutionalized world cultural structures—cultural structures that are global in scope. In this view, the 'diffusion of norms' is the working out of global events constituting situated actors' purposes. Norms thus are not essentially instrumental solutions to problems among rational actors but are performative.

What is a Norm?

A norm commonly is understood to be a rule about behavior that actors construct and adopt. This understanding leads to debates about why they would do so. The prevalent answer is that actors create norms for functional, pragmatic reasons (e.g., Berger and Luckmann, 1966). For theories that explain structures in terms of rational actors, the interpretation is that states create and agree to rules to manage complexity by coordinating and controlling each other's actions, making it possible to optimize interests (e.g., Keohane and Nye, 2001; Keohane, 1993; see Coleman, 1990 for a general form of this argument). A criticism of this explanation is that norms seem to proliferate with no strong relationship to complexity or material interests (e.g., Drori et al., 2006). Moreover, it is well known in sociology of organizations research that formal rules are decoupled to varying extents from practices, making it a logical fallacy to explain formal rules in terms of functionality when they are not actually practiced (e.g., Meyer and Rowan, 1977; Thomas, 2010). Decoupling is pervasive in international organizations and apparent in gaps between formal state adoption and implementation.

A commonly proposed alternative interpretation is that non-state actors, labeled norm entrepreneurs, create norms because of value motivations, a line of interpretation labeled a cultural turn in IR theory (e.g., Finnemore and Sikkink, 1998). This loosens the presumption of material rationalism but does not fully pursue the embeddedness of actors and their values. More generally, taking non-state actors seriously, actors such as NGOs (Risse-Kappen, 1995; Boli and Thomas, 1997; Risse, 2002; Koppell, 2010) and social movement organizations and networks (Keck and Sikkink, 1998; Smith and Wiest, 2006), is important, but the tendency is to simply add them to the pantheon of interested actors and debate whether they are as value-oriented and democratic as they claim. The influence of international NGOs suggest a distinct authority, a rational moral (or rational voluntaristic, Boli and Thomas, 1997) authority that calls into question both methodological rationalism and individualism.

Critical social theorists (constructivists in IR) critique actor-centeredness and rationalism. They argue that power is built into institutional practices (following, for example, Foucault or Bourdieu), and by implication any norm has to be interpreted in its institutional context. Many constructivist studies, however, tend to explain institutionalized practices in terms of powerful actors, thereby slighting institutional cultural structures.

It is important to underscore the embeddedness of not only actors but also of norms. Most uses of the term 'norm' lack precision by conflating ideas, values, and behavior (Cancian, 1975). It is common, for example, to point to states' violations of international treaties to argue that a norm does not exist or has not diffused. The obvious shortcoming of this argument is that a norm is not marked by conformity to it but rather by whether others treat an action as a violation. Similarly, we would not presume a norm merely because we observe behavior consistent with it. The imprecision stems in part from treating a norm as an isolated, singular rule reducible to practice. That an international norm is embedded is commonly acknowledged but rarely pursued (e.g., Finnemore and Sikkink, 1998). Treating a norm in isolation has a long history in the social sciences, even as it has been thoroughly critiqued. The quintessential puzzles in classical social theory involved trying to understand sacred dietary laws: Why did God tell Moses to forbid the eating of pigs? Why do Hindus not eat cows? There are a number of extant explanations for each law in its singularity. Pigs, for example, are an inefficient resource, and eating them is unhealthy. To paraphrase Mary Douglas (1966), it is a shame to treat Moses as an early public health administrator; more generally, each singular rule requires a unique explanation.

A norm is embedded (Berger and Luckmann, 1966; Douglas, 1966, 1973; Geertz, 1973; Cancian, 1975; Bourdieu, 1977; Wuthnow, 1987; Robertson, 1992; Zerubavel, 1997). Structuralism and post-structuralism in particular, following Durkheim and Mauss (1903), pressed the idea that any rule is embedded in a cultural order of things—a set of bounded categories or identities. A categoric identity is constituted by rules that define it by drawing a boundary between it and other categories. Rules simultaneously constitute an identity and locate it relative to other identities. Any given rule makes sense only as part of the order of things and relative to bounded, categoric identities. A rule thus always carries implicitly the reality of the larger order. To violate a rule is to violate a categoric identity, to dislocate who one is, resulting in danger and threat. The embeddedness of norms requires that we shift our focus from a particular rule in isolation to the cultural order of things, to institutional contexts. These institutionalized structures have both cognitive and moral aspects and have been referred to as classification systems (e.g., Douglas, 1966, 1986), ontologies (Meyer, Boli and Thomas, 1987), moral orders (e.g., Wuthnow, 1987), and social imaginaries (Taylor, 2004). All of these appellations for 'culture' attempt to get at the conceptualization of culture as a structured order of things. These conceptualizations have parallels with the body of work of Foucault, and they are distinct from viewing culture primarily as values that are internalized.

An international norm thus cannot be understood apart from its cultural context; it is part of an institutional package: a set of categories, an order of things, a structure of identities and associated practices. For example, religious rights and the separation of state and religion are aspects of a model of the nation-state; yet, there is great variation in the actual constitutional rules and practices of religious rights. There is great variability among even Western states in the actual rules (e.g., compare the USA, France, and the Netherlands), but they are accounted as instances of the general model (Thomas, 2010). From another angle, even with very different particular rules and practices across national polities and across religious traditions, religious rights constitute general models of religion, individuality, and groups (Thomas, 2004). This is so because rights and categoric identities are part of the same order of things.

Diffusion or Global Event?

In an important sense, then, it is a cultural package or model that diffuses, not a singular norm (Strang and Meyer, 1993). Content and substance are important, and world institutionalized cultural structures comprise a global rationalism: actorhood ascribed to states, individuals, and corporations authorize and compel rational action, nature is rationalized as a passive field for action, and action is highly theorized. Actors are authorized and compelled to create the good society through rational actions, programs, and organizations, and thereby are open to model programs.

The establishing of a model globally can be viewed as a global event. Models are institutionalized globally and elements of them are adopted (or not) by particular states. There is much agency and diversity here, resulting in the empirical observations of hybridity and differences. This is not quite the same thing as diffusion. A state's policy might be directly copied by others because it is a successful embodiment of a globally established model. Consider the international testing of students on math and science such as the Programme for International Student Assessment (PISA) tests. Such testing is based on presumptions of the nature of math and science, on individual age-appropriate learning (and the theories behind them), and mass schooling, all of which tacitly are integral to nation-state purposes and globally mandated responsibilities. States throughout the world participate in this testing, and thereby take on these presumed global models. When students of a country such as Finland repeatedly score at the top, many states examine what Finland 'did right' and possibly adopt particular practices, curricula, and organizational designs. This copying is not precisely one country copying the model of another nor is it precisely the diffusion from one country to another. Rather, it is one state copying how another has successfully implemented a global model. A state copying how Finland performed so well makes sense only given the existence in the first place of the abstract, institutionalized cultural model and its association with nation-state identity and purpose. This shifts attention from isolated norms and policies to the creation and adoption of the international testing regime as a global model and its sources in the prior global establishment of science authority, schooling, human capital theories, and state purposes.

One might focus on a norm not as a singular entity but more as a foreground. In a picture, a foreground figure is an integral part of the whole and gains its identity and meaning from its relationship to the background. We can focus on it only relative to the background; that is, only relative to understanding its location in the whole. The adoption of a particular rule or policy such as Finnish math instruction (the foreground) is interpreted in the context of other already institutionalized cultural models (the background) such as state identities and purposes of developing human capital through mass schooling, and the presumed causal relationship between knowing how to do algebra and economic development. With other research purposes, we might want to explain the rise and diffusion of those models and we would then foreground them (for this usage of foreground and background, see Thomas, 1989).

One implication is that a norm will be adopted within a locale when the local culture or ontology is one in which the rule makes sense (Alasuutari and Qadir, 2013). A norm will diffuse into a locale if the local culture has an affinity to the cultural context of the norm. There is no suggestion that they must be identical or homogenized. There nevertheless needs to be an affinity between the structured orders, an 'elective affinity' of ontologies (Thomas, 1989). And again, this means that diffusion is really a working out of already present abstract models.

The Limits of Functional Differentiation and Disjuncture

Scholarly resistance to considering the presence of a global consciousness or world culture is reinforced by prevalent theoretical conceptualizations of modernity and globalization. Scholars across disciplines working from a variety of perspectives define modernity in terms of functional differentiation, information networks, disjunctures, and difference. Scholars working within phenomenology (Berger and Luckmann, 1966; Berger et al., 1973), post-structuralism (Douglas, 1966), and modern systems theory (Luhmann, 1996; Albert et al., 2010), view the defining characteristic of modernity as functional differentiation. Social life is marked by functionally differentiated spheres: public/private, politics, economics, law, religion, culture. The assumption is that functional differentiation results from objective, rational adaptation to increased complexity and density of population, exchange, and interdependencies. Formal organizations within the different spheres take on distinctive forms and logics. The prevalent interpretation is that these are highly compartmentalized, even autopoietic, spheres with distinctive logics (see Albert et al. 2013 for a comprehensive discussion). The different logics and grounds of organization, it is argued, preclude overarching cultural structures.

Yet, we observe across distinct functionally differentiated spheres common organizational forms and discourse. All reflect an instrumental rationalism marked by the dominance of science authority, professional experts, rationalized bureaucracies, and cost-benefit and outcome metrics. To explain this, scholars rely on some form of methodological rationalism: there is an isomorphism of organizational forms and discourse across differentiated spheres because these are objective adaptions to complexity. That is, the commonality among spheres that would account for these crosscutting similarities is not culture but nature. There are several problems with this style of explanation. One is that the degree to which rationalism dominates is out of proportion to the degree of complexity observed in different spheres and geographical locales (e.g., Drori et al., 2006). Also, there is a pervasively observed gap between formal organization and actual practices; this makes untenable functional explanations of formal organization in terms of its practical effects. The different spheres, moreover, show high levels of interpenetration. This sometimes is celebrated for knowledge diffusion while in other cases it is decried, such as when states or corporations compromise civil society (e.g., Alexander, 2006) or when religion and state are intermingled (Thomas, 2010). The fragility of spheres such as the civil sphere or separation of religion and state is puzzling if they are objective adaptations but expected if they are cultural projects.

Studies of transnational networks of experts and professionals document their emergence within specialized spheres, but they also show a universalistic rationalism. Modernity, globalization, and functional differentiation generally are marked by specialization and the professionalization of technocrats and intellectual elites, and these increasingly are transnational. Within each differentiated sphere (politics, development, law, education, child welfare, health) we can identify networks of intellectual elites, professional experts, who develop and press actors (states, organizations, individuals) to take efficient lines of action and follow 'best practices.' Scholars focus on socialization and network-based power and on developing objectively adaptive policies, whether they be functionally meeting systemic needs or functioning to protect elite interests. Yet, detailed studies and histories of professionalization and transnational experts show that they are dominated by rationalism (e.g., Kauppi and Madsen, 2013). They all marshal scientific authority and technical analysis to identify and legitimate rational policies and programs, best practices, and measured outcomes. They justify models in terms of efficiency and success. This work on transnational experts is consistent with more general sociological evidence that professionalization and a cadre of experts emerge in a system of professions and abstract rationalistic knowledge (Abbott, 1988).

Thus, the evidence suggests that functional differentiation and transnational intellectual, technocratic elites are found in a common cultural context. Global rationalism prescribes specialization and functional differentiation as modern rational organizing, even when objectively such abstract rationalism might not be (and sometimes obviously is not) appropriate. Functional differentiation and professionalization thus are projects and models for action.

Many scholars who focus on the importance of culture in globalization processes also tend to foreground disjuncture and compartmentalization. Appadurai (1996), for example, argues that we find distinct 'scapes' (e.g., mediascapes, ethnoscapes) highly differentiated and compartmentalized from each other and each internally marked by disjunctures. This captures much of what we observe worldwide. The conclusion is drawn that it is impossible to speak of a crosscutting or overarching global culture.

Despite the insights of this line of work, this conclusion is wrong for several reasons. First, it misses the fact that across these different scapes, there is an identifiable rationalism. There at times is explicit borrowing, a cultural arbitrage. Business best practices are applied to the arts and religion, and therapists apply scientific models to family relations. More generally, no sphere is immune to movements to reform, evaluate, measure, and rationally plan. The results certainly include tensions, contradictions, and resistance, not to mention differences and disjunctures. But this points to the second error: to conclude from differences that there is no overarching cultural context is to labor under the notion that culture is a container in which everyone is homogenized. The innovations in our understanding of culture over the last half-century make it clear that differences, contradictions, tensions, and resistance mark the presence of culture, not its absence. Culture is a set of claims about external boundaries; that everything within is the same and the only difference is inside and outside. Culture simultaneously is a set of claims about internal lines that categorize and order. These claims often are contradictory, contested, and highly situated. This approach to culture is not new and is somewhat commonplace, but it needs to be applied with some precision to global rationalism.

Conditions and Processes for Diffusion

Given the importance of considering world historical cultural contexts, it is useful to identify factors or conditions that promote the adoption of models in different locales and the kinds of tensions, contradictions, resistance, and hybridity generated. The general condition for adoption of models and norms locally is an affinity between global models and locales. Particular cultural factors include the constituting and maintenance of actorhood identity and purpose, the authorization of non-state actors both domestic and international, global events, the abstractness of institutionalized global models, and sites of contention within which the global and local are articulated (see Meyer et al., 1997; Strang and Meyer, 1993).

The Constituting of Actor Identities: States and Individuals

The categoric identity 'nation-state' constituting state authority and *raison d'*état is embedded in world cultural contexts. The nation-state emerged historically within the context of Christendom and subsequently the Westphalian interstate-system. States as externally legitimated civilizational projects created their societies as nations and constructed the individual largely through citizenship and rights (Strayer, 1970; Boli, 1987). In the current era of globalization, the world is a dense set of institutional structures constituting states and individuals. Nation-states are externally constituted with mandates and obligations, including mandates to generate economic development and to educate and develop their citizens. They often are reluctant to take on such obligations because of the costs involved and the often built-in failure to meet expectations and standards. In state-centered political sociology and IR what is external to the nation-states is simply other states. Here, however, the external is understood to be a polity and global institutional structures (Thomas et al., 1987) including what English School theorists refer to as master primary institutions (e.g., Buzan, 2004). States are oriented to the order of things and have rational and moral purpose (Reus-Smit, 1999). Nation-state identity thus is embedded in the same world cultural and world polity contexts as are international norms, and many of these norms are constitutive; consequently, there is a ready-made, structured predisposition to adopt them. This process accounts for the isomorphism among states and the often rapid diffusion of models and norms throughout the world.

Similarly, the constituting of persons as individuals creates a degree of individuality throughout the world. The nature of the individualism varies dramatically, but nevertheless the individual with value and rights is a categoric identity found throughout the world. Individuality is promoted globally by myriad international organizations that define a panoply of rights and needs, with responsibility for meeting them devolving onto the state, largely through national institutions such as mass schooling. Individuality also is promoted by other factors such as the incorporation of everyday life into capitalist markets and development programs. Moreover, one aspect of individualism is the obligation of individuals and their associations to others globally. In short, the individual is constituted by cultural structures, global in scope, that facilitate the diffusion of models and norms associated with individual identity and purpose. This process reinforces and is reinforced by mandates placed on the state to promote the flourishing of their citizens, and increasingly that of individuals who are not their citizens.

Norms that are constitutive and legitimating or that evidence good, moral, successful claims are likely to be practiced by actors in part because their practice legitimates actors' claims. Put simply if somewhat dryly, a state adopts such norms because it is a state; individuals act like individuals as ways of claiming individuality. This might seem circular or trivial, but it is useful when considering attempts to convince armed corporate kinship groups to adopt norms constitutive of nation-states. Discourse promoting the adoption of a model or norm will cast it in terms of the rational, moral requirements of the actors. Resisting the imposition of a model or norm often takes the form of delegitimating the associated identities: rejecting the 'Western state' or 'Western or decadent individualism.' Indeed, contentions over a specific norm might actually be over the ontological baggage that it carries. Locales in which identities of rational actorhood are already salient are relatively open to the adoption of aspects of abstract global models.

The Authorization of Non-State Actors

Because the world is a stateless society, the mandate to implement social and individual development devolves onto the rational-legal state, and also myriad actors are authorized to promote these purposes. These are voluntaristic associations, local NGOs, and INGOs. Many claim to have authority to act in the interest of others. These 'rationalized others' (Meyer, 1994) function as lobbyists and as experts (Boli and Thomas, 1997). They lobby IGOs to pressure states, and they target states directly through lobbying, boycotts, shaming, and protests. They include organizations of professional experts, many working in academia, that carry the rational, moral mandates of the world polity elaborating established principles and models, documenting newly identified shortcomings of existing institutions and policies, and presenting new reforms and rational programs. These actors articulate discourse that appeals to objective, scientific, technical necessities that compel actors to adopt a norm, policy, program, or reform. This rationalism also is highly moralistic: actors have a moral responsibility to pursue objective rational solutions to problems.

Non-state actors as rationalized others thus manage the scripts that are constitutive of rational actorhood. Many are technicians identifying appropriate practices and moral managers that delineate obligations. In the case of IGOs, states often are agents for implementing international agreements and purposes. INGOs and IGOs promulgate standards, responsibilities, and new programs, but it is the state that incurs the costs. In this sense, inverting the common scholarly understanding, states are agents of international organizations.

There is ample evidence for the influence of these non-state actors in getting states to adopt and even comply with international standards. For example, regarding the environment, studies document the power of discourse (Epstein, 2008), the role of INGOs in state compliance with standards (Prakash and Potoski, 2006) and their effects on environmental outcomes (Schofer and Hironaka, 2005). They seem to play a key role in getting states to comply with human rights instruments. While there is a well-documented gap between signing a treaty and implementing it, a record of compliance seems to be positively influenced by the density or structuration of international non-state actors (e.g, Hafner-Burton and Tsutsui, 2005).

One thus could argue generally that the presence of non-state actors increases the likelihood of diffusion, but this must be qualified. Many non-state actors are perceived as outsiders, agents of power from a distance, and they can produce resistance. Their authorization and the power of their discourse are rooted in a world culture that generates particular norms and standards. Thus resistance to a norm or to the influence of international non-state actors necessarily involves engaging the world cultural structures and one's own identity relative to them.

Global Models and Events

Cultural structures are institutionalized globally, and thus an argument has been made here to conceptualize the adoptions of a particular norm as instances of the working out of one global event. Andrew Abbott has conceptualized and attempted to develop statistical procedures for identifying an event associated with a sequence of occurrences (2001). An event might be the global creation of a type of welfare program or a set of rights and the event plays out through their adoptions by states (Abbott and DeViney, 1992).

To illustrate the approach, consider people leaving a movie theater at the end of a movie. This is commonly understood as a singular event and can be analyzed as such. It also can be analyzed as a series of individual actions; individuals' leaving a room is a common illustration of rational-actor theories and agent-based modeling. There is one person who leaves his or her seat and the theater first, and another is second. There are laggards who leave the latest even as employees are beginning the cleanup. If we were interested in individual behavior, then we would make much of individual motivations, interests, and preferences (why are some people so interested in the credits or why do others want to be the first out). If, however, we are interested in the event, we would focus on when the movie ends and thus on the movie schedule, how it is set, and how the schedule, rules of personal space, and ecology of movement shape the time pattern of people leaving. Clearly these levels are interrelated. The example is not meant to imply a strict correspondence to norm diffusion, but only that there are characteristics of an event as a whole over and above the actions and preferences of particular actors.

International conferences, IGO resolutions and programs, and other global events can establish and frame a problem that demands action, resulting in states adopting norms, policies, and programs and in activist mobilization. For example, the UN's inclusion of consumer rights in its 1969 statement on development was followed by nearly all nation-states in the world establishing national consumer rights agencies in the 1970s (Mei and Thomas, 1997). Similarly for activist organizations, the Stockholm Conference of 1972 established 'the environment' as a frame for myriad movements (such as clear air, clean water) and was followed by an increase in the rate of founding of environmental organizations and in change generally (Wapner, 1996; Frank et al., 1999; see Epstein, 2008 for the role of discourse in this process and Hironaka, 2014 for conceptualizing the institutional creation of 'workspaces').

The Abstractness of the Cultural Models and their Reification

Strang and Meyer argue that the degree of abstraction or the degree to which a model is theorized affects its diffusion. By theorized or theorization, they mean a self-conscious elaboration and abstraction of categories and relationships (1993, p. 492) consistent with global rationalism—a highly theorized rationality oriented to abstract ends. Science authority plays an important role in the reification of this theorization by locating it in nature. It, moreover, depicts nature as a mechanical system that is passive and open to human action. It thereby casts expert, technical knowledge as objective, as something independent of actors and culture. The sociology of science shows, of course, that science in practice operates in interested and culturally informed ways, whether in terms of professional interests or in terms of penetration by interested actors. Nevertheless, the nexus of professional experts and abstract knowledge are an integral part of science's authority and what is constituted as objective, unbiased knowledge (e.g., Drori et al., 2003), usefully conceptualized as epistemic governance (Alasuutari and Qadir, 2014).

Abstract models, moreover, are constitutive of civilization, and they legitimate claims to actorhood. The arts and sciences were associated with civilization early in the emergence of the state (e.g., Wuthnow, 1987) and continue to be associated with development and progress. As another example, Donnelly (1998) suggests that the purposes and model of human rights became in the latter half of the twentieth century a standard of civilization.

Consequently, programs and norms are more likely to be adopted by actors if the models in which they are embedded are (1) abstract and theorized, (2) reified through science authority, and (3) markers of civilization. This is mutually reinforcing with actor identities to the degree that these same models constitute nation-state identity and purpose. Given high levels of abstraction, actors are authorized to specify and adapt models, resulting in great potential for contention over not so much whether or not to adopt the models but how and in what form. Again consider religious rights and the separation of state and religious organization: The abstractness of the principles of religious freedom and separation of state and religious organization results in great variations and in much contention, as witnessed by international debates in the United Nations and by court cases in national and international courts.

Sites of Contention: Affinity of Locales and World Cultural Structures

Local actors and states are embedded in local and national cultural contexts, and greater affinity between these and global rationalism will increase the likelihood and degree of diffusion. Historically, from the origins of the modern nation-state, states have been legitimated by external sovereignty (sovereignty constituted and recognized externally) and then have faced long fights over establishing internal sovereignty (recognition by authorities, groups, and actors internally) (see for example Strayer, 1970; Geary, 2002). Since World War II states enact externally sourced mandates (e.g., mass education, population policy, gender equality, development), requiring the expansion of state authority into society in the face of varying degrees of local openness and resistance.

State policies and interventions domestically vary in the degree to which they are in sync with national society. While state adoption of a norm, policy, or program might be taken as diffusion, decoupling implementation might be due to being out of sync with the population and locale. International organizations that pressure the state to implement such policies also find themselves at odds with local institutional structures. Yet, national and local populations are themselves very likely to be highly connected to world cultural models, through education, media, markets, diaspora and transnational communities, professional networks, and participation in INGOs. In most countries banal domestic issues and debates already include world models and institutions such as development, instrumentality, individualism, and rights (Alasuutari and Qadir, 2013). Even in local sites, many global cultural elements are already presumed and most of the major players likely are present: agents of IGOs, INGO members, state officials, municipal officials, and community members including kin and religious leaders. Those claiming actorhood eagerly negotiate the design of policies and organizations. Those claiming disinterested expertise and moral authority ('otherhood' in Meyer, 1994) eagerly advise and support, lobby and pressure.

Thus, policymaking, debates, contentions, and decisions are situated in sites that to varying degrees articulate the local and national with global rationalism. The adoption of abstract global models means not just the global confronting the local or national nor a mechanical diffusion; it means the establishing of discursive sites in which actor identities, lines of action, policies, programs, and discourse are framed, articulated, and contested. In identifying conditions for adoption of global models and norms, one needs to better understand the characteristics of these sites.

Çevik (2015) in a study of Islamic resurgence in Turkey develops the concept of 'cultural sites of hybridity' which are institutional locations in which actors apply, articulate, contest, and innovate institutional models. Çevik identifies national political institutions, entrepreneurial production and middle-class consumption, and civic associations among others as such sites. Global pressures toward neo-liberalization in Turkey resulted in an emergence of a new globally oriented bourgeoisie that was rooted in Muslim sensibilities. Eschewing both secular and

Islamist (fundamentalist) orientations, they worked out rationalized, individuated Islam (what Çevik terms Muslimism) with modern institutions in cultural sites of hybridity that produce civic participation, Muslim-sensitive consumer goods, and predispositions for liberal state policies.

Alasuutari and associates identify national decision-making arenas such as parliaments and analyze the discourse surrounding the adoption of policies that are pressed by international organizations, such as child-centered educational reform. Discourse supporting the proposed policy relies heavily on epistemic governance (Alasuutari and Qadir, 2014), the objective scientific expertise behind the new reforms and the various organizations and experts. Supportive discourse points to reforms adopted by other countries with positive results. This is a synchronization (Alasuutari and Qadir, 2013) in which one country synchronizes its policies to those of other countries not as bilateral imitation but rather as adopting a successful implementation of an established global model. At the same time, such policies rooted externally can seem foreign and as interference, and they thus are framed as being nationalistic and consistent with national identity. This can require nuanced discourse and politicking: supportive actors simultaneously rely heavily on international epistemic governance and distance the policy or norm from the foreignness of international organizations and other states (Boyle, 2002). The result is what Alasuutari and Qadir refer to as domestication (2013).

Hironaka (2014) argues that international institutions create multi-scale sites, what she terms 'workspaces' in which myriad actors contest and negotiate issues. International institutions often do not have linear, causal effects on outcomes, often interpreted as ineffectiveness. Yet they establish workspaces embedded in global rationalism, and the resulting contentions and negotiations are steered however tacitly in rationalistic directions. She shows for several environmental issues how international institutions created workspaces that generated chaotic issues and tangents and contentions among a myriad of actors but out of which emerged in unintended ways a coherent framing and subsequent cumulative change.

Sites thus are scaled from the local to the global with state and national institutions often but not always mediating between the global and local; all scales can be, and arguably are, in some way present in every other site. Consider again religious rights and the separation of state and religious organization. Sites of policymaking and contention range from the United Nations to international courts to various nation-state agencies to municipal zoning laws to local communities. Highly personal issues of religious expression and conversion involve religious communities, immediate family and kinship systems. For example, a large percentage of court cases over religion, including international courts such as the European Court of Human Rights, involve children and schools. Consequently, the European Court and local sites of interaction among parents, children, teachers, and school boards are not merely interconnected but are interwoven with identities and meanings.

Cultural Analysis and Critical Theory

It has been argued that human freedom lies in the ambiguities, contradictions, and tensions of culture and is threatened by the presumed necessities of technique (Ellul, 1985, 1967). If theories rooted in methodological rationalism and individualism were able to explain patterns of globalization, there would be little room for critiquing global rationalism. If there is one set of material conditions that are determinative, and if there is one matrix of technical means 'discovered' by experts that determine 'best practices,' then we would be in the realm of necessity. There would be no distance between our consciousness, reflection, and decision-making on the one hand and the supposed objective conditions. Global rationalism promises human sovereignty to create the global good society, but it requires that we do only what needs to be done. The propensity of states to adopt all sorts of policies and norms results from their drawing on global cultural structures to formulate practices that stake claims to sovereignty and civilization. Any adequate critique of global rationalism therefore must problematize the modern subject and its claim to sovereignty, thereby connecting with a central concern of critical theory (e.g., Walker, 2010).

Merely accepting the now commonplace that globalization is a technological-economic juggernaut entails the acceptance, however unconscious, of modern identities and subjectivities. This view embodied in methodological rationalism and individualism, however, has problems explaining empirical patterns of globalization and the diffusion of norms. Taking seriously the operation of a global culture is better able to explain such phenomena. By analyzing globally institutionalized cultural ontologies, we undermine the reification of technique, instrumentalism, and modern sovereign subjects, and press for analysis of otherwise taken-for-granted modern identities and subjectivities.

References

Abbott, A. 1988. *The System of Professions*. Chicago, IL: Chicago University Press.

Abbott, A. 2001. *Time Matters: On Theory and Method*. Chicago, IL: University of Chicago Press.

Abbott, A., and S. DeViney. 1992. 'The Welfare State as Transnational Event: Evidence from Sequences of Policy Adoption.' *Social Science History* 16(2): 245–74.

Alasuutari, P., and A. Qadir (eds). 2013. *National Policy Making: Domestication of Global Trends*. London: Routledge.

Alasuutari, P., and A. Qadir. 2014. 'Epistemic Governance: An Approach to the Politics of Policy-Making.' *European Journal of Cultural and Political Sociology* 1(1): 67–84.

Albert, M., B. Buzan, and M. Zürn (eds). 2013. *Bringing Sociology to International Relations: World Politics as Differentiation Theory.* Cambridge: Cambridge University Press.

Albert, M., L. Cederman, and A. Wendt (eds). 2010. *New Systems Theories of World Politics.* New York: Palgrave.

Alexander, J.C. 2006. *The Civil Sphere.* Oxford: Oxford University Press.

Appadurai, A. 1996. 'Disjuncture and difference in the Global Cultural Economy.' In *Modernity at Large: Cultural Dimensions of Globalization,* 27–48. Minneapolis: University of Minnesota Press.

Barnett, M., and M. Finnemore. 2004. *Rules for the World: International Organizations in Global Politics.* Ithaca, NY: Cornell University Press.

Berger, P., and T. Luckmann. 1966. *The Social Construction of Reality.* Garden City, NY: Anchor Books.

Boli, J. 1987. 'Human Rights or State Expansion? Cross-National Definitions of Constitutional Rights, 1870–1970.' In *Institutional Structure: Constituting State, Society and the Individual,* edited by G.M. Thomas, J.W. Meyer, F.O. Ramirez, and J. Boli, Chapter 6. Newbury Park, CA: Sage.

Boli, J., and G.M. Thomas. 1997. 'World Culture in the World Polity: A Century of International Non-Governmental Organization.' *American Sociological Review* 62(April): 171–90.

Boli, J., and G.M. Thomas (eds). 1999. *Constructing World Culture: International Nongovernmental Organizations since 1875.* Stanford, CA: Stanford University Press.

Bourdieu, P. 1977 [1972]. *Outline of a Theory of Practice.* Cambridge: Cambridge University Press.

Boyle, E.H. 2002. *Female Genital Cutting: Cultural Conflict in the Global Community.* Baltimore, MD: The Johns Hopkins University Press.

Buhari-Gulmez, D. 2010. 'Stanford School on Sociological Institutionalism: A Global Cultural Approach.' *International Political Sociology* 4(3): 253–70.

Buzan, B. 2004. *From International to World Society? English School Theory and the Social Structure of Globalization.* Cambridge: Cambridge University Press.

Cancian, F. 1975. *What are Norms?* Cambridge: Cambridge University Press.

Çevik, N. 2015. *Muslimism in Turkey and Beyond: Religion in the Modern World.* New York: Palgrave.

Coleman, J.S. 1990. *Foundations of Social Theory.* Cambridge, MA: Harvard University Press.

Donnelly, J. 1998. 'Human Rights: A New Standard of Civilization?.' *International Affairs* 74(1): 1–23.

Douglas, M. 1966. *Purity and Danger.* London: Penguin.

Douglas, M. 1973. *Rules and Meanings: The Anthropology of Everyday Knowledge.* London: Penguin.

Douglas, M. 1986. *How Institutions Think.* Syracuse. NY: Syracuse University Press.

Drori, G.S., J.W. Meyer, and H. Hwang. 2006. *Globalization and Organization: World Society and Organizational Change.* New York: Oxford University Press.

Drori, G.S., J.W. Meyer, F.O. Ramirez, and E. Schofer. 2003. *Science in the Modern World Polity: Institutionalization and Globalization.* Stanford, CA: Stanford University Press.

Durkheim, E., and M. Mauss. 1963[1903]. *Primitive Classifications.* Chicago, IL University of Chicago Press.

Ellul, J. 1967. *The Political Illusion.* New York: Knopf.

Ellul, J. 1985. *The Humiliation of the Word.* Grand Rapids, MI: Eerdmans.

Epstein, C. 2008. *The Power of Words in International Relations: Birth of an Anti-Whaling Discourse.* Cambridge, MA: MIT Press.

Finnemore, M., and K. Sikkink. 1998. 'International norm Dynamics and Political Change.' *International Organization* 52(4): 887–917.

Frank, D., A. Hironaka, J.W. Meyer, E. Schofer, and N. Tuma. 1999. 'The Rationalization and Organization of Nature in World Culture.' In *Constructing World Culture*, edited by J. Boli and G.M. Thomas, 81–99. Stanford, CA: Stanford University Press.

Geary, P.J. 2002. *The Myth of Nations: The Medieval Origins of Europe.* Princeton, NJ: Princeton University Press.

Geertz, C. 1973. *The Interpretation of Cultures.* New York: Basic Books.

Hafner-Burton, E., and K. Tsutsui. 2005. 'Human Rights in a Globalizing World: The Paradox of Empty Promises.' *American Journal of Sociology* 110(5): 1373–411.

Hironaka, A. 2014. *Greening the Globe.* Cambridge: Cambridge University Press.

Kauppi, N., and M.R. Madsen (eds). 2013. *Transnational Power Elites: The New Professionals of Governance, Law and Security.* London: Routledge.

Keck, M., and K. Sikkink. 1998. *Activists Beyond Borders: Advocacy Networks in International Politics.* Ithaca, NY: Cornell University Press.

Keohane, R.O. 1993. 'Institutional Theory and the Realist Challenge after the Cold War.' In *Neorealism and Neoliberalism: The Contemporary Debate*, edited by D.A. Baldwin, 269–300. New York: Columbia University Press.

Keohane, R.O. and J.S. Nye. 2000[1977]. 'Realism and Complex Interdependencies.' In *Power and Interdependence*, 3rd edn, Chapter 2. New York: Longman.

Koppell, J.G.S. 2010. *World Rule: Accountability, Legitimacy, and the Design of Global Governance.* Chicago, IL University of Chicago Press.

Luhmann, N. 1996. *Social Systems.* Stanford, CA: Stanford University Press.

Mei, Y., and G.M. Thomas. 1997. 'International Non-Governmental Organizations and the Global Spread of Consumer Rights Organizations and Models.' Paper presented at the Annual Meetings of the American Sociological Association, Toronto, Canada.

Meyer, J.W. 1994. 'Rationalized Environments' in *Institutional Environments and Organizations: Structural Complexity and Individualism*, edited by W.R. Scott and J.W. Meyer, 28–54. London: Sage.

Meyer, J. W., and B. Rowan. 1977. 'Institutionalized Organizations: Formal Structure as Myth and Ceremony.' *American Journal of Sociology* 83(1): 340–63.

Meyer, J.W., J. Boli, and G.M. Thomas. 1987. 'Ontology and Rationalization in the Western cultural Account.' In *Institutional Structure: Constituting State, Society and the Individual*, edited by G.M. Thomas, J.W. Meyer, F.O. Ramirez, and J. Boli, 12–27. Newbury Park, CA: Sage.

Meyer, J.W., J. Boli, G.M. Thomas, and F.O. Ramirez. 1997. 'World society and the Nation-State' *American Journal of Sociology* 103(1): 144–81.

Prakash, A., and M. Potoski. 2006. 'Racing to the Bottom? Trade, Environmental Governance, and ISO 14001.' *American Journal of Political Science* 50(April): 350–64.

Reus-Smit, C. 1999. *The Moral Purpose of the State: Culture, Social Identity, and Institutional Rationality in International Relations*. Princeton, NJ: Princeton University Press.

Risse, T. 2002. 'Transnational Actors and World Politics.' In *Handbook of International Relations*, edited by W. Carlsnaes, T. Risse, and B. Simmons. Chapter 13. Newbury Park, CA: Sage.

Risse-Kappen, T. 1995. *Bringing Transnational Relations Back In*. Cambridge: Cambridge University Press.

Robertson, R. 1992. *Globalization: Social Theory and Global Culture*. Newbury Park, CA: Sage.

Schofer, E., and A. Hironaka. 2005. 'The Effects of World Society on Environmental Protection Outcomes.' *Social Forces* 84(1): 25–47.

Smith, J., and D. Wiest. 2006. 'National and Global Foundations of Global Civil Society,' In *Global Social Change*, edited by C. Chase-Dunn and S. Babones, 289–313. Baltimore, MD: The Johns Hopkins University Press.

Strayer, J. 1970. *On the Medieval Origins of the Modern State*. Princeton, NJ: Princeton University Press.

Taylor, C. 2004. *Modern Social Imaginaries*. Durham, NC, and London: Duke University Press.

Thomas, G.M. 1989. *Revivalism and Cultural Change*. Chicago, IL: University of Chicago Press.

Thomas, G.M. 2004. 'Constructing World Civil Society through Contentions over Religious Rights.' *Journal of Human Rights* 3(2): 239–51.

Thomas, G.M. 2010. 'Differentiation, Rationalization, and Actorhood in New Systems and World Culture Theories,' In *New Systems Theories of World Politics*, edited by M. Albert, L.-E. Cederman, and A. Wendt, 220–48. New York: Palgrave.

Thomas, G.M. 2013. 'Rationalized Cultural Contexts of Functional Differentiation.' In *Bringing Sociology to International Relations: World Politics as Differentiation Theory*, edited by M. Albert, B. Buzan, and M. Zürn, 27–49. Cambridge: Cambridge University Press.

Walker, R.B.J. 2010. *After the Globe, Before the World*. New York: London.

Wapner, P. 1996. *Environmental Activism and World Civic Politics*. Albany, NY: SUNY Press.

Wuthnow, R. 1987. *Meaning and Moral Order: Explorations in Cultural Analysis.* Berkeley: University of California Press.

Zerubavel, E. 1997. *Social Mindscapes.* Cambridge, MA: Harvard University Press.

Chapter 6

Rationalizing Global Consciousness: Scientized Education as the Foundation of Organization, Citizenship, and Personhood

Gili S. Drori

Studies of global or comparative education have offered ample evidence for the global and worldwide expansion of education. Indeed, now in the second decade of the twenty-first century, global youth literacy rate has reached 89 percent and over 150 countries have enshrined education as a right by including constitutional provisions for free and nondiscriminatory education. And although many countries are falling far short of the progress targets set for education and literacy in the Millennium Development Goals, the core features of education—from schools, to curricula, to excellence measures, to teacher training—are increasingly similar worldwide and are made further uniform through processes of benchmarking and the homogenizing effect of education experts. Much of this worldwide expansion and uniformity is driven by the exemplar of Western leadership, and, in spite of many decades of critique of Western domination and a growing number of development success cases outside the West, the principal features of education remain Western in character. Scientization is prime among such features. Scientization is the penetration of science-like logics and scientific-like practices into everyday life in general and into the everyday life of education in particular. The result is the global expansion, diffusion, and prominence of *scientized education*, where education is colored by scientization. Therefore, it is the notion of scientized education in particular, rather than education in general, that best captures the global and worldwide trends repeatedly documented. And it is scientized education that has become a global institution, or a sacred cultural element of contemporary society, and legitimates global forms of both connectivity and consciousness.

In this essay, I explore the impact that the global expansion of scientized education bears on the nature of societies worldwide. I argue that scientization, occurring primarily through education, permeates all spheres of hypermodern life and, by changing modes of thinking and consciousness, also changes modes of organization, social engagement and thus connectivity. Building on Drori and Meyer's (2006) description of scientization as a lever for formal organization, I herein describe scientized education as also a lever for a new mode of citizenship and personhood. I argue that scientized education is a rationalizing mechanism and a mechanism for empowerment, which constitutes the organization and the person as purposive, as bounded even if embedded, and as a universal entity. To support these claims, this chapter describes the cultural tenets of scientized education, thus outlining the themes of global consciousness that scientized education carries and constitutes. Following, the chapter describes the manner by which these features of global consciousness imprint the principal features of globalization. In this way, the arguments brought here challenge conventional descriptions of globalization as interdependencies by pointing to the cultural and institutional foundations of globalization.

Scientized Education

Even before designating the current state of affairs as 'knowledge society' or 'knowledge economy,' in which the role of knowledge production is reserved for education and science, education and science were regarded as the foundation for progress. Since the Enlightenment era, and more dramatically since the late nineteenth century in the West and the post-World War II era worldwide, both education and science were given the task of building human capital capacity, socializing into modernity, and thus allowing for the harnessing of human capacity toward improvement of natural and human conditions (Chabbott and Ramirez, 2000; Drori, Meyer, Ramirez and Schofer, 2003). Regardless of the actual contribution of science and education to human development, this utilitarian, developmentalist, and functionalist agenda has constituted the synergy between education and science (Drori, 1998, 2000; Carter, 2005). Education and science are assumed to be linearly connected into the 'pipeline' of human capital formation (see Figure 6.1). In this scheme, science and education are inseparable institutions: much like the linguistic turn in STS scholarship to increasingly rely on the term 'technoscience,' the term 'scientized education' represents such synergy.

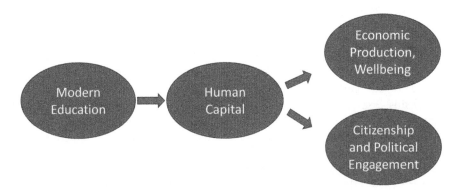

Figure 6.1   Science and education as foundations for social development: A realist approach

The global dimensions of scientized education are a result of two intertwined processes: the dramatic expansion of education worldwide and global scientization. First, the worldwide diffusion of education (Meyer, Ramirez, and Soysal, 1992), which is delivering a consolidated model of primary, secondary, and increasingly also tertiary education to national education systems worldwide (Ramirez and Ventresca, 1992), is evident in the expanding reaches and scope of education. As Meyer and Ramirez argue, '[s]chooling the masses is a core theme on national agendas, and any erosion in primary educational enrollments is everywhere treated as evidence of severe national crisis' (2000, p. 121). The institutionalization of formal education is driven by the shared belief that education is both an individual and collective good (Meyer and Ramirez, 2000), the panacea for every social ill or crisis (see, for example, Uriah and Wosu, 2012), and recently also a universal human right (see, for example, Spring, 2000; Grover, 2004; McCowan, 2010). As such, the massification of schooling is directly inspired by the global normative pillars of progress and justice (Meyer, Ramirez and Soysal, 1992; Ramirez and Ventresca, 1992; Meyer and Ramirez, 2000; Ramirez, 2012).

Second, into this global expansion of education comes science, with both an expansion of science education activities and with the penetration of science logic into social definitions of erudition, knowledge, and learning. Most evidently, STEM (science, technology, engineering, and math) curricula became a core component of education practices (Benavot et al., 1991; Kamens et al., 1996; McEneaney and Meyer, 2006) and has taken a similar form and content in spite of the differentiating characteristics of education systems worldwide (McComas and Olson, 2002; Baker and LeTendre, 2005). Also, methods of governing the education sector rely on scientized instruments, mainly for assessment of student performance, pedagogical efficacy, and system efficiency. From a cultural perspective, the notion of scientized education goes far beyond the current emphasis of 'science for all' initiatives of adding science-related subjects and demanding competency in science-like methods. Rather, scientization highlights the infusion of modern and contemporary education with scientization. This means that 'scientific literacy' is institutionalized as an unopposed component of erudition and that science logic has transformed the character of learning and the practice of schooling. The most obvious example for this intense scientization of education is the invasion of education systems' standardized testing to evaluate educational progress (Kamens and McNeely, 2010). Such tests, which are now routine in education systems at national, state, city, and other levels, are developed upon scientized schemes, which are thick with assumptions about optimal methods for evolution and result in a series of scientized outputs, such as ranking of student performance and school success (see, Pizmony-Levy et al., 2014). In these ways, and in many others, education is scientized to its core: education is organized around the scientized scripts that 'convey an epistemology of method and facts, systematic analysis and proof, order and verification' and whose authority takes 'precedence over moral, political, or authoritarian judgments' (Drori and Meyer, 2006, p. 61). Overall, scientization has permeated into, and also constituted, this world of expanded education.

The worldwide and global institutionalization of scientized education defies functionalist and utilitarian explanations. Scientized education is commonplace in societies where the functional utility of such educational capacity or of such human capital skills is, at best, unclear. For example, Benavot (1992) shows that, in comparison with other world regions, African countries devote the highest share of their primary and secondary school hours to science and math instruction regardless of prospects for science training in higher education or of labor force prospects in science-related professions in this world region. Therefore, the strong appeal of scientized education comes because it is a source of legitimacy. Indeed, 'adherence to rational myths can influence the ability of educational development INGOs to marshal resources' (Bromley, 2010, p. 597) and reliance on scientized forms of operation, evaluation, and action, which are captured in such common practices as strategic planning and data-driven assessments, speaks to the authority of science as an analytic grid of modernity (Drori, Meyer, Ramirez and Schofer, 2003). In these many ways, the scientization of education, while multifaceted and comprehensive, is giving body to global culture and consciousness. And as a global cultural force, scientized education bears a wide-ranging, both concrete and abstract, impact on hypermodern global society.

Scientized Education and Organization

The corresponding processes of the scientization of society and the socialization of science (Schofer, 1999), which blurred the boundaries between science and society, are enabling the impact of scientized education on multiple and diverse sets of social institutions. In previous work co-authored with John W. Meyer (Drori and Meyer, 2006), which itself drew upon our study of the global institutionalization of science (Drori, Meyer, Ramirez and Schofer, 2003), we explored the mechanisms by which scientization gives rise to organization. Specifically, we outlined three such mechanisms – professionalization, rationalization, and actorhood – each highlighting a unique dimension of scientization and thus having a distinct impact on organization. In the following section, I explain the role of scientized education plays in driving organization.

Organization stands not only for a singular and formal social entity but also highlights the preferred mode of authority. Formal organization is, therefore, both a bureaucratized set of operations and a logic of operation and governance. Formal organization has expanded enormously worldwide: more than ever before, social activities of various sorts and in various sectors have become formally organized. Yet, unexpectedly, much of this dramatic expansion of formal organization comes with webbed and diffuse coordination and with emphasis on 'soft law' and voluntary compliance measures, rather than on central control and enforcement. This hypermodern and global organization is uniquely professionalized, rationalized, and empowered and, central to this discussion, builds on scientized education to further its grip on world society.

First, scientized education bears a direct and concrete impact on organization through professionalization. The scientized nature of professional education constructs professional tools and solidifies professional ethos around such tools; the profession of accounting is defined by the terminology and methods for measuring, processing, and reporting of financial information, whereas psychologists are trained to describe and guide the mental capacity and behavior of humans in accordance to their professional taxonomies and strategies. In this regard, scientized education is very much a guild practice that involves instruction and often also apprenticeship in the 'tools of the trade.'

Second, scientized education constitutes rationalization, which is a prime feature of organization. Rationalization, defined by Meyer and Jepperson as 'the cultural accounting of society and its environments in terms of articulated, unified, integrated, universalized, and causally and logically structured schemes' (2000, p. 102), is the process of applying a systematized and standardized scheme that links cause with effect and means with ends. Through rationalization, scientized education establishes order in nature and in society. Most chaotic elements of life, such as risk and uncertainty, are tamed through scientized education and its tools; we restate risk in terms of 'error terms' and 'statistical margins' and uncertainty in terms of 'scenario planning' and 'futures exchange.' These scientized terms are at the core of management professionalization and, consequently, organization has become highly rationalized.

Third, scientized education constitutes organization by imbuing the organization with agency. The cultural theme of actorhood, which instills a sense of agency into the constituted social actor, is central to world society in numerous ways. Specific to organization, the most obvious and direct impact of scientized education is through the expansion of access to the world of authoritative knowledge; the massification of access to what once was reserved for 'the Mandarin' is allowing for scientized education to drive the 'professionalization of everybody' (Wilensky, 1964).

Overall, scientized education affects organization in an indirect and abstract manner by constituting modes of thinking that rationalize organization and infuse it with agency (see following sections). Scientized education—through its role as a mechanism of professionalization, rationalization, and actorhood—'allows organizations to be manageable units and forms the cadre of managers as taking charge of this real and empowered social actor' that is the organization and is the 'core process in the hyper-organization of world society' (Drori and Meyer, 2006, pp. 64, 53). The effect of scientized education on organization is self-propelling; the professionalization of professional education escalated scientization by reinforcing scientized education as a principle of all professional training. In other words, once trained as professionals, the 'guild,' or profession, is then charged with imparting its professional knowledge and practices onto the world of organization; some professions, most pronouncedly professional managers, are defined as a transnational social category, and, therefore, management is given generic responsibilities as administrators of organizations. Last, scientized education changes the organization by bringing together the cultural-normative with the cognitive-behavioral, thus reinforcing the link between culture and identity (Erez and Drori, 2009), constructing both organizations and the people in them as social agents (Meyer and Bromley, 2013) and preparing them to partake in society as citizens.

Scientized Education and Citizenship

By imbuing organizations and people with agency, scientized education constructs citizenship. From a functionalist perspective, education is a mechanism of socialization into the role of citizen and much of the discussion about the relationship between scientized education and citizenship revolves around the notion of 'scientific citizenship.' Education, even a liberal arts curriculum (Nussbaum, 2002), nurtures the human capacity to compile information, reason through it, and thus reach informed decisions, all of which are critical for political action and democratic involvement (see Figure 6.1). Building upon earlier discussions of literacy and citizenship, specifically of science and democracy (see, for example, Ezrahi, 1990), scientific citizenship focuses on the acquisition of scientific literacy to affect involvement in public life (Elam and Bertilsson, 2003). The notion of 'scientific citizenship' is used to understand the involvement of informed yet 'ordinary' laypeople that rely on scientized data to organize campaigns and politicize scientific endeavors (Gofen, 2012, 2013). Therefore, scientific citizenship comes into play in debates concerning genetically modified organisms (Goven, 2006; Horst, 2007), home-schooling and other parental entrepreneurship in education (Gofen and Blomqvist, 2013), global warming (Frank, 2013), and anti-vaccination campaigns (Gofen and Needham, 2014). Such acts of scientific citizenship are among the modes of utilization of research for public policymaking (Weiss, 1979; Eyal and Levy, 2013).

At the same time, these acts of challenging state dictates and other noncompliance reveal that '[a]renas once reserved to the sole judgment of scientists now await professionalized science-based judgment from laypeople under the assumption that people can all be scientifically literate' (Drori and Meyer, 2006, p. 52). More importantly, the scientization of politics in such acts expresses a profound sense of agency: through scientization the organization-citizen and the person-citizen engage with their role as citizens in a rationalized manner, involving themselves in public life in an informed, ordered, and calculative way (Figure 6.2). Scientific citizenship is, therefore, a part of the hypermodern redefinition of authority and a redrawing of authority relations. First, authority relations are contractualized. Specifically, the relationship between public administration and the citizen is formalized through citizen contracts, turning the citizen into a client and the public administrator into a service provider (Andersen, 2007). Second, authority is asserted in scientific, rather than moral, ethical, or charismatic terms. Specifically, whereas decisions regarding the sanctity of the Sabbath or the virtues of euthanasia could have relied on the eminence of pious figures, such forms of authority are overshadowed by the rationalized, professionalized and agentic—or scientized—mode of governmentality (Drori and Meyer, 2006). Scientized governmentality means that science-based and science-like practices are the basis for administration, management and other forms of exercising power and order. In its appearance as 'soft law,' scientized governmentality is a cultural and abstract, rather than directly political or economic, mode of control. For example, the statistical formulas that relate data into categories and rank universities for excellence, countries for corruption, or corporations for their social responsibility initiatives, construct categories of good or bad, worthy or shameful, valuable or useless. In this way the scientized practices of quantification and valuation (see Espeland and Stevens, 2008; Lamont, 2012) also serve as a mechanism for institutionalizing governance.

Moreover, this scientized mode of governance spills over the brim of professional epistemic authority (see, for example, Seabrooke, 2014) to the lay-yet-informed citizen-agent. This defines scientized, rather than scientific, citizenship. Yet, while scientized citizenship privileges experts over lay citizens, potentially deterring civil involvement (Bromley, 2010, p. 598), the drama of hypermodern authority comes from the importance given to the voice of the informed layperson. Much of this empowerment of the informed, enabled layperson is a product of the information revolution (Shapiro, 1999) and the balance it brings to so-called 'information asymmetries.' And yet, over and above the platform afforded by information and communications technology, scientization continuously defines new taxonomies, and by attributing interests and agency to these categories scientization constructs them as social entities (Meyer and Jepperson, 2000; Drori, Meyer, Ramirez and Schofer, 2003). Over the course of the twentieth century and accelerating at the turn of the twenty-first century, the ontological place of such entities came to be redefined, as citizenship was redefined in universalistic terms, giving rise to the notion of the 'global citizen' (Buckner and Russell, 2013), whose rights and responsibilities are predicated not solely on national law but rather draw upon universal principles. 'The progressive inclination today,' writes Ramirez about education (2006, p. 380), 'is to think in terms of persons and their rights independent of their citizenship status.'

Scientized Education and Personhood

Personhood, or actorhood in general, is the theme that runs through the relations between scientization and both organization and citizenship. This means that what is understood as entrepreneurial initiative or citizen activism, both of which are based upon education and information, is essentially an expression of actorhood, the logic of constituting the social entity as an empowered agent. Seeing that an actor is commonly defined as a person who is infused with a sense of agency and a responsibility to act (see Elliott, 2007), actorhood is essentially personhood, even when referring to collective entities such as corporations, associations, or nation-states (see, for example, Matten and Crane, 2005; Kruecken and Meier, 2006).

The defining characteristic of personhood is agency or action: Meyer and Jepperson refer to the constructed person as the 'legitimated agent and carrier of authority, responsibility, and capacity to act' (2000, p. 106). As noted earlier in regard to scientized citizenship, the definition of the person through her action drives much the intervention by citizens. It accounts for the intervention demanded of the literati (which is captured in the discussions of the social role of 'public intellectuals' and the role of expertise in the public sphere; Eyal and Bucholtz, 2010) and it is increasingly also expected of laypersons. Action is also extended from personhood to otherhood, namely 'from agency for the self to agency for other actors' (Meyer and Jepperson, 2000, p. 107). Such personhood also breeds formal organization: 'Structured social organizations arise to pursue, with great legitimacy, validated individual and collective purposes and responsibilities' (Meyer and Jepperson, 2000, p. 105; see also, Frank and Meyer, 2002). The resulting intensity of action and the elaboration of displays of agency is most consuming: Meyer and Bromley comment about the irony that '[b]eing an actor in the contemporary world can take up practically all one's time, and the displays involved can dramatically interfere with action capability' (2013, p. 377). Also ironic is the extent of standardization of such displays of personhood and agency, as is captured by Robertson's phrase 'the universalism of particularism' (1992).

Scientized education constitutes personhood and accounts for both its prevalence and isomorphism. First, as argued in detail by Drori, Meyer, Ramirez and Schofer (2003, pp. 268–9), scientized education serves to constitute social entities. Specifically, categorization of objects constructs both the object and the category, allowing for claims on behalf of the 'category;' for example, a sociological study of inequality constitutes both 'the poor' and the claimant, and therefore such constitution is consequential for policymaking (see Ferguson, 1990; Schneider and Ingram, 1993). In addition, scientized education serves as a mechanism of empowerment. Some such empowerment is direct: McEneaney (2003) describes the shift in the textual and visual content of science textbooks in primary schools worldwide from descriptive to peopled scripts, thus tracing the thematic changes in the definition of participation in science (from leisure activity to individualist, everyday activity and from awe to fun) and the definition of authority (from the scientist-expert to everybody, where nature is also redefined from untamed to benign). This impact of scientized education on the constitution and empowerment of personhood is amplified in human rights education, in which, unlike the formal agenda of STEM curricula, the intention is formally to constitute and empower the universalized category of the person. Human rights education, in particular, reorients empowerment towards the human individual and towards cultural, rather than legal, initiative (Meyer, Bromley and Ramirez, 2010, p. 113).

Second, the worldwide institutionalization of scientized education carries notions of personhood worldwide and with little variation. Meyer and Jepperson (2000), while detailing the dominant features of world-regional models of personhood, also argue that American hegemony has swept through the world to institutionalize a western, now global, notion of the person. Therefore, in spite of the nuanced differences between a corporatist model of personhood (typically German and Scandinavian, where entities are trapped 'in explicitly articulated roles and hierarchic structures, and less in scripted agency—placing more emphasis on direct training, control, and discipline'; Meyer and Jepperson, 2000, p. 109) and Anglo-American liberal model (where personhood is 'organized more directly around agency' and as 'more an action system than a control structure'; Meyer and Jepperson, 2000, p. 110), the dominant global model is one of embedded autonomy that is highly scripted. Such scripting of personhood produces similarity even where traditions or conditions of wealth and politics would have otherwise created variation; for example, increasingly constitutional legal provisions for rights, which are a prime site for constitution of claims and responsibilities, are remarkably similar across very different polities (Beck, Drori, and Meyer, 2012). In this sense, common social theory, which is itself highly scientized, often overstates the essentialist character of the person-actor and the functionalist role of social action. This furthers the hubris that is personhood, especially scientized.

In The Era of (Hyper-)Globalization

The worldwide processes of rationalization of organization, citizenship, and personhood that are facilitated by scientized education are hallmarks of the current era of globalization. And while the nature of such rationalized logics is rooted in Enlightenment-era discussions of purpose and action, the globalization of scientized education is driven specifically by nineteenth-century nation-statehood and the mid-twentieth-century emergence of the world polity. Throughout these centuries, and through the exponential rates of expansion in scope and reaches, it is made evident that globalization is primarily the consolidation of a global imagined community, or the setting of the global as the social horizon, rather than merely the intensification of global transference and transformation. In accordance with world society theory (Drori, 2008; Buhari-Gulmez, 2010), globalization is primarily the cultural process of recognizing the global scale and meaning of social life (see, Drori, Meyer, and Hwang, 2006, p. vii) more than they are patterns of international exchange and interdependence.

The recognition of hypermodern society as global and of social action and actors as universal is the essence of global scripts; and such global scripts are the inspiration for all embedded entities. As a result, scientized education is cross-nationally isomorphic, as are its imprints on organization, citizenship, and personhood. Such cross-national isomorphism does not equal uniformity; rather, it is interlaced with both loose coupling and glocalization. First, scientized education is riddled with multiplicity and internal inconsistency. Specifically, various practices related to scientized education, although they are considered to be linearly connected into a pipeline of human capital enhancement or a link chain between basic to applied science, are only loosely connected, especially in developing and newly-independent countries (Shenhav and Kamens, 1991; Drori,

Meyer, Ramirez and Schofer, 2003). This disjunction is a result of the ritualistic affirmation of the authority or legitimacy of scientized education. Indeed, scripts of scientized education are enacted worldwide, obviously by governments but also by corporations that build 'corporate universities' and other forms of in-house training (Luo 2006; Lui Abel and Li, 2012). Seeing the tight discursive link between scientized education on the one hand and notions of organization, citizenship, and personhood on the other hand, much of the globalization of scientized education is also fueled by the value assigned to nation-statehood and the importance assigned to development. These are all bundled together, or conflated into, the neoliberal model of society/market/democracy, which has dominated world affairs in the post-World War II era and fully confirmed American hegemony since the 1990s.

Second, much like the variations among models of organization, of citizenship and of personhood, scientized education too is glocalized. Although 'to a large extent the grammar of schooling is global' (Baker and LeTendre, 2005, p. 9), science and education historically vary greatly—by polity type (see, Josephson, 1998), development level (see, for example, Ynalvez and Shrum, 2011), culture (see, Cobern and Loving, 2000), and by their impact on societies in which they become institutionalized (Shenhav and Kamens, 1991; Schofer, Ramirez and Meyer, 2000). Therefore, beyond the geo-political differences in science or education practices (see Drori, Meyer, Ramirez and Schofer, 2003), scientized education embodies a global model of national agenda (see Baker and LeTendre, 2005). Scientized education also serves as a cultural model of political and economic motivations. Still, wrestling with the extent of such particularity and the place of each such locale within a global context reveals that the glocalization of scientized education creates a mosaic of local differences and global similarities. And, these degrees of the variation in glocalization of scientized education account for the corresponding cross-national variation in the rationalization of organization, citizenship, and personhood (see, Drori, Höllerer and Walgenbach, 2014).

Concluding Comments: The Rationalizing Impact of Scientized Education

The massive expansion of primary, secondary, and lately also tertiary education declares schools and universities as the central arena for socialization into world society. The scientized character of such education, which emphasizes rationality and is increasingly standardized, is further reinforced by the transition into a global knowledge economy. The cultural tenets of this now global institution of scientized education are the main forces in shaping economies and politics internationally and globally. Specifically, scientized education bears an impact on organization (and with that on governance and labor), on citizenship (and with that on community and the state), and on personhood (and with that on identity and action). In the absence of concentrated global command or tight international law to indicate social order, it is scientized education that allows for social order in the loosely organized, Tocquevillianly associational, global society. In other words,

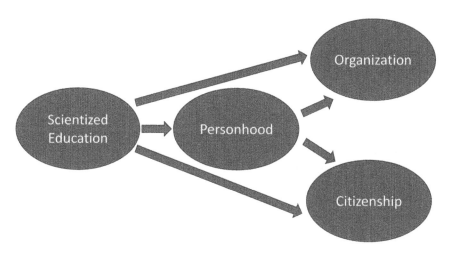

Figure 6.2 The role of scientized education in constituting contemporary world society: An institutionalist approach

in the contemporary world that is described in terms of contingency, uncertainty, and instability, scientized education is the authoritative global mechanism for conferring order and constituting transnational governance. By transporting notions of rationality and agency, scientized education declares its Western epistemology though it is now a thoroughly global institution.

Following Beck's discussion of cosmopolitan identity, Beck and Sznaider (2006) specifically consider the important place that is reserved for social issues—which are often titled 'social problems' or 'risk' and are exemplified by environmental care, poverty, or human rights—and action around them in forming cosmopolitanism. In this way, issues of global concern are becoming a part of people's moral life-worlds (2006, p. 11) and are central to the formation of a world community. Scientization comes into play in such acts of cosmopolitanism because any discussion of socially constructed problems is heavily infused with causal logic, evidence-based argumentation, and professionalism.

As the discussion here makes clear, the prime theme of the globalization of scientized education is the change to the nature of social authority, furthering a sense of profound agency. As a result, all contemporary institutions—even some as different as governance, family, health, and happiness—presuppose the existence of an autonomous, rational, and informed social actor. Specifically regarding organization, Meyer and Bromley conclude, 'Organizations require the depiction of sovereign decision making and accountability but also incorporate an interpenetrated array of goals and have very weak levels of actual coordination or control' (2013, p. 384). Seeing the pervasive nature of world society and with it of global culture, such rationalized empowerment is part of an overall move towards embedded autonomy, wherein both organizations and people are understood to act within the context, not merely the confines, of their environment. The global social environment nowadays situates scientized education as the predominant institution, endowing it with the position to constitute agents. As such, scientized education is a core cultural element in the constituted, or imagined, world society.

Acknowledgements

I thank my colleagues Patricia Bromley, Anat Gofen, and John W. Meyer for their thoughtful comments on earlier drafts.

References

Lui Abel, A., and J. Li. 2012. 'Exploring the Corporate University Phenomenon: Development and Implementation of a Comprehensive Survey.' *Human Resource Development Quarterly* 23(1): 103–28.

Andersen, N.Å. 2007. 'Creating the Client Who Can Create Himself and His Own Fate: The Tragedy of the Citizens' Contract.' *Qualitative Sociology Review* 3(2): 119–43.

Baker, D., and G.K. LeTendre. 2005. *National Differences, Global Similarities: World Culture and the Future of Schooling*. Stanford, CA: Stanford University Press.

Beck, C.J., G.S. Drori, and J.W. Meyer. 2012. 'World Influences on Human Rights Language in Constitutions: A Cross-National Study.' *International Sociology* 27(4): 483–501.

Beck, U., and N. Sznaider. 2006. 'Unpacking Cosmopolitanism for the Social Sciences: A Research Agenda.' *The British Journal of Sociology* 57(1): 1–23.

Benavot, A. 1992. 'Curricular Content, Educational Expansion, and Economic Growth.' *Comparative Education Review* 36(2): 150–74.

Benavot, A., Y. Cha, D. Kamens, J.W. Meyer, and S. Wong. 1991. 'Knowledge for the Masses: World Models and National Curricula, 1920–1986.' *American Sociological Review* 561(1): 85–100.

Bromley, P. 2010. 'The Rationalization of Educational Development: Scientific Activities among International Non-Governmental Organizations.' *Comparative Education Review* 54(4): 577–601.

Buckner, E., and S. Garnett Russell. 2013. 'Portraying the Global: Cross-national Trends in Textbooks' Portrayal of Globalization and Global Citizenship.' *International Studies Quarterly* 57(4): 738–50.

Buhari-Gulmez, D. 2010. 'Stanford School on Sociological Institutionalism: A Global Cultural Approach.' *International Political Sociology* 4(3): 253–70.

Carter, L. 2005. 'Globalisation and Science Education: Rethinking Science Education Reforms.' *Journal of Research in Science Teaching* 42(5): 561–80.

Chabbott, C., and F.O. Ramirez. 2000. 'Development and Education.' In *Handbook of the Sociology of Education*, edited by M.T. Hallinan, 163–187. New York: Springer US.

Christensen, T. 2012. 'Global Ideas and Modern Public Sector Reforms: A Theoretical Elaboration and Empirical Discussion of a Neoinstitutional Theory.' *The American Review of Public Administration* 42(6): 635–53.

Cobern, W.W., and C.C. Loving. 2005. 'Defining 'Science' in a Multicultural World: Implications for Science Education.' *Science Education* 85(1): 50–67.

Djelic, M. 2011. 'From the Rule of Law to the Law of Rules.' *International Studies of Management and Organization* 41(1): 35–61.

Drori, G.S. 1998. 'A Critical Appraisal of Science Education for Economic Development.' In *Socio-Cultural Perspectives on Science Education: An International Dialogue*, edited by W.W. Cobern, 49–74. Dordrecht, The Netherlands: Kluwer Academic Publishing.

Drori, G.S. 2000. 'Science Education and Economic Development: Trends, Relationships, and Research Agenda.' *Studies in Science Education* 35(2): 27–58.

Drori, G.S. 2008. 'Institutionalism and Globalization Studies.' In *Handbook of Organizational Institutionalism*, edited by R. Greenwood, C. Oliver, K. Sahlin, and R. Suddaby, 798–842. Los Angeles: Sage.

Drori, G.S., and J.W. Meyer. 2006. 'Scientization and Organization.' In *Globalization and Organization: World Society and Organizational Change*, edited by G.S. Drori, J.W. Meyer, and H. Hwang, 50–68. Oxford, UK: Oxford University Press.

Drori, G.S., M.A. Höllerer, and P. Walgenbach. 2014. 'The Glocalization of Organization and Management: Issues, Dimensions, and Themes.' In *Global Themes and Local Variations in Organization and Management: Perspectives on Glocalization*, edited by G.S. Drori, M.A. Höllerer, and P. Walgenbach, 3–36. New York: Routledge.

Drori, G.S., J.W. Meyer, F.O. Ramirez, and E. Schofer. 2003. *Science in the Modern World Polity: Institutionalization and Globalization*. Stanford, CA: Stanford University Press.

Elam, M., and M. Bertilsson. 2003. 'Consuming, Engaging and Confronting Science The Emerging Dimensions of Scientific Citizenship.' *European Journal of Social Theory* 6(2): 233–51.

Elliott, M. 2007. 'Human Rights and the Triumph of the Individual in World Culture.' *Cultural Sociology* 1(1): 343–63.

Erez, M., and G.S. Drori. 2009. 'Global Culture and Organizational Processes.' In *Handbook of Culture, Organizations, and Work*, edited by R.S. Bhagat and R.M. Steers, 148–79. Cambridge: Cambridge University Press.

Espeland, W.N., and M.L. Stevens. 2008. 'A Sociology of Quantification.' *European Journal of Sociology* 49(3): 401–36.

Eyal, G., and L. Buchholz. 2010. 'From the Sociology of Intellectuals to the Sociology of Interventions.' *Annual Review of Sociology* 36(1): 117–37.

Eyal, G., and M. Levy. 2013. 'Economic Indicators as Public Interventions.' *History of Political Economy* 45(1): 220–53.

Ezrahi, Y. 1990. *The Descent of Icarus: Science and the Transformation of Contemporary Democracy.* Cambridge, MA: Harvard University Press.

Ferguson, J. 1990. *The Anti-Politics Machine: 'Development,' Depoliticization, and Bureaucratic Power in Lesotho.* Cambridge: Cambridge University Press.

Frank, A. 2013. 'Welcome to the Age of Denial.' *New York Times*, August 21, pp. A–27.

Frank, D.J., and J.W. Meyer. 2002. 'The Profusion of Individual Roles and Identities in the Postwar Period.' *Sociological Theory* 20(1): 86–105.

Gofen, A. 2012. 'Entrepreneurial Exit Response to Dissatisfaction with Public Services.' *Public Administration* 90(4): 1088–106.

Gofen, A. 2013. 'Citizens' Entrepreneurial Role in Public Service Provision.' *Public Management Review* 17(3): 404–24.

Gofen, A., and P. Blomqvist. 2013. 'Parental Entrepreneurship in Public Education: A Social Force or a Policy Problem?.' *Journal of Education Policy* 29(4): 546–69.

Gofen, A., and C. Needham. 2014. 'Service Personalization as a Response to Noncompliance with Routine Childhood Vaccination.' *Governance*. [Available online Feb2014; DOI: 10.1111/gove.12082].

Goven, J. 2006. 'Processes of Inclusion, Cultures of Calculation, Structures of Power: Scientific Citizenship and the Royal Commission on Genetic Modification.' *Science, Technology & Human Values* 31(5): 565–98.

Grover, S. 2004. 'Secondary Education as a Universal Human Right.' *Education and the Law* 16(1): 21–31.

Horst, M. 2007. 'Public Expectations of Gene Therapy Scientific Futures and Their Performative Effects on Scientific Citizenship.' *Science, Technology & Human Values* 32(2): 150–71.

Josephson, P.R. 1998. *Totalitarian Science and Technology.* Amherst, NY: Humanity Books.

Kamens, D.H., J.W. Meyer, and A. Benavot. 1996. 'Worldwide Patterns in Academic Secondary Education Curricula.' *Comparative Education Review* 40(2): 116–38.

Kamens, D.H., and C.L. McNeely. 2010. 'Globalization and the Growth of International Educational Testing and National Assessment.' *Comparative Education Review* 54(1): 5–25.

Krücken, G., and F. Meier. 2006. 'Turning the University into an Organized Actor.' In *Globalization and Organization: World Society and Organizational Change*, edited by G. S. Drori, J.W. Meyer, and H. Hwang, 241–57. Oxford: Oxford University Press.

Lamont, M. 2012. 'Toward a Comparative Sociology of Valuation and Evaluation.' *Sociology* 38(1): 201–21.

Mata, T., and S.G. Medema. 2013. 'Cultures of Expertise and the Public Interventions of Economists.' *History of Political Economy* 45(1): 1–19.

Matten, D., and A. Crane. 2005. 'Corporate Citizenship: Toward an Extended Theoretical Conceptualization.' *The Academy of Management Review* 30(1): 66–79.

McComas, W.F. and J.K. Olson. 2002. 'The Nature of Science in International Science Education Standards Documents.' In *The Nature of Science in science Education*, edited by W.F. McComas, 41–52. Dordrecht, Netherlands: Springer.

McCowan, T. 2010. 'Reframing the Universal Right to Education.' *Comparative Education* 46(4): 509–25.

McEneaney, E. H. 2003. 'Elements of a Contemporary Primary School Science.' In *Science in the Modern World Polity: Institutionalization and Globalization*, edited by G.S. Drori, J.W. Meyer, F.O. Ramirez, and E. Schofer, 136–54. Stanford, CA: Stanford University Press.

McEneaney, E.H., and J.W. Meyer. 2000. 'The Content of the Curriculum: An Institutionalist Perspective.' *Handbook of the Sociology of Education*, edited by M.T. Hallina, 189–212. New York: Springer.

Meyer, J.W., and P. Bromley. 2013. 'The Worldwide Expansion of "Organization."' *Sociological Theory* 31(4): 366–89.

Meyer, J.W., and R.L. Jepperson. 2000. 'The 'Actors' of Modern Society: The Cultural Construction of Social Agency.' *Sociological Theory* 18(1): 100–120.

Meyer, J.W., and F.O. Ramirez. 2000. 'The World Institutionalization of Education.' In *Discourse Formation in Comparative Education*, edited by J. Schriewer, 111–32. Frankfurt: Peter Lang.

Meyer, J.W., P. Bromley, and F.O. Ramirez. 2010. 'Human Rights in Social Science Textbooks Cross-national Analyses, 1970–2008.' *Sociology of Education* 83(2): 111–34.

Meyer, J.W., F.O. Ramirez, and Y. Nuhoğlu Soysal. 1992. 'World Expansion of Mass Education, 1870–1980.' *Sociology of Education* 65(2): 128–49.

Pizmony-Levy, O., J. Harvey, W.H. Schimdt, R. Noonan, L. Engel, M.J. Feuer, C. Santorno, I. Rotberg, H. Braun, P. Ash, J. Torney-Purta, and M. Chatterji. 2014. "On the Merits of and Myths about International Assessments." *Quality Assurance in Education* 22(4): 319–38.

Ramirez, F.O. 2006. 'From Citizen to Person: Rethinking Education as Incorporation.' In *International Perspectives on Education and Society*. Vol. 7, *The Impact of Comparative Education Research on Institutional Theory*, edited by D.P. Baker and A.W. Wiseman, 367–87. Oxford, UK: Elsevier JAI.

Ramirez, F.O. 2012. 'The World Society Perspective: Concepts, Assumptions, and Strategies.' *Comparative Education* 48(4): 423–39.

Ramirez, F.O., and M. Ventresca. 1992. 'Building the Institution of Mass Schooling: Isomorphism in the Modern World.' In *The Political Construction of Education*, edited by B. Fuller and R. Rubinson, 47–59. New York: Praeger.

Robertson, R. 1992. *Globalization: Social Theory and Global Culture*. London: Sage.

Schneider, A., and H. Ingram. 1993. 'Social Construction of Target Populations: Implications for Politics and Policy.' *American Political Science Review* 87(2): 334–47.

Schofer, E. 1999. 'Science Associations in the International Sphere, 1875–1990: The Rationalization of Science and the Scientization of Society.' In *Constructing World Culture: International Nongovernmental Organizations Since 1875*, edited by J. Boli and G.M. Thomas, 249–66. Stanford, CA: Stanford University Press.

Schofer, E., and J.W. Meyer. 2005. 'The Worldwide Expansion of Higher Education in the Twentieth Century.' *American Sociological Review* 70(6): 898–920.

Schofer, E., F.O. Ramirez, and J.W. Meyer. 2000. 'The Effects of Science on National Economic Development, 1970 to 1990.' *American Sociological Review* 65(6): 866–87.

Seabrooke, L. 2014. 'Epistemic Arbitrage: Transnational Professional Knowledge in Action.' *Journal of Professions and Organization* 1(1): 49–64.

Shapiro, A.L. 1999. *The Control Revolution: How the Internet is Putting Individuals in Charge and Changing the World We Know*. New York: The Century Foundation.

Shenhav, Y.A., and D.H. Kamens. 1991. 'The Costs of Institutional Isomorphism: Science in Non-Western Countries.' *Social Studies of Science* 21(3): 527–45.

Spring, J. 2000. *The Universal Right to Education: Justification, Definition, and Guidelines*. New York: Routledge.

Uriah, O.A., and J.I. Wosu. 2012. 'Formal Education as a Panacea for Sustainable National Development: A Theoretical Discussion.' *International Journal of Scientific Research in Education* 5(2): 130–37.

Weiss, C.H. 1979. 'The Many Meanings of Research Utilization.' *Public Administration Review* 39(5): 426–31.

Wilensky, H.L. 1964. 'The Professionalization of Everyone?.' *American Journal of Sociology* 70(2): 137–58.

Ynalvez, M.A., and W.M. Shrum. 2011. 'Professional Networks, Scientific Collaboration, and Publication Productivity in Resource-constrained Research Institutions in a Developing Country.' *Research Policy* 40(2): 204–16.

Chapter 7
Jesuits, Connectivity, and the Uneven Development of Global Consciousness since the Sixteenth Century

José Casanova

In the early modern phase of human globalization, during the so-called era of 'Great Navigations,' the Jesuits were pioneers both, in global connectivity and in global consciousness.[1] A few decades after their official foundation in 1540 they had 'missions' literally all over the globe, not only over the lands of Christian (Catholic, Protestant and Orthodox) Europe, but over the Americas, Africa and Asia. Following Roland Robertson's broad definition of globalization as the set of processes involving the world becoming a single place with increasing global connectivity and, not least, global consciousness; and taking the globe as a focus for human activities, one could argue that the Jesuits have been the first organized group in history to think and to act globally, before there were institutionalized global structures that would sustain such global practices. In a sense, the Jesuits' global consciousness transcended existing patterns of global connectivity, but their own global practices constructed novel forms of global connectivity that contributed, at times directly but mostly indirectly, to the formation of global structures.

The aim of this paper is to examine the Jesuits through the prism of globalization and globalization through the prism of the Jesuits in order to explore three interrelated sets of questions: Firstly, what were the conditions of possibility for the emergence of such an NGO of global missionaries and global educators before the existence of the kind of global structures that could sustain such practices? Secondly, what was peculiar to the global practices pioneered by the Jesuits? How were those practices intertwined with the emerging global structures of colonial capitalism and the Westphalian imperial system of nation-states? What explains the clash between the Jesuit project of globalization and other global projects that led to the progressive expulsion of the Jesuits from many areas of the globe until the final suppression of the Society of Jesus by the Pope in 1773? Finally, what

---

1   This paper builds upon and develops further some of the arguments elaborated in José Casanova, 'The Jesuits Through the Prism of Globalization, Globalization Through a Jesuit Prism,' in Thomas Banchoff and José Casanova, eds, *The Jesuits and Globalization* (Washington, DC: Georgetown University Press, 2015).

can the Jesuit global story teach us about the complex and contingent processes of globalization, which have led to our contemporary global age? One of the main assumptions of this paper is that an examination of Jesuit global practices before the triumph of European global hegemony may help to illuminate in fruitful ways some of the newly emerging structures of a more decentered global culture after Western hegemony.

The Jesuits as Global Missionaries and Global Educators

Three interrelated historical development shaped the opportunity structures that made possible the rapid transformation of the small group of companions that gathered around Ignatius of Loyola at the University of Paris in the early 1530s into a prodigiously successful global missionary enterprise. Those interrelated processes were: a) the Iberian colonial expansion into the newly discovered 'Indies,' b) the early modern Catholic revival, and c) Renaissance Humanism. All three evolving manifestations had been operative for well over half a century before the official foundation of the *Societas Iesu* in 1540. All three helped to shape the institutional development and the global expansion of the new society in the following decades.

The Iberian Colonial Expansion

In the literal sense of the term, modern processes of globalization began historically with the 'discovery' of the 'New World' by Europeans, with the circumnavigation of the globe and with the ensuing Iberian global colonial expansion. It was global in that it incorporated for the first time the new Columbian exchange formed by the transatlantic triangle of Europe, Africa and the Americas as well as the new transpacific realm linking for the first time Asia and the Americas (Crosby, 1972; Wolf, 1982).

Certainly, well before 'the rise of the West' and 'before European hegemony' there had existed already an interdependent world system linking all the cultures and civilizations of Eurasia, the Middle East and Africa (McNeill, 1963; Abu-Lughod, 1989; Chaudhuri, 1990). Prior to the sixteenth century Western Europe had constituted a rather marginal and peripheral peninsula of such a system.

The Iberian colonial expansion made possible the connection of this Old World and the New World, thus forming for the first time one truly global world. This is the world within which the Jesuits emerged to become pioneer globalizers. Indeed, no other group took the entire globe as eagerly as the focus of their activities, taking inspiration from Jerónimo Nadal's famous slogan, 'the world is our home' (O'Malley, 2013).

They sailed around the world in the same ships as *conquistadores*, traders, migrants, and colonial administrators. Many of the Jesuit missions were sponsored by colonial administrators. The Jesuit Portuguese Assistancy, 'a vast complex of administrative units that included the kingdom of Portugal and its empire, portions of the Indian subcontinent, Japan, China, Southeast Asia, and certain lesser territories,' constituted undoubtedly the core of the global Jesuit enterprise in the sixteenth century (Alden, 1996; see also Boxer, 1978).

But from its inception, the Jesuit global 'enterprise' (*empresa*) had primarily a 'religious' missionary meaning. Indeed, as pointed out by O'Malley, the Jesuits were among the first to use the term 'mission' in our modern sense and were 'the group initially perhaps most responsible for its widespread propagation' (O'Malley, 2013, p. 217). Yet, also from the outset, the Jesuit religious *empresa* could not but accrue a very 'worldly' and secular connotation, that of being somehow also an economic and political 'enterprise.' The historian C.R. Boxer has claimed that the Jesuits could be considered 'the first multinational corporation' in that their 'economic activities were ... far greater in scope than those of either the Dutch or the English East India Companies' and unlike the national directors of those companies 'the Jesuit Generals at Rome, and the Provincials, superiors, and heads of the missions abroad were truly international' (cited in Alden, 1996, p. 668). Moreover, the Jesuits were also maligned as the first and paradigmatic 'international' secret organization bent on gaining global political power (Pavone, 2005).

Yet, the Jesuit global salvific enterprise ought not to be reduced to the globalizing logic of the emerging capitalist 'world system' or to the equally globalizing logic of the emerging Westphalian system of European territorial states competing in their colonial expansion throughout the world (Clossey, 2008; Broggio, 2004). Its primary mission and its ultimate end was the universal salvation of 'souls' *ad majorem Dei gloriam*. To reduce the Jesuit mission to something else is not only to miss what clearly motivated Ignatius and the Society he founded, but also to misunderstand the very source of the globalizing dynamic of the Jesuit enterprise.

Early Modern Catholicism

Ignatius' spiritual journey and the foundation and dramatic expansion of the Society of Jesus need to be viewed in the context of the broad and widespread manifestations of the early modern Catholic renewal which flourished in Italy and the Iberian Peninsula before the Protestant Reformation. It is thus misleading to characterize such broad Catholic reform movement as 'Counter Reformation.'[2] But irrespective of the name one prefers to use, what is relevant is the fact that this is the era when Catholicism attained global reach from East Asia to North

---

2   New historiography in the last two decades has challenged traditional interpretations. See John O'Malley, *Trent and All That: Renaming Catholicism in the Early Modern Era* (Cambridge, MA: Harvard University Press, 2000); Jean Delumeau, *Le Catholicisme entre Luther et Voltaire* (Paris, 1971); and Robert Bireley, *The Refashioning of Catholicism, 1450–1700: A Reassesment of the Counter Reformation* (Washington, DC: Catholic University of America Press, 1999).

America, from the Philippines to South America. R. Po-Chia Hsia has argued that 'the centuries of Catholic renewal formed the first period of global history,' in that the Early Modern era was shaped by 'the encounter between Catholic Europe and the non-Christian world'(2005, p. 7).

The Jesuits were neither the only nor the first global missionaries. In fact, they followed literally in the steps of other older Catholic orders, Franciscans, Dominicans, Augustinians, etc., who had preceded them in colonial Spanish America as well as in Portuguese India. In this respect, the Jesuit global mission was part and parcel of the Golden Age of global Catholic missions that flourished throughout the sixteenth and seventeenth centuries, well before the emergence of global Protestant missions towards the end of the eighteenth century. As every Christian mission before and after, this global Catholic mission was a response to Jesus 'great commission' to his followers 'go and make disciples of all nations,' (Matthew, 28: 19).

This should serve as a reminder that the missionary impulse of the so-called 'world religions' which have their remote origins in the axial age, such as Buddhism, Christianity and later Islam, have been important carriers of trans-cultural and trans-political civilizational dynamics which have contributed in manifold ways[3] to processes of globalization throughout history (Casanova, 2011).

The mission of Franciscan Friars to China beginning in 1245 preceded the much more famous Jesuit mission by several centuries and even preceded by a few decades the voyages of the Venetian merchants Nicoló, Maffeo and Marco Polo who simply used the well-trodden Muslim Silk Road, made now safe by the Mongol world empire (Foltz, 2010; Boulnois, 2005). Marco Polo's travelogues were to play an important role in the increased globalizing awareness of Asia and the Indies in the European imagination, inspiring Columbus and other early modern globalizers. Francis of Assisi's 1219 mission of peace to the Muslim Sultan of Egypt, Malik al-Kamil, in the midst of the Fifth Crusade also preceded the interreligious encounter and dialogue that were to become such an important dimension of the Jesuit globalizing mission.

Nonetheless, the Jesuit missionary expansion of the sixteenth century can only be understood properly if one takes into account the fact that global mission became the specific foundational mission or ministry of the Jesuits from its very inception in a way in which it had not been the case of the mendicant or other Catholic orders. As expressed explicitly in the *Formula of the Institute*, the 1539 foundational charter of the order, Jesuits took an oath, 'to travel to any part of the world where there was hope of God's greater service and the good of souls' in order to minister to 'the Turks or any other infidels, even those who live in the regions called the Indies, or ... any heretics whatever, or schismatics, or any of the

---

3 This should also alert us that perhaps the revival of all religious traditions that we are witnessing in the contemporary age of globalization may not be reducible to 'fundamentalist' rejections of globalization, and may constitute today also a globalizing dynamic in its own right.

faithful' (*Constitutions*, 68). Global mobility was culturally encoded, as it were, into the make-up of the Jesuit order from its conception.

Renaissance of Christian Humanism

The Jesuits were not only the first Catholic 'teaching' order but the first transnational professional organization of schoolmasters. Originally teaching had not been envisioned as a particular Jesuit ministry. But the establishment of the first Jesuit school in Messina, Sicily, in 1548, was to have immense repercussions on the character and development of the Society (O'Malley, 2000, p. 199).

If the charisma of Ignatius and his early companions may explain the rapid initial growth of the Society, it is the dramatic growth of Jesuit colleges that accounts for the steady stream of recruits thereafter. At the death of Ignatius in 1556, the order that had been made up of ten companions in 1540 had grown to over 1,000 members and administered already 46 colleges. In 1579 the Society had 5,164 members and 144 colleges. By 1626 the respective numbers were 15,544 members and 444 colleges plus 56 seminaries. In 1749, ten years before the expulsion from Portugal and its empire, the order had over 22,000 members and over 800 colleges spread throughout Europe, Latin America and Asia, as seen at the Table I.I 'Growth of the Society of Jesus, 1556–1749' published in Alden (1996, p. 17).

The Jesuits played a crucial role in developing a model of humanist liberal arts education, institutionalized in the 1599 *Ratio studiorum*, or plan of studies, that was to become globalized through their extensive network of colleges throughout the world (Duminuco, 2000; Giard, 1995). The Jesuit College was a combination of two competing systems of education, the university system with its scholastic and professional training paradigmatically represented by the University of Paris and the humanistic college that had emerged in fifteenth-century Renaissance Italy. The first Jesuits were themselves products of both institutions. But as they appropriated them, they imbued them with distinctive characteristics and particularly they gave them a global orientation shaped by what the historian of science Steven Harris has called 'the Jesuit geography of knowledge' (Harris, 1999; Feingold, 2003).

The Stanford 'world polity' school of globalization, led by John W. Meyer, has stressed the surprising isomorphic character of institutional and organizational structures throughout the world: from constitution and state bureaucracies, to universities and health systems, to normative scripts of economic development, environmentalism and gender equality (Meyer et al.,1997).

The central assumption is that all these isomorphisms derive from models embedded in an overarching world culture which is exogenous to all the particular societies of the world, a world society as it were, which shapes the particular societies. The central question then becomes: What processes in world society construct and shape these 'actors' to produce such isomorphisms? But the prior question they do not ask is how has this so-called 'world society' or 'world polity' come about, through which processes was it constructed and by whom? One of the claims of this paper is that the Jesuits as pioneer cultural brokers and translators between North and South and East and West were important actors in the construction of the early phases of such a world society.

Education and schooling present a relevant case because it is undoubtedly one of the most isomorphic institutions of our globalized world. Today, it is an institution controlled, regulated, and authorized by the nation-state and yet each nation-state reproduces increasingly the same educational modules. For that very reason, the development of Jesuit education in early modernity presents an interesting case, because the Jesuit 'college' was developed at a time when there was an obviously rising demand for education from the nobility and the emerging middle classes well before the state took over the control of schooling.

There was a particular historical window of opportunity which the Jesuits exploited: they were the pioneer constructors of a model of educational institution, which they themselves reproduced isomorphically around the world. Of course, one could expect that their very success both, stimulated many imitations but also provoked the envy and enmity of competitors who wanted to take over education from them. In fact, conflicts over education and schooling were central to the conflicts, on the one hand, between Jesuits and enlightened philosophes, many of whom had been educated in Jesuits colleges, and, on the other, between the religious order and the absolutist state that wanted to take over the role of *pater et magister* from the 'mother' church.

But the most important contribution of the Jesuits to the formation of a world society was in their advancement of what according to Roland Robertson are two of the four major aspects, or reference points of the global field, namely, a) *individuals* or *selves*, which in Jesuit-Christian parlance were called *souls*; and b) *humankind* or global humanity (Robertson, 1992, p. 25). As is in so many other things, the Jesuits were not so much the originators but the effective carriers of a wider culture of universal Christian humanism that emerged from the confluence of Aristotelian-Thomist scholastic philosophy and Renaissance humanism, and crystallized in the 'School of Salamanca and Coimbra.' The founding and leading figure, Francisco de Vitoria, was a Dominican, as were the other leading theologians, Domingo de Soto and Melchior Cano. Two Jesuit theologians, Francisco Suárez and Luis de Molina, became equally influential figures. Most importantly, in their encounters with the non-Christian 'other,' Jesuit global missions and colleges became the effective global disseminators of this culture of Christian humanism (See Padgen, 1982; Stamatov, 2013; Wilde, 2011).

The Jesuit Project of Globalization and its Tensions with the Colonial Capitalist and Westphalian Projects

The Jesuit 'catholic' missionary impulse had naturally, as a matter of course, the hegemonic purpose of universal conversion to the true Catholic faith. But what makes Jesuit global missionary practices particularly relevant is the fact that, under certain 'circumstances,' their controversial method of 'accommodation' took a form which we would call today 'nativist inculturation' or Christian 'glocalization.' One should avoid, of course, anachronistic interpretations of early modern Jesuit practices from our contemporary global perspective of cultural and religious pluralism. Nevertheless, the famous instruction of Alessandro Valignano, the influential administrator of the Jesuit missions in India, Japan, and China, that their task was not to 'Portugalize' the Chinese converts, but to make Christianity Chinese through their own 'Sinicizing,' points to a formula of globalization which rejects unidirectional Westernization and opens itself to multicultural encounters and reciprocal learning processes (Schütte, 1980; Ücerler, 2009; Standaert, 2003).

Even in Spanish colonial America, where conquest, colonization, reduction of the indigenous peoples, and conversion to Christianity were so inextricably intertwined, José de Acosta already insisted that 'hispanización' was not necessary to 'preach the Gospel' to the Indians nor to 'procure their salvation' (de Acosta, 1999). This was the rationale behind the simultaneous publication (i.e. translation from Latin) of the trilingual Lima Catechism (1583) in Spanish, *Quechua* and *Aymara*. It amounts to a formula of globalization of Christianity through the particularization of the universal, by going 'local' or 'native' through a process of reflexive inculturation and acculturation, which theologically amounts to a formula of ever renewed Christian 'incarnation.'

This is the famous and controversial formula of Jesuit cultural accommodation which led to the adoption of the Confucian 'habitus' in China by Matteo Ricci, the Brahmin 'habitus' in India by Roberto de Nobili, the Guarani 'habitus' in the 'Reducción de Paraguay,' but also the for us today less commendable accommodating 'habitus' of slave-owner in the Jesuit plantations in Brazil or Maryland. It was the differentiation of true universal *religion* and particular *culture*, as well as that between *civilization* and *idolatry*, introduced by the Jesuits that allowed the various accommodating syntheses of supposedly Christian universalism and cultural particularism (Rubiés, 2005). The fact that the method was so vehemently attacked by the other missionary orders and even by other Jesuits in India and China, before it exploded into the Chinese and Malabar Rites controversies in Rome and Paris indicates the extent to which it challenged Eurocentric notions of a uniform Roman Catholic globalization.[4]

As the classificatory scheme of the *Formula of the Institute* indicates, the Jesuits initiated their mission with the traditional and customary distinction between 'the true Christian faith' or 'Catholic religion' and all others: Christian 'schismatics' and 'heretics,' Jewish and Muslim 'infidels,' and the remaining 'pagans' and 'idolaters.' The Jesuits at first in their missionary encounters with the religious other followed somewhat reluctantly the already established practices

---

4 On the internal Jesuit disputes concerning missionary methods in India see Ines G. Županov, *Disputed Mission. Jesuit Experiments and Brahmanical Knowledge in Seventeenth-century India* (New Delhi: Oxford University Press, 1999).

of the Portuguese Inquisition in Goa and the destruction of pagan Hindu temples, as well as the Catholic campaigns for the 'extirpation of idolatry' in the Spanish Viceroyalty of Peru (Županov, 2005; Maldavsky, 2012). But soon the Jesuits, or at least some of their prominent members, 'under certain circumstances,' began to adopt a more ambiguous and open, at times even dialogical, but more importantly dia-practical relation with the religious 'other' which began, eventually and mostly unwittingly, to undermine the old religious taxonomy, thus initiating the long historical process of transformation in the direction of the still unsettled contemporary pluralist global system of religions.

Particularly in the encounter with the multifaceted religions of Asia the old catch-all category of 'pagan,' 'heathen' or 'infidel' began to collapse and a new plural system of what later would be called 'world religions' began to emerge. It is undeniable that the Jesuits served as pioneer interlocutors in the religious, cultural, scientific and artistic encounter between East and West and between Old and New World. Particularly, pioneer Jesuits in Japan, China, Tibet, Vietnam, and India played an important role in transmitting and mediating the first knowledge about the foundational texts, religions, cultures and civilizations of the 'Orient,' which would later develop into full-fledged academic 'orientalism' (Jensen, 1997; Rule, 1986; Mungello, 1985; Caraman, 1997; Phan, 1998; de Nobili, 2000).

José de Acosta's developmental theory of Amerindian religions as well as his comparative reflections on Amerindian cultures and the religions and cultures of Asia, presented in *De Procuranda Indorum Salute* (1588) and in *Historia Natural y Moral de las Indias* (1590), mark the point of departure of modern comparative ethnology and anticipate many of the later Euro-centric stadial theories of human development, both being forms of imagining global humanity (de Acosta, 2002; Burgaleta, 1999; del Pino Díaz, 1992). In fact, despite their Christo-centric assumptions and their frequent recourse to divine and satanic devices as explanatory keys to all forms of cultural and religious diversity, the Jesuit early modern imaginary of global humanity and their dia-praxis of cultural 'accommodation' and local inculturation appears less Euro-centric, less racist and less unilinear than later imaginaries associated with the cosmopolitan Enlightenment or with the 19th and 20th centuries' *mission civilisatrice* and imperial 'White Man's Burden.'

Historically, with their final defeat in the 'rites controversy' at the beginning of the eighteenth century, the Jesuit accommodating way of proceeding lost the battle within the Church and within the wider world. Their ethical contextualism was ridiculed as opportunistic 'casuistry.'[5] Critics within the Church, particularly Dominicans and Franciscans, accused the Jesuits of using a cunning strategy of relativist 'accommodation' that compromised the universality of Christianity (Mungello, 1994; Cummins, 1993). The Eurocentric perspective and uniform Romanization prevailed within the Church. Externally, the transnational papal order also lost the battle against the triumphant Westphalian model of sovereign

---

5   Pascal's *Provincial Letters* offers the most famous and influential critique of Jesuit casuistry.

territorial states and against the absolutist Catholic kings who one after another, beginning with Portugal in 1759 expelled the Jesuits from their realms and conspired in the papal dissolution of the order in 1773.

Standard accounts of processes of globalization tend to view the dynamics of expansion of the world system of capitalism as the primary globalizing logic. Yet the parallel and intertwined logic of the global expansion of state territorialization have been and still are, despite all the misleading talk about the end of nationalism or the fading away of the state, of equal relevance in the historical formation of our contemporary world system or world society, which now encompasses all peoples and all territories of the entire globe. The process of state territorialization had from the very beginning two intertwined dynamics, the internal dynamics of territorial nation-state formation within Europe that led to the consolidation of the Westphalian system of competing sovereign territorial states, and the external dynamics of overseas colonial territorial expansion of the European states.

The Jesuits were intimately implicated in both 'political' processes, the internal European and the external colonial, playing ambiguous and relatively autonomous roles in both. It is for this very reason that Anti-Jesuitism as a critique of Jesuit 'meddling in politics,' of their location as 'a state within the state,' and of the dread of a 'Jesuit Republic' or a 'global Jesuit empire,' supposedly based on a secret Jesuit project of global domination, had so much traction and could persist for so long (On Jesuit politics, see Bertrand, 1985; Höpfl, 2004; Bireley, 2003; Mörner, 1953).

Although there were always particular grievances or concerns connected with specific Jesuit practices which may explain any anti-Jesuit outburst at any particular time, the persistence, the recurrence and the broad character of the many accusations that fed into the Black Legend are only comprehensible if one takes into account the ambivalent even contradictory location occupied by the Jesuits, as a transnational and 'papal' order, within the early modern dynamics of globalization. Equally important was the ambiguous and equivocal significations that the Jesuits, as a *hermaphrodite* 'religious' order actively engaged in worldly 'secular' affairs, elicited with their peculiar 'way of proceeding.' Furthermore, their character as a highly centralized and hierarchic transnational organization with a highly flexible and mobile structure, with ambiguous and overlapping loyalties to various authorities and jurisdictions, well-fitted to accommodate the most diverse local contexts, gave the Jesuits certain global structural advantages in the early modern phase of globalization which elicited much envy, dread, and competition from friend and foe alike (Fabre and Maire, 2010; Burke, 2001; Pavone, Monreal and Zermeno, forthcoming).

At the end, all the accusations and stereotypes about Jesuit conspiratorial politics, internal as well as external, would converge and merge in 'the final solution,' first to expel them from every Catholic Kingdom and then to force the Pope to suppress the order once and for all. Anti-Jesuitism was apparently shared by Protestants, Jansenists, and enlightened *philosophes* alike, by Catholic sovereigns, national ecclesiastical hierarchies and national *bourgeoisies*, by Catholic religious orders and even by the papal curia. All the different sources of anti-Jesuitism now had merged into one. At the end, nobody came to their public defense. Even the infamously polemicist Jesuits accepted their cruel fate silently and obediently *ac perinde cadaver*. Only by becoming *normal* persons—either regular clergy, secular clergy, or laity—and only by abandoning their interstitial transnational status and becoming *normal* subjects of some sovereign territorial state, could the Jesuits escape their fate of becoming stateless displaced persons and refugees.

Potential Lessons of the Failed Jesuit Globalization Project for our Contemporary Global Age

The uncontested suppression of the Jesuits in the second half of the eighteenth century would seem to indicate that their global practices were in fundamental tension with all the ascending global forces: a) with the triumphant structural forces of capitalist and Westphalian globalization which now were being carried by Protestant powers, b) with the alternative secular cosmopolitan project of the Enlightenment, which thereafter would inform global educational systems and c) even with the two other Catholic models competing over the direction of global Catholicism, namely plural national Catholic churches under royal patronage (the equivalent to the Protestant Erastian Landeskirche) versus a uniform transnational Catholic regime under centralized Roman control, a project that had been gaining traction since the establishment of the Holy Congregation for the Propagation of the Faith (*Propaganda Fidei*) in 1622, in order precisely to gain Roman curial control over the global Catholic missions which the Jesuits had done so much to establish precisely in places which the national Catholic colonial powers (Portugal, Spain, France) could not reach.

But for over two centuries, from the 1540s to the 1760s, no other group contributed so much to the advancement of global connectivity and global consciousness linking the four quadrants of the world. They did it not only through their ubiquitous missions but through their prodigious production and global circulation of annual letters and edifying mission reports, scientific and ethnographic descriptions, mapping and cartographic exercises, through the construction of numerous scripts, lexicons and grammars of non-Western languages, through the translation of classical Greek and Latin texts into non-Western languages and the translation of non-Western classical texts into Latin, through the production of Catechisms in every possible vernacular, and through the global circulation of all kind of objects, from scientific instruments to printing presses and type scripts, from medicinal plants (Jesuits bark or quinine) to all kinds of sacred objects, icons, and paintings, church architectural styles, music, drama and ballet (See O'Malley et al., 2006; Bailey, 1999; de Castelnau et al., 2011; Gagliano and Ronan, 1997; Wilde, 2011). Even the 1689 Sino-Russian Treaty of Nerchinsk, the first official diplomatic encounter setting the territorial borders between the Chinese and the expanding Russian empires, was written in

Latin and mediated by the Jesuits Tomé Pereira and Jean-François Gerbillon, with close links to the imperial courts in Peking and Moscow (Sebes, 1962).

It is of course misleading to speak of a Jesuit project of globalization that was supposedly defeated by the triumphs of the world capitalist system and the Westphalian international system, with the implication that the Jesuits may have had an alternative project of either economic or political globalization, or any particular vision of an alternative world order or world society that they tried somehow to implement. Despite the conspiratorial myths of a Jesuit project of global domination, there is no evidence that the Jesuits had such a vision or such a project. Their project was one of 'world evangelization' (Donnelly, 1988).

In the same way that they adapted flexibly to different circumstances and to the various political structures in different countries in Europe and in overseas colonies, their method of accommodation in non-Western contexts also implied flexible adaptation to the most diverse socio-political and cultural systems they encountered. They adapted to the *daimyo* warring states system in Japan, the centralized imperial mandarin system in China, the Muslim Mughal Empire in Northern India and the Hindu Tamil kingdoms of Southern India, the tribal chiefdoms in Congo, etc. Even the most famous of the Jesuit missionary enterprises, the Guaraní Reductions or the so-called 'Paraguay Jesuit State,' that so fascinated Voltaire, Montesquieu and other Enlightenment *philosophes*, ought not to be understood as a rational experiment in the construction of a Christian social order, but rather as a complex historically contingent process of encounters, accommodations and adaptations in which *guaraní* and other indigenous groups, Jesuits and other missionary clerics, colonists and imperial agents participated to construct a dynamic, ambiguous and conflictive sociopolitical order (See Wilde, 2009; Ganson, 2003).

While some individual Portuguese or Spanish Jesuits may have supported the competing imperial projects of their respective nations, in general the Jesuits were not the advocates of a Universal Christian Monarchy (Bosbach, 1998). Prominent Jesuits often found themselves in vehement disagreement about all kinds of geopolitical, national political and internal issues of Jesuit organizational policy. The well-known and public polemics between two prominent Spanish Jesuits, José de Acosta and Alonso Sánchez, particularly their disagreements concerning the proposal of a Spanish military invasion of China from the Philippines, are a case in point (Catto, 2011; Bourdon, 1960). If one may speak at all of a Jesuit political vision or ultimate political *ratio*, it is to be found in a rather conventional Thomist scholastic moral and political concern for 'justice' and 'the common good' in internal affairs and for their defense of the early modern *Jus Gentium* in international affairs.

Jus Gentium or *Derecho de Gentes*, the moral laws and rights that allow and promote the peaceful coexistence and just interactions of the open world society of nations, was the basis for the Jesuit vision of a world society. Francisco Suárez, the most influential Jesuit political theologian, wrote in *De Legibus* (1612) in a passage reminiscent of Francisco de Vitoria:

> The human race, howsoever divided into various peoples and kingdoms, always has a certain unity, not only specific, but also as it were political and moral, which is indicated by the natural precept of mutual love and mercy, a precept extended to all, even strangers and of whatsoever reason. Therefore, although each perfect city, state or kingdom constitutes in itself a perfect community consisting of its own members, nevertheless each of them is also a member in a certain fashion of this universe, so far as it concerns the human race. (Francisco Suárez cited in Clossey, 2008, p. 254; see also, de Vitoria, 1964)

This paragraph already contains the four elements which according to Robertson (1992) constitute the global field of world society: *selves* or individuals who are supposed to follow the natural (not Christian) precept of mutual love and mercy, *humankind* or the human race, *national societies* or the various peoples, cities, states or kingdoms, and *the world system of societies* or the universe of which each of them is also a member. This paragraph can serve to alert us to the particular and contingent institutionalization of the isomorphic Westphalian world system of national societies. World society could have developed differently more in the direction of a system that accommodated the diverse pre-existing civilizational forms and cultures and less in the isomorphic direction it took once the colonial imposition of Western hegemony forced all societies to follow the Westphalian territorial model.

The Jesuit project of world evangelization was predicated on a vision of an open world system of societies in which the right to evangelize and therefore open access was taken for granted. But as the debate between Sánchez and Acosta concerning the evangelization of China indicates, their fundamental disagreement rested on the legitimacy or illegitimacy of the use of force (*ius belli*) in order to guarantee open access. Valignano's method of accommodation presupposed the missionary's need to adapt to the cultural habitus, civic customs and political conditions of other civilizations, which were to be treated as equal to European civilization. Evangelization did not imply necessarily straightforward or unidirectional Europeanization.

The right to commerce presupposed the same right to access. Strenski (2004) has traced the modern legitimation of economic globalization back to its religious roots in the early modern project of world evangelization. In this respect the right to evangelize and the right to commerce went hand in hand. Western colonial powers reserved for themselves the use of gunboats to guarantee their right to commercial open access. But in the same way as globalization could have happened without the imposition of the Westphalian territorial state system, open world trade could have developed without the colonial imposition of unfair treaties which forced all Chinese walls to open.

This is the most important lesson of an analysis of the Jesuit story of globalization before the triumph of Western hegemony. Globalization did not need to happen through the imposition of Western modernization. Western modernity is a contingent historical process, not a functional necessity. It could have been otherwise. Thus, countering theorists of Western modernity such as Anthony Giddens, one may insist that globalization is not simply 'a consequence of modernity,' or *an enlargement* of modernity, from society to the world,' as if 'modernity is inherently globalizing' (Giddens, 1990, pp. 29, 63, 177). Globalization is not simply Western 'modernity on a global scale.' Globalization is not necessarily Westernization.

It is one of the central analytical assumptions of this paper that there were relevant historical processes of globalization before the hegemonic triumph of Western modernity, and that to speak of a contemporary 'global age' implies making the judgment that we are entering a new phase in human history which is characterized by qualitative differences with the preceding 'modern age' or with the age of hegemonic Western modernization.

If, as Giddens explains, 'modern organizations are able to connect the local and the global in ways which would have been unthinkable in more traditional societies,' then one could argue that the Society of Jesus may have been the first paradigmatic modern organization. But alternatively one could also argue that the Society of Jesus was a 'global' organization before the hegemonic triumph of Western modernity. Their organizational character as a transnational global NGO before the establishment of an international system was predicated on the possibility of a de-territorialized Christian evangelization which assumed a form of Christian religious universalism disembedded from any particular culture and which therefore could become inculturated anew in any culture, the way in which early Hebrew Christianity became inculturated in ancient Greece and ancient Rome.

Given their own cultural roots in Renaissance humanism, for the early modern Jesuits the Christianization of pagan antiquity served as implicit model for such a process of inculturation. After the so-called Jerusalem compromise, Gentiles did not need to become Jews in order to become Christians. Pagans were to become Christians. But it happened through a complex process of inculturation, which entailed deep theological, metaphysical and epistemic transformations, through which Christianity also became in the process Greek-Hellenic and Roman-Latin. This was the practical experiment in Christian inculturation that Jesuits, following Valignano's instructions, were willing to probe in Japan, in China and in the Madurai mission. All three missions ultimately failed for a combination of geo-political, civilizational, and ecclesiastical reasons.

But if one takes seriously the argument that processes of globalization are contingent historical processes, not functionally necessary processes or consequences of modernity, then the most important lesson from the Jesuit global story is that different historical processes, that is, different outcomes in the Jesuit Christian encounter in Japan, China or India could have led to a different age of globalization. One enters thereby into the highly problematic yet illuminating field of speculative fictional yet theoretical 'what if' story. The merit of such a theoretical exercise or thought experiment resides not so much in its ability to construct rational social structures freed from any particular practical constraint but rather in facilitating the critical reflexivity which is required to free ourselves from what Charles Taylor calls 'the untought,' namely to allow us to reflect critically upon the deep taken for granted structures of our own epistemic and metaphysical presuppositions.

Every dialogical process of inculturation and every deep and open intercivilizational encounter creates the possibility for such critical reflexivity concerning the character of all four components of our global field: individual selves or persons, humankind, societies and the world system of societies. One may presuppose that the particular determination of each of these components has been and remains historically contingent. As we are entering a new decentered global age after Western hegemony the Jesuit global story of dialogic inculturation and deep intercivilizational encounters still contains valuable lessons for us. Most of the issues they grappled with and their attempts to find viable resolutions to the tensions between universality and particularity, and between the global and the local are still with us.

References

Abu-Lughod, J.L. 1989. *Before European Hegemony: The World System A.D. 1250–1350*. Oxford: Oxford University Press.

Alden, D. 1996. *The Making of an Enterprise. The Society of Jesus in Portugal, Its Empire and Beyond, 1540–1750*. Stanford, CA: Stanford University Press.

Bailey, G.A. 1999. *Art on the Jesuit Missions in Asia and Latin America, 1542–1773*. Toronto: Toronto University Press.

Bertrand, D.S.J. 1985. *La politique de Saint Ignace de Loyola*. Paris: Les Éditions du CERF.

Bireley, R. 1999. *The Refashioning of Catholicism, 1450–1700: A Reassesment of the Counter Reformation*. Washington, DC: Catholic University of America Press.

Bireley, R. 2003. *The Jesuits and the Thirty Years War. Kings, Courts, and Confessors*. Cambridge: Cambridge University Press.

Bosbach, F. 1998. *Monarchia Universalis. Storia di un concetto cardine della politica europea (secoli XVI-XVIII)*. Milan: Vita e Pensiero.

Boulnois, L. 2005. *The Silk Road: Monks, Warriors and Merchants*. New York: Norton.

Bourdon, L. 1960. 'Un projet d'invasion de la Chine par Canton à la fin du XVIe siècle.' In *Actas do III Colóquio Internaciona de Estudos Luso-Brasileiros*, 97–121. Lisbon: Imprenta de Coimbra.

Boxer, C.R. 1978. *The Church Militant and Iberian Expansion, 1440–1770*. Baltimore, MD: The Johns Hopkins University Press.

Broggio, P. 2004. *Evangelizzare il mondo: Le missioni della Compágnia di Gesú tra Europa e America (secoli XVI-XVII)*. Roma: Carocci.

Burgaleta, C.M., S.J. 1999. *José de Acosta, S.J. (1540–1600)*. Chicago IL: Loyola Press.

Burke, P. 2001. 'The Black Legend of the Jesuits: An Essay in the History of Social Stereotypes.' In, *Christianity and Community in the West: Essays for John Bossy*, edited by S. Ditchfield, 175–7. Aldershot: Ashgate.

Caraman, P.S.J. 1997. *Tibet: The Jesuit Century*. St Louis: Institute of Jesuit Sources.

Casanova, J. (forthcoming) 2015. 'The Jesuits through the Prism of Globalization, Globalization through a Jesuit Prism.' In *The Jesuits and Globalization*, edited by T. Banchoff and J. Casanova. Washington, DC: Georgetown University Press.

Casanova, J. 2011. 'Religion, the Axial Age, and Secular Modernity in Bellah's Theory of Religious Evolution.' In *The Axial Age and Its Consequences*, edited by R.N. Bellah and H. Joas, 191–221. Cambridge, MA: Harvard University Press.

Catto, M. 2011. 'Una cruzada contra la China: El Diálogo entre Antonio Sánchez y José de Acosta en torno a una guerra justa al celeste imperio (1857).' In *Saberes de la conversion*, edited by G. Wilde, 441–63. Buenos Aires: Editorial Sb.

Chaudhuri, J.L. 1990. *Asia before Europe: Economy and Civilization of the Indian Ocean from the Rise of Islam to 1750*. Cambridge: Cambridge University Press.

Clossey, L. 2008. *Salvation and Globalization in the Early Jesuit* Missions. Cambridge: Cambridge University Press.

The Constitutions of the Society of Jesus. 1970. Trans. George S. Gans. St Louis: The Institute of Jesuits Sources.

Crosby, A.W. 1972. *The Columbian Exchange: Biological and Cultural Consequences of 1492*. Westport, CT: Greenwood.

Cummins, J.S. 1993. *A Question of Rites: Friar Domingo Navarrete and the Jesuits in China*. Aldershot: Ashgate.

de Acosta, J. 1999. *De Procuranda Indorum Salute o Predicación del Evangelio en las Indias* (1588). Alicante: Biblioteca Virtual Miguel de Cervantes.

de Acosta, J. 2002. *Natural and Moral History of the Indies*. Edited by J. Mangan and translated by F. López-Morillas. Durham, NC: Duke University Press.

de Castelnau, C., M.L. Copete, A. Maldavsky, and I. Županov (eds). 2011. *Missions d'évangelisation et circulation des saviors. XVIe-XVIIIe siècle*. Madrid-Paris: Casa de Velasquez-EHESS.

Delumeau, J. 1971. *Le Catholicisme entre Luther et Voltaire*. Paris: Presses Universitaires De France.

de Nobili, R.S.J. 2000. *Preaching Wisdom to the Wise. Three Treatises by Roberto de Nobili, S.J., Missionary and Scholar in 17th Century India*. Translated and Introduced by A. Amaladass, S.J. and F.X. Clooney, S.J. St Louis: Institute of Jesuit Sources.

Donnelly, J.P. 1988. 'Antonio Possevino's Plan for World Evangelization.' *Catholic Historical Review* 74(2): 179–98.

Duminuco, V.J. (ed.). 2000. *The Jesuit Ratio Studiorum: 400th Anniversary Perspectives*. New York: Fordham University Press.

del Pino Díaz, F. 1992. 'Humanismo renacentista y orígenes de la etnología: a propósito del P. Acosta, paradigma del humanismo antropológico jesuita.' In *Humanismo y visión del otro en la España moderna: cuatro estudios*, edited by B. Ares, Chapter 4. Madrid: CSIC.

de Vitoria, F. 1964. 'De Indis et de iure belli relectiones.' In *Classics in International Law*, edited by E. Nys. New York: Oceana.

Fabre, P., and C. Maire (eds). 2010. *Les Antijésuites: Discours, figures et lieux de l'antijésuitisme à l'époque modern*. Rennes: Presses Universitaires de Rennes.

Feingold, M. (ed.). 2003. *Jesuit Science and the Republic of Letters*. Cambridge: Cambridge University Press.

Foltz, R. 2010. *Religions of the Silk Road. Premodern Patterns of Globalization*, 2nd edition. New York: Palgrave Macmillan.

Gagliano, J.A. and C.E. Ronan (ed.). 1997. *Jesuit Encounters in the New World: Jesuit Chroniclers, Geographers, Educators, and Missionaries in the Americas, 1549–1767*. Rome: IHSI.

Ganson, B. 2003. *The Guaraní under Spanish Rule in the Río de la Plata*. Stanford, CA: Stanford University Press.

Giard, L. (ed.). 1995. *Les Jésuites à la Renaissance: Système éducatif et production du savoir*. Paris: PUF.

Giddens, A. 1990. *The Consequences of Modernity*. Stanford, CA: Stanford University Press.

Harris, S. 1999. 'Mapping Jesuit Science: The Role of Travel in the Geography of Knowledge.' In *The Jesuits: Cultures, Sciences and the Arts, 1540–1773*, edited by J.W. O'Malley, G.A. Bailey, S.J. Harris and T.F. Kennedy, 212–40. Toronto: University of Toronto Press.

Höpfl, H. 2004. *Jesuit Political Thought. The Society of Jesus and the State, c. 1540–1630*. Cambridge: Cambridge University Press.

Jensen, L. 1997. *Manufacturing Confucianism: Chinese Tradition and Universal Civilization*. Durham, NC: Duke University Press.

McNeill, W.H. 1963. *The Rise of the West: A History of the Human Community*. Chicago, IL: University of Chicago Press.

Maldavsky, A. 2012. *Vocaciones Inciertas: Misión y misioneros en la provincia jesuita del Perú en los siglos XVI y XVII*. Sevilla: CSIC.

Meyer, J.W. J. Boli, G.M. Thomas, and F.O. Ramirez. 1997. 'World Society and the Nation-State.' *American Journal of Sociology* 103(1): 144–81.

Mungello, D.E. 1985. *Curious Land: Jesuit Accommodation and the Origins of Sinology*. Honolulu: University of Hawaii Press.

Mungello, D.E. (ed.). 1994. *The Chinese Rites Controversy: Its History and Meaning*. Nettetal: Steyler Verlag.

Mörner, M. 1953. *The Political and Economic Activities of the Jesuits in the La Plata Region: The Habsburg Era*. Stockholm: Victor Petersons Bokindustri Aktiebolag.

O'Malley, J.W., G.A. Bailey, S.J. Harris, and T.F. Kennedy (eds). 2006. *The Jesuits II: Cultures, Sciences and the Arts, 1540–1773*. Toronto: Toronto University Press.

O'Malley, J.W. 2013. 'To Travel to Any Part of the World: Jerónimo Nadal and the Jesuit Vocation.' In *Saints or Devils Incarnate? Studies in Jesuit History*, 147–64. Leiden: Brill.

O'Malley, J. 2000. *Trent and All That: Renaming Catholicism in the Early Modern Era*. Cambridge, MA: Harvard University Press.

Padgen, A. 1982. *The Fall of Natural Man: The American Indian and the Origins of Comparative Ethnology*. Cambridge: Cambridge University Press.

Pavone, S. 2005. *The Wily Jesuits and the Monita Secreta*. St. Louis, MO: Institute of Jesuit Sources.

Pavone, S., S. Monreal, and G. Zermeno (eds). 2014. *Antijesuitismo y Filojesuitismo. Dos identidades ante la restauración*. Mexico, CF.: U. Javeriana.

Phan, P.C. 1998. *Mission and Catechesis: Alexandre de Rhodes and Inculturation in Seventeent-Century Vietnam*. Maryknoll: Orbis Books.

Po-Chia Hsia, R. 2005. *The World of Catholic Renewal, 1540–1770*. Cambridge: Cambridge University Press.

Robertson, R. 1992. *Globalization: Social Theory and Global Culture*. London: Sage.

Rubiés, J.P. 2005. 'The Concept of Cultural Dialogue and the Jesuit Method of Accommodation: Between Idolatry and Civilization.' *Archivum Historicum Societati Iesu LXXIV* 147: 237–80.

Rule, P. 1986. *K'ung-tzu or Confucius? The Jesuit Interpretation of Confucianism*. Sydney: Allen & Unwin.

Schütte, J.F. 1980. *Valignano's Mission Principles for Japan* 2 volumes. St. Louis: The Institute of Jesuits Sources.

Sebes, J. 1962. *The Jesuits and the Sino-Russian Treaty of Nerchinsk (1689): The Diary of Thomas Pereira*. Rome: IHSI.

Stamatov, P. 2013. *The Origins of Global Humanitarianism. Religion, Empires and Advocacy.* Cambridge: Cambridge University Press.

Standaert, N. 2003. *L'autre' dans la mission. Leçons à partir de la Chine.* Bruxelles: Lexius.

Strenski, I. 2004. 'The Religion in Globalization.' *Journal of the American Academy of Religion* 72: 631–52.

Ücerler, S.J., M.A.J. (ed.). 2009. *Christianity and Cultures: Japan & China in Comparison*. Rome: Institutum Historicum Societatis Iesu.

Wilde, G. 2009. *Religión y poder en las misiones de guaraníes*. Buenos Aires: Editorial Sb.

Wilde, G. (ed.). 2011. *Saberes de la Conversión. Jesuítas, Indígenas e Imperios Coloniales en las Fronteras de la Cristiandad*. Buenos Aires: Editorial Sb.

Wolf, E. 1982. *Europe and the People without History*. Berkeley: University of California Press.

Župnov, I.G. 1999. *Disputed Mission. Jesuit Experiments and Brahmanical Knowledge in Seventeenth-century India.* New Delhi: Oxford University Press.
Župnov, I.G. 2005. *Missionary Tropics. The Catholic Frontier in India (16th-17th Centuries)*. Ann Arbor: The University of Michigan Press.

Chapter 8
Glocalization and Global Sport

Richard Giulianotti

Globalization has become one of the most important analytical themes in the sociological investigation of sport. This paper examines some of the key contemporary sociological issues surrounding sport culture within the global context. It is argued that socio-cultural approaches, which recognize the critical engagement of social actors in making and adapting transnational phenomena, provide the most insightful ways of understanding global processes in sport. Particular attention is paid to the concept of glocalization, as an explanatory sociological device and as a 'social fact' within global sports culture. Glocalization processes are considered as shaping sports culture in two broad ways: first, through a tendency towards cross-cultural homogenization with regard to sport 'forms'; second, through a tendency towards cross-cultural heterogenization in regard to sport 'contents'. Key literature on the glocal aspects of sport is discussed. Throughout, the paper explores these processes and issues with empirical reference to prominent substantive features and aspects of global sport culture, such as the 'global game' of football and the Olympic Games.

According to Robertson's (1992, p. 8) famous definition, 'Globalization as a concept refers both to the compression of the world and the intensification of consciousness of the world as a whole'. The sub-title of this book captures these defining qualities. 'Compression' points to the complex and diverse forms of 'connectivity' associated with globalization, most obviously in recent years in the rise of transnational social media. 'Consciousness' of the world, as a single place, is reflected in part in discourses and policies relating to universal rights and environmentalism, as well as in themes associated with the inevitability of divisions within the world (Barber, 1992; Huntington, 1996).

Sport provides some exceptionally vivid and vibrant manifestations of these defining aspects of globalization. In terms of compression and connectivity, we may consider the hundreds of millions of television viewers who watch, at the same time, sport mega-events, such as the Olympics or World Cup finals; the advertising images and messages associated with top athletes, such as Usain Bolt, Roger Federer, or David Beckham, which reach transnational markets; or, the social media (Facebook, Twitter, Instagram and so on) which are used to connect the supporters of different sports clubs who are scattered across the world. In terms of consciousness of the world, we might highlight the rhetoric and imagery of major international sport federations in associating their respective sports with a global humanity, or their tournaments with forms of world unity;

such global references are also evident in sport-related marketing campaigns by major corporations. Sport is, therefore, one of the most compelling fields for social scientific inquiry in regard to the study of global processes.

In this chapter, I explore the intersections of sport and globalization in three main sections, with reference to three key sociological issues. First, I introduce the concept of glocalization to examine how the global aspects of sport show tendencies towards cultural convergence and divergence; the idea of the 'duality of glocality' captures these dual trends. Second, I explore how global sport is marked by processes of relativization and differentiation, particularly in the construction of local and national identities. Third, in the longest section, I turn to address cultural identities and practices within global sport, in particular how globalization gives rise to complex, hybrid, 'glocal' sport cultures. I conclude by arguing that studies of glocalization should draw more on sport and on case-study approaches in order to understand and explain more effectively the complexities of cultural globalization.

Glocalization and Sport

The concept of glocalization was introduced by Robertson to enable the social scientific study of the socio-cultural aspects of globalization. The approach which I follow here draws heavily on Robertson's pioneering work on this concept (see, for example, Robertson, 1992, 1994, 1995; Robertson and White, 2004), and also our subsequent collaborative work on football and sport in general which applies and develops glocalization theory (Giulianotti and Robertson, 2004, 2005, 2007a, 2007b, 2009, 2012a).

In short, the concept of glocalization registers how individuals, social groups and organizations seek to create, interpret, adapt, and transform global phenomena at the everyday level (Robertson, 1992, pp. 173–4). The concept thus reflects how routinely diverse social groups encounter ideas, information, images, objects, and products that circulate across different borders. Accordingly, 'glocalization projects' – which involve the process of engaging with these global phenomena – are increasingly common practices, and indeed may be understood as the 'constitutive features of contemporary globalization' (Robertson, 1995, p. 41).

Two important points follow from these initial observations, on the 'postbinary' appeal of glocalization. First, glocalization theory helps us to move beyond the rather crude binary oppositions between 'the local' and 'the global'. Instead, the local and the global should be seen instead as within a 'mutually implicative' relationship, as fundamentally interdependent. Second, theories of glocalization also require us to move beyond the old binary oppositions that centre on convergence and divergence, or homogenization and heterogenization, or sameness and difference. Instead, we should understand that these polar opposites – such as between convergence and divergence – are again interdependent.

In passing, we might note that glocalization theory has tended to be associated mostly with the heterogenization or divergence set of arguments – that is, with how global culture is adapted and transformed by social actors at the everyday level, thereby leading to a growing diversity of cultural practices and products (see, for example, Ritzer, 2004). Such an emphasis is understandable, in serving to challenge more deterministic, top-down analyses that emphasize forms of cultural convergence, as advanced for example by arguments on the 'Americanization' or 'Westernization' of global culture (Beck, 2004; Latouche, 1996; Said, 1978).

Conversely, elsewhere, we have reiterated that glocalization inevitably involves the twin possibilities and trends of convergence *and* divergence, by advancing the concept of the *duality of glocality* (Giulianotti and Robertson, 2007, 2009, 2012a). In other words, there is an inherent duality in the theory of glocalization, pointing to both sameness and difference, in the continuous interplay of local-global processes.

The Duality of Glocality and Sport

There are distinctive patterns within the duality of glocality, in regard to how and when tendencies towards convergence and divergence take hold, with reference to cultural forms and cultural contents. Tendencies towards cultural sameness or convergence occur particularly in regard to cultural *forms* and *institutions*, for example in how film, literature, painting, and specific sports have spread across the world. Conversely, tendencies towards difference or divergence relate primarily to the *contents* and *practices* of social groups, for example in how societies engage with or create diverse themes, techniques, and styles within the arts or sports.

What does all this mean for sport? The first side of the duality of glocality leads us to examine tendencies towards the convergence of sport forms in different societies. We may begin by recognizing that processes of homogenization have been at the heart of the global diffusion of sport; that is, the spread of particular sporting *forms* into new territories across the planet, through the nineteenth and twentieth centuries, to become strongly embedded within different societies. Obvious examples here are football, as well as athletic disciplines (notably in 'track and field', such as sprint and distance running, hurdle races, or javelin and shot putt); across the Commonwealth countries and parts of Europe, we might point to rugby union and cricket as further instances – all of these are sports that have become relatively 'globalized'.

The spread of such 'global sport' has been, of course, underpinned by significant forces of cultural imperialism, notably as the British inculcated their sports within the colonies, often to the exclusion of indigenous body cultures, and also used trade and educational influences to promote football among Europeans and Latin Americans in particular (Bale and Sang, 1996; Mangan, 1986). Latterly, the international spread of the American sports such as baseball and basketball has been greatly assisted by the assiduous work of their respective elite governing bodies (and marketing machines), namely MLB and the NBA.

While these sporting forms have undergone extensive globalization in terms of reaching and engaging different populations, so too have they benefited from powerful processes of transnational *institutionalization*. International sport governing bodies – such as the International Olympic Committee (IOC), the Fédération Internationale de Football Association (FIFA), the International Cricket Council (ICC), and the International Rugby Board (IRB) – have sought to establish and to develop their sports in different nations and regions, in part through requiring the foundation of specific organizational structures, such as representative national sport bodies (Meyer et al., 2006).

The second side of the duality of glocality leads us to consider aspects of divergence in sport at transnational level. We should appreciate that, to begin with, sport does have instances, somewhat unusually, when the actual sporting forms undergo a radical transformation. Consider the case of American baseball – in which a variant of the English game of rounders was adapted to create, ultimately, an iconic American sport (Henderson, 2001, pp. 153–4). Consider also the more spectacular case of Trobriand cricket: celebrated by anthropologists, through the famous 1970s film about the game, and demonstrating how the famously quintessential English sport could be transformed into a local ritual in the Pacific Islands that bears little resemblance to its original form (Kildea and Leach, 1976).

Notwithstanding these instances, we find that tendencies towards divergence or heterogenization in sport are most evident in regard to sporting *content*: that is, at the everyday level, where individuals and social groups creatively engage with the lore and language, techniques and tropes of specific sports, in part as sites for exploring and constructing their own cultural values, meanings and identities. There are so many instances of such activities that to pick specific ones may appear trite and arbitrary. However, we might consider, for example, how different football clubs or nations undergird their distinctive histories and mythologies with reference to heroic players and epic moments, whether in victory or defeat; and, also understand their collective football identities with reference to particular playing styles, or the customary ways in which the game is played. To choose some specific cases from South America: Uruguay is sometimes regarded as having been 'made', in terms of national identity, in part through its epic football successes in the early twentieth century (winning two Olympic gold medals, and two World Cup finals); in Argentina, a national masculine identity is associated with the preferred national playing style in football, particularly focusing on highly technical and dribbling skills; and, in Brazil, more spectacular and acrobatic football skills are viewed as favoured by spectators and players, and despite winning several World Cup finals, the national football culture continues to reference, as a defining moment, its loss in the 1950 World Cup final, played in Rio before 200,000 fans (Archetti, 1998; Bellos, 2002; Giulianotti, 2000).

Similar points might be made about cricket in regard to Indians, West Indians, Australians, and other cricketing nations. As Appadurai (1996) notes, cricket is a relatively 'hard' cultural form, resistant to significant adaptation. Yet, when considering India, the game was 'hijacked', becoming 'an emblem of Indian nationhood at the same time that it became inscribed, as practice, into the Indian (male) body' (1996, p. 45). Indian players are known for particular playing techniques, notably spin bowling and, latterly, fluent shot-making when batting; India has also come to dominate cricket's governance and finance, through influence within the ICC and the inauguration of cricket's richest tournament, the Indian Premier League (IPL) (Rumford, 2007).

Elsewhere, cricket in the West Indies has been historically associated with the empowerment and expression of Afro-Caribbean identity within the colonial and post-colonial contexts; in terms of technique, West Indian players have been renowned for exceptional skills in fast bowling and in fast-scoring batting. This confluence of politics and practice on the cricket field was perceptively identified by the great West Indian historian and cricket-writer, CLR James, when discussing the skills of the great Gary Sobers, whose 'command of the rising ball in the drive, his close fielding and his hurling himself into his fast bowling are a living embodiment of centuries of a tortured history' (quoted by Stoddart, 1989, p. 144). Finally, the Australian way of playing cricket is often presented as reflecting wider aspects of white male Australian culture, with a focus on playing the game 'tough' (notably through the 'sledging' or verbal abuse of opponents) and with a strong 'mateship' culture among team-mates.

In all of these instances and many more, we find that global sport is party to the dual components of glocalization in different social contexts – convergence, as the sporting form itself 'takes off', and becomes embedded, within these diverse milieu; and divergence, as the content of the sport is adapted and transformed, to give it meaning and relevance vis-à-vis local or national identities.

Relativization, Differentiation and Sport

Following from these latter observations, we need also to register the wider context in which these distinctive sporting cultures are constructed. These processes of identity-making occur within the international or global context, for example at major sport tournaments such as the World Cup finals in individual sports, in football, rugby union, and cricket (in the case of tennis, we might consider also the nations-based competition, the Davis Cup). These events allow for a kind of collective looking-glass to be brought into play, for a national version of George Herbert Mead's (1934) idea of the 'me' to be explored, as nations imagine how others see them, in the light of their particular sporting successes or disasters. Thus, for the football fans of relatively small nations, part of the attraction of attending the tournament is a collective pride in seeing their 'little nation' on a global stage, being watched and discussed by global sport audiences (Giulianotti, 1996).

At the same time, this world context for the making and playing of sport points the participants towards processes of *relativization* and differentiation. Relativization occurs as different social groups become more conscious of their position within a broader world context, and thus respond by identifying themselves and marking themselves off in distinctive and elaborate ways. Relativization is also enhanced by intensified global compression and connectivity, as greater levels of transnational connection, interaction, and commingling lead to more extensive ways in which social identities are more sharply defined and 'marked off' vis-à-vis other groups.

Also, there has been a long-term, growing expectation that individuals and social groups will mark themselves off in extensive ways, usually according to particular common reference points. In other words, the idea of 'identity-as-differentiation' has been normalized and standardized at global level, to the extent that it is a decisive way of being 'in the world'. It has been reflected, for example, in the growth and cultivation of national identity and nationalism since at least the eighteenth century; and, in the classification of all individuals as 'belonging' to specific nations. Common reference points for establishing these national identities include, for example, citizenship status, national passports, and registration with national taxation systems; such identities are also conveyed through identification with common symbols and cultural resources, such as national flags, anthems, institutions, historical narratives on the 'making' of the nation, and of course national sport teams.

In sport, such relativization and differentiation are manifested in ritualized, Durkheimian ways at international events: the national teams and spectator groups are bedecked in national emblems and colours; and, pre-game ceremonies may include the airing of national anthems, unfurling of national flags, and the presentation of national teams to national VIPs in attendance. Indeed, there is an expectation in sport that such identity differentiation will occur, and in increasingly pronounced ways. Moreover, sport mega-events such as the Olympic Games or various World Cup finals tend to draw together spectator groups from a wide variety of nations. The social compression that occurs at such events – as these different nationalities commingle and interact, in public squares, bars, parks, and stadiums – leads to greater relativization, as these diverse collective national groups seek to express and to distinguish themselves in evermore elaborate ways.

These forms of identity-as-differentiation are evidenced, of course, at other levels, such as the civic and regional, or the continental; also, in ethnic terms, such as in the stronger expression of indigenous or 'first nation' identities, or in transnational religious terms; and, through association or identification with particular subcultural groupings and formations, as in the cases of youth movements. In sport, these patterns of differentiation have tended to be most apparent in supporter identification with specific club-level sport teams that are based in particular locations.

Glocal Identities and Cultures

Having set out the concepts of glocalization and relativization with regard to sport, I turn now to address how glocal identities are constructed in sport and more widely at the everyday level. The emphasis here is on the 'glocal': that is, we should recognize that all cultural identities and practices are now glocal rather than local. Otherwise put, no matter how localized they may appear, these identities and practices are unavoidably engaged with and inextricably embedded within broader global processes, and thus represent forms of response to globalization.

In passing, we might note that other scholars have understood glocalization as encompassing such multi-scalar processes. For example, the Mexican anthropologist Néstor García Canclini (1995, pp. 749–50) uses the idea of glocalization to describe cities that contain mixtures of local, national and international culture. Additionally, urban geographers such as Swyngedouw (1992) and Brenner (1999) view glocalisation (this time, spelling with an 's' not 'z') as a process that involves the partial shifting of nation-state powers upwards to supranational bodies such as the EU and downwards to sub-national or regional institutions.

In the socio-cultural context, the making of such glocal cultures and identities reflects the long-term influences and impacts of complex cultural mixtures, the 'hybridization' or 'creolization' of diverse cultural meanings and practices through processes of melding and fusion (Hannerz, 1992; Pieterse, 2001). In this sense, it becomes increasingly problematic to demonstrate or to reveal aspects of 'original' culture or 'fundamental' identity, although paradoxically we find that processes of relativization lead diverse social groups into seeking out or manufacturing these essences. In the following discussion, I explore how these glocal cultures are constructed before examining their impacts and manifestations within the sport.

Migration, Media and Commerce

Three important processes are at play in the making of glocal cultural identities and practices. First, since the early nineteenth century, the mass migration of diverse populations across the world has had a profound impact upon local, regional and ethno-national identities. In effect, such identities have become more and more disembedded, deterritorialized and mobile (Friedman, 2002; Tomlinson, 1999); if these identities are 'imagined communities' of peoples, as Anderson (1991) argued, then these forms of common identification are increasingly imagined across disparate territories. Thus, of course, more and more contemporary 'glocal cities' have populations that are drawn from across the planet, and which are sometimes differentiated into particular ethno-national neighbourhoods. In these settings, diverse ethnic groups are able to reintroduce their sport clubs and cultures, albeit in 'glocalized' versions that are adapted to the 'host' settings.

Second, we have the multifarious cultural influences of transnational media upon identities, tastes, meanings and practices. On one hand, there is the transnational structure and distribution of media products, wherein a common suite of films, television programmes, music, news, and televised sport is transmitted through global networks such as the Sky/Star/Fox conglomerate to reach audiences worldwide. Indeed, global sport has played a crucial role in the foundation of these media networks: for example, Sky TV was effectively built through the 1990s and 2000s on exclusive access to live English football matches which were beamed worldwide.

On the other hand, there are transnational media platforms and media content which enable disparate audiences to pursue or to strengthen their forms of cultural differentiation. For example, this process is facilitated through programmes and stations on satellite or digital television platforms that are aimed at households speaking minority languages; this also occurs through televised sport, for example as specialist television stations or online platforms provide live coverage of Portuguese league football or south Asian cricket tournaments to migrant groups that live in North America.

In addition, we have to consider the as-yet poorly understood and weakly theorized influence of contemporary social media upon identity construction. Overall, these diverse forms of mediatized connectivity have complex and competing cultural impacts: they allow for the construction of relatively homogenized or 'mass' forms of cultural consumption and identification, for example as the world's richest sport teams have become global 'brands'; they allow for a 'longer-tail' of small-scale or minority cultural identities and practices to be pursued, for example as minority sports are able to reach bigger audiences at transnational level; and, they allow for new, relatively niche forms of cultural identification to emerge at transnational level, such as with subcultures that follow particular clothing or musical styles, or sport teams.

Following from this, and third, we have the wider transnational commercialization of culture to consider. For example, we have an array of transnational corporations which fill the world's shopping malls and drive contemporary global consumer culture; in the fashion and leisurewear sectors, we have Gap, H&M, Abercrombie & Fitch, and Levis, and in the sportswear areas we have Nike, Adidas, Reebok, Puma, and many others (Lash and Lury, 2007). Brand endorsements by global celebrities – particularly from film, music, fashion and sport – play critical roles in accelerating product consumption; major examples in sport here include Beckham with Adidas, Michael Jordan with Nike, and Djokovic with Uniqlo (Cashmore, 2002; LaFeber, 2002).

Glocal Identities in Sport: Diasporas, Subcultures, Flâneurs

Sport is deeply embedded within glocal cultural processes that are driven by migration, media, and commerce. These glocal processes in turn have profound impacts on the construction and transformation of sport identities. Here, I outline three such varieties of sport identity which emerge.

First, we have the *glocalized sport cultures of diasporic groups*. Here, I am referring in particular to cases where migrant ethnic groups are able to establish their 'home town' sport clubs, or to develop 'supporters clubs' for their home teams, in the new host societies. For example, south Asians living in Scandinavia or North America create their own cricket clubs and tournaments, despite these settings having relatively little historical interest in the sport; and, Turks living in

Germany, or Italians in Australasia, establish football supporters' clubs for their preferred teams 'back home'.

To pick a further illustration, I conducted research in North America and Australasia into the migrant Scottish fans of Scotland's leading two teams, Celtic and Rangers. In North America in the early 2000s, these fans had established over 40 Celtic supporters' clubs, and over 25 Rangers clubs; some of these clubs had over 400 members, and many had their own licensed premises. A key driver for the foundation of many clubs had been a mix of transnational media and social connectivity: specifically, the network of North American clubs established a partnership with an Irish-based satellite television company which held a contract with the Scottish football league, to beam live coverage of these fixtures into North American clubhouses or households. Accordingly, supporters would typically meet on weekend mornings in clubhouses to watch live football fixtures. The supporter identities and practices which emerged were 'glocalized', in terms of mixing influences from the host and home societies: for example, many fans argued that, due to the different contexts In North America, they had less 'bitter' or sectarian rivalries with the other football team, while many of the old symbols associated with the club history and culture were retained (Giulianotti and Robertson, 2005, 2007a).

Second, a growing range and number of *transnational sport subcultures* has emerged, in which significantly strong forms of identification with specific sport teams or sport practices have occurred among different social groups at the global level. For example, in terms of sport club identification, we might consider the tens of thousands of Norwegians who identify strongly with different football clubs in England (Hognestad, 2006). These allegiances have been inspired largely by the live Norwegian television coverage of English fixtures since the 1960s, and by the later emergence of leading Norwegian players in the English game from the late 1980s onwards. Certainly, many of these Norwegian fans do not see themselves as transient supporters (see below), but as having lifelong commitments to their favoured club, as reflected in part by their flying visits to English games; research in Finland suggests similar processes at play elsewhere in the Nordic region (Heinonen, 2002). Illustrations from other sports are found in East Asian supporter allegiances with North American baseball teams, or Nordic support for Canadian ice-hockey teams. In terms of sport participation, we might also point to the rise of transnational subcultures that engage in 'extreme' sports and new sporting activities such as snowboarding or skateboarding (Langseth, 2012; Thorpe, 2011).

Third, we have also witnessed the rise of much looser, fleeting and transient forms of sport identification, in large part through the confluence of processes of commercialization and mediatization in the broad 'sport industry'. Such developments are manifested in manifold ways.

In broad terms, we might note the long-term penetration of the leisurewear marketplace by sport merchandise companies, so that sport training apparel – such as trainers/sneakers, sweatshirts, hooded tops, and shellsuits – has become standard attire in public and private spaces. In addition, various High Street fashion retailers have produced clothing ranges which play heavily on sport, and forms of sport identification – for example, tracksuit-style tops which are emblazoned with national names ('Italy', 'Brazil', 'England', 'Argentina' and so on).

More specifically, we might point to highly transient, consumerist, and *flâneur*-like associations with sport clubs by different individuals and consumers (Giulianotti, 2002). Leading sport club 'brands' seek to attract new 'consumers' at global level through diverse forms of promotion; hence, clubs such as New York Yankees, Manchester United, Real Madrid, Dallas Cowboys, and LA Lakers will promote themselves in foreign markets through, for example, the 'marquee signing' of celebrity players, relentless advertising, opening shops and selling fashion-focused club merchandise, special tours of key target nations and regions, and running television stations devoted to their teams. While such activities may serve to increase the scale and range of transnational sport subcultures (as discussed above), they also lead towards the representation of sport club brands as 'commodity signs', which consumers may obtain and discard at whim, with relatively low levels of identification or club-based 'solidarity'. These transient forms of consumption may be based, for example, on the sport team's level of success ('always back a winner'), association with celebrity players (buy into 'brand Jordan'), or effective marketing of products (think, for example, of the ubiquitous 'NY' baseball cap, which unbeknown to many wearers is specifically tied to the New York Yankees baseball team).

This intersection of sport, commodification and consumer culture is a prominent part of the globalization of contemporary sport. It is also significantly influenced by on-going processes of postmodernization, notably in the growing systemic significance of popular culture, and the rise in fleeting, consumer-based cultural practices and identifications. Additionally, we witness a growth in neo-tribal forms of identification, which are less focused on strong forms of solidarity, and more on fluid emotional sites and spaces, into which diverse groups might move and cluster. Social media perhaps shows the most prominent recent examples of such neo-tribalism, in regard to 'trending' issues or topics that are suddenly and momentarily very popular on Twitter or YouTube: sport incidents, celebrities, and teams feature strongly in the top 'trending' items.

Glocal Sport in the Mix: Banal Cosmopolitanism and Cultural Exchange

We need also to recognize that greater levels of transnational connectivity and consciousness have impacted significantly on sport in the adaptation and transformation of cultural meanings, practices and techniques. In effect, this leads to the construction of glocal sport cultures. There are two main everyday processes that might be highlighted as underlying such cultures.

First, the social experience of sport and other forms of popular culture has been characterized by increasing levels of *banal cosmopolitanism* (Giulianotti and Robertson, 2009). By banal cosmopolitanism, I am referring to how significant varieties and volumes of non-national and international culture are increasingly encountered in routine and mundane ways at the everyday level, particularly in mega-cities and in most locations in the global North. For example, the food shops and courts in shopping malls typically feature foodstuffs and varieties of cuisine that are drawn from across the world. In sport, banal cosmopolitanism is strongly driven through sport-related media, for example through the vast array of different sport tournaments that are routinely available to viewers, such as on pay-television or through online platforms (such as sopcast, Acestream, Flash, and VLC); and, on social media, through access to information and comment on global sport. In addition, the global consumer marketplace promotes the mundane intermingling, in diverse public settings, of products associated with world sport brands. For sport spectators, banal cosmopolitanism is also manifested in how athletes from across the world are routinely encountered in professional and semi-professional contests, particularly in the global North. This reflects the rapid growth and complexity of the international division of sport labour over the past two decades, primarily due to the liberalization of athlete markets and the increasing revenues and profits to be derived from such mobility (Miller et al., 1999).

Second, there are the long-term impacts and influences of the transnational movements of athletes, experts, capital, ideas, information, owners, practices, products, symbols, and technologies. In short, sport at the everyday level has become increasingly marked by *cultural exchange*, in the form of transnational mixing and creolization at the social and cultural levels. Accordingly, the simple binary opposition of the 'local versus global', always problematic, becomes more and more absurd, particularly if we seek to talk about distinctive, stand-alone local and national sport 'traditions'. Rather, sport cultures should be come to be seen as 'glocal', to register their different experiences and responses to transnational influences and processes. That said, we should be clear on the subtleties of glocalization. Glocal processes and cultures will not be manifested in identical ways; individuals and social groups will engage with different aspects of transnational culture, making the latter their own in different ways.

How do these different forms of glocal culture play out in the sport context? We might turn to football, as a brief case study. In broad terms, in football, we find that, increasingly, many teams from across the world will draw upon a range of globally-recognized playing formations (most obviously, 4-4-2 or 4-3-3) and a mix of similarly familiar playing styles (such as fast attacking, or counter-attacking, or high-tempo pressing, or slow-quick build-up, or multi-pass possession play). In effect, many of these formations and styles have spread across the world, notably as the methods that are favoured by the most successful teams and coaches are shared or copied in different settings, and as the influences of different international coaches or players come to have a significant impact on specific sides. What this means is that, particularly at club level, many teams are able to change radically their playing styles and formations according to the coach. For example, in the 1970s, 1980s and much of the 1990s, the successes of the Arsenal side in England were built primarily on very tight defensive performances, to the extent that the team was derided by opposing fans (and celebrated by their own) through chants of 'boring, boring Arsenal'. That football tradition was largely transformed when the French coach, Arsène Wenger, took charge and placed a long-term focus on a highly-technical, fluid, and attacking style, largely driven by the recruitment of French and other non-UK players; indeed, at various times since, the Arsenal team has contained no UK players. In England, other leading clubs whose playing styles have been significantly influenced or transformed by foreign coaches have included Chelsea (under the Portuguese, Mourinho), Liverpool (under the Frenchman, Houllier, then the Spaniard, Benitez), and Manchester City (under the Italian, Mancini, and the Chilean, Pellegrini).

We might also look at *tiki-taka*, arguably the most successful playing style in football since the early 2000s, and associated in particular with the Barcelona club side and the Spanish national team. *Tiki-taka* is characterized by high levels of ball possession, many short passes and continuous player movement, as an attacking opportunity is patiently explored. Importantly, this style has its origins in the arrival of former top player, Johan Cruyff, at Barcelona as coach in the late 1980s, who introduced what was then regarded as a Dutch style of play, and established a youth academy which taught these principles to future star players. Thus, in the cases of both Arsenal and Barcelona, we find that the distinctive and indeed world-renowned playing styles of these clubs are derived from the influences of international coaches. These playing styles are highly glocalized, in terms of how such international influences are absorbed and adapted at club and national levels.

However, there are some areas of football in different countries, in which processes of glocalization are firmly weighted towards the idea of retaining particular identities and practices vis-à-vis perceived transnational influences. Often, such responses represent conscious ways of marking out specific identities, as motors of relativization. For example, much of Italian football continues to be associated with highly disciplined defensive methods; and, in English football, the game is high-tempo, combative, and marked by a stated (if, now more often, unobserved) opposition to player 'diving' and the feigning of injuries. The reproduction of these forms of cultural identity is facilitated in part by discourses in the wider public spheres and lifeworlds of football in these locations, where typically such playing methods and ethics are subject to critical normative discussion. Moreover, in marked contrast to the examples of Arsenal and Barcelona, we find that even world-leading coaches who go to work in these countries will make reference to the fact that the 'football culture is different here', and that they have had to 'adapt' to this, such as by favouring more defensively-aware tactics in Italy or more combative players and methods in England. Thus, glocalization processes in football, or in sport more generally, are themselves a complex process, of absorption, adaptation, blending, differentiation and rejection. Indeed, even in cases where particular transnational practices are rejected at everyday level – such as in England, where players are heavily criticized for obvious 'dives' or for possibly feigning injuries – these critical responses further establish a particular type of 'glocal' football culture, as they serve to sharpen these sport identities within the global context.

Concluding Comments

Glocalization processes are central to the making of global sport, and global sport is itself a key driver of processes of globalization. The concept of the 'duality of glocality' captures how the forms and contents of global sport are marked by different tendencies of convergence and divergence between different sporting societies and cultures. The concept of relativization helps to explain how globalization serves to underscore and to sharpen, rather than to 'abolish', forms of local identity in sport and other cultural fields. Migration, media and commerce play critical roles in the making and reshaping of contemporary 'glocal' identities; in sport, as I have argued, these processes serve to produce diverse types of identity and solidarity, which I have characterized as subcultures, diasporas and *flâneurs*. Banal cosmopolitanism and cultural exchange serve to intensify forms of cultural mixing and creolization, though the resulting 'glocal cultures' in sport are marked by significant differences in how social groups borrow, adapt or reject cultural phenomena.

Where next might glocalization processes take social scientists, in terms of examining the making of sport cultures and the shaping of sport's broader contribution to global cultures? Two brief observations may be made here. First, researchers may move from exploring broad issues and general questions on the glocalization of sport (an approach that has certainly been adopted in this chapter), to examine instead, with the use of case studies and in far greater detail, how these processes are played out in more complex terms at the everyday level. More specifically, social scientists may turn to explore the glocal politics of specific sport cultures and identities, to consider in particular the types of consensus and conflict that surround key sport institutions, and how they engage with glocal processes, whether these might be sport clubs, national sport teams, sport governing bodies, and sport-related corporations.

Second, social scientists might consider how glocalization theory, as employed in the study of sport, might also be used to explain other fields of culture and society. On one hand, such a strategy may draw social scientists into recognizing the importance of sport in the global context, and thus the need to utilize glocalization theory in this and other areas. For example, many emerging nations – such as the 'BRICS' as well as Qatar – are hosting sport mega-events, as a crucial aspect of their glocal political strategies; any social scientist interested in these nations thus needs to take very seriously the role of sport and, I would argue, glocalization theory as a tool for analysis and explanation. On the other hand, sport provides an ideal case study of wider cultural processes, in which glocal identities and practices are constructed at everyday level, for example through migration, the creation of diasporic communities, and the complex mixing and blending of diverse cultural influences. Study of these processes inevitably peeks our interest in how such processes may play out in other cultural spheres, such as in religion, music, literature, cuisine, dance, sexuality, and festivals. Future comparative studies between sport and these other cultural spheres would significantly advance our understanding of the complexities of contemporary glocal cultures.

References

Anderson, B. 1991. *Imagined Communities*. London: Verso.
Appadurai, A. 1995. 'Playing with Modernity: The Decolonization of Indian Cricket'. In *Consuming Modernity*, edited by C.A. Breckenridge, 23–48. Minneapolis, MN: University of Minnesota Press.
Archetti, E. 1998. *Masculinities*. Oxford: Berg.
Bale, J., and J. Sang. 1996. *Kenyan Running*. London: Frank Cass.
Barber, B. 1992. 'Jihad versus McWorld'. *Atlantic Monthly*, 1 March. http://www.theatlantic.com/magazine/archive/1992/03/jihad-vs-mcworld/303882/.
Beck, U., N. Sznaider, and R. Winter (eds). 2004. *Global America?*. Liverpool: Liverpool University Press.
Bellos, A. 2002. *Futebol: The Brazilian Way of Life*. London: Bloomsbury.
Brenner, N. 1999. 'Globalisation as Reterritorialisation: The Re-scaling of Urban Governance in the European Union'. *Urban Studies* 36(3): 431–51.
Canclini, N.G. 2001. *Consumers and Citizens*. Minneapolis: University of Minnesota Press.
Cashmore, E. 2002. *Beckham*. Cambridge: Polity.
Friedman, J. 2002. 'From Roots to Routes: Tropes for Trippers'. *Anthropological Theory* 2(1): 21–36.
Giulianotti, R. 1996. 'Back to the Future: An Ethnography of Ireland's Football Fans at the 1994 World Cup Finals in the USA'. *International Review for the Sociology of Sport* 31(3): 323–43.
Giulianotti, R. 2000. 'Built by the Two Varelas: Football Culture and National Identity in Uruguay'. In *Football Culture: Local Conflicts, Global Visions*, edited by G.P.T. Finn and R. Giulianotti, 134–54. London: Frank Cass.
Giulianotti, R. 2002. 'Supporters, Followers, Fans and *Flâneurs*'. *Journal of Sport and Social Issues* 6(1): 25–46.
Giulianotti, R., and R. Robertson. 2004. 'The Globalization of Football: A Study in the Glocalization of the "Serious Life"'. *British Journal of Sociology* 55(4): 545–68.
Giulianotti, R., and R. Robertson. 2005. 'Glocalization, Globalization and Migration: The Case of Scottish Football Supporters in North America'. *International Sociology* 21(2): 171–98.
Giulianotti, R., and R. Robertson. 2007a. 'Forms of Glocalization: Globalization and the Migration Strategies of Scottish Football Fans in North America'. *Sociology* 41(1): 133–52.
Giulianotti, R., and R. Robertson. 2007b. 'Recovering the Social: Globalization, Football and Transnationalism'. *Global Networks* 7(2): 144–186.
Giulianotti, R., and R. Robertson. 2007c. 'Sport and Globalization: Transnational Dimensions'. *Global Networks* 7(2): 107–12.
Giulianotti, R., and R. Robertson (eds). 2007d. *Globalization and Sport*. Oxford: Wiley-Blackwell.
Giulianotti, R., and R. Robertson. 2009. *Globalization and Football*. London: Sage.

Giulianotti, R., and R. Robertson. 2012a. 'Glocalization and Sport in Asia: Diverse Perspectives and Future Possibilities'. *Sociology of Sport Journal* 29(4): 433–54.

Giulianotti, R., and R. Robertson. 2012b. 'Mapping the Global Football Field: A Sociological Model of Transnational Forces within the World Game'. *British Journal of Sociology* 63(2): 33–58.

Heinonen, H. 2002. 'Finnish Soccer Supporters Away From Home'. *Soccer & Society* 3(3): 26–50.

Henderson, R.W. 2001 [1947]. *Ball, Bat and Bishop: The Origin of Ball Games*. Urbana: University of Illinois Press.

Hognestad, H. 2006. 'Transnational Passions: A Statistical Study of Norwegian Football Supporters'. *Soccer and Society* 7(4): 439–62.

Huntington, S.P. 1996. *The Clash of Civilizations and the Remaking of World Order*. New York: Simon & Schuster.

Kildea, G., and J. Leach. 1976. *Trobriand Cricket: An Ingenious Response to Colonialism* (film/documentary).

LaFeber, W. 2002. *Michael Jordan and the New Global Capitalism*. New York: Norton.

Langseth, T. 2012. 'BASE Jumping: Beyond the Thrills'. *European Journal for Sport and Society* 9(3): 155–76.

Lash, S., and C. Lury. 2007. *Global Culture Industries*. Cambridge: Polity.

Latouche, S. 1996. *The Westernization of the World*. Cambridge: Polity.

Mangan, J.A. 1986. *The Games Ethic and Imperialism*. London: Viking.

Mead, G.H. 1934. *Mind, Self and Society from the Standpoint of a Social Behaviorist*. Chicago, IL: University of Chicago Press.

Meyer, J.W., G.S. Drori, and H. Hwang. 2006. 'World Society and the Proliferation of Formal Organizations'. In *Globalization and Organization: World Society and Organizational Change*, edited by G.S. Drori, J.W. Meyer and H. Hwang, 25–49. Oxford: Oxford University Press.

Miller, T., G. Lawrence, D. Rowe, and J. McKay. 1999. *Globalization and Sport*. London: Sage.

Pieterse, J.N. 2007. *Ethnicities and Global Multiculture*. Lanham, MD: Rowman and Littlefield.

Ritzer, G. 2004. *The Globalization of Nothing*. Thousand Oaks, CA: Pine Forge.

Robertson, R. 1992. *Globalization: Social Theory and Global Culture*. London: Sage.

Robertson, R. 1994. 'Globalisation or Glocalisation?'. *Journal of International Communication* 1(1): 33–52.

Robertson, R. 1995. 'Glocalization: Time-Space and Homogeneity-Heterogeneity'. In *Global Modernities*, edited by M. Featherstone, S. Lash and R. Robertson, 25–44 London: Sage.

Robertson, R., and K.E. White. 2004. 'La Glocalizzazione Rivisitata ed Elaborata. [Glocalization Revisited and Elaborated]' in *Glocal*, edited by F. Sedda. Roma: Luca Sossella Editore.

Rumford, C. 2007. 'More Than a Game: Globalization and the Post-Westernization of World Cricket'. *Global Networks* 7(2): 202–14.

Said, E. 1978. *Orientalism*. New York: Vintage.

Stoddart, B. 1989. 'Gary Sobers and Cultural Identity in the Caribbean'. *Sporting Traditions* 5(1): 131–46.

Swyngedouw, E. 1992. 'The Mammon Quest: 'Glocalization', Interspatial Competition and the Monetary Order: The Construction of New Scales'. In *Cities and Regions in the New Europe: The Global-Local Interplay and Spatial Development Strategies*, edited by M. Dunford and G. Kafkalis, 39–67. London: Belhaven Press.

Thorpe, H. 2011. *Snowboarding Bodies in Theory and Practice*. Basingstoke: Palgrave.

Tomlinson, J. 1999. *Globalization and Culture*. Oxford: Wiley.

Chapter 9
Global Culture in Motion

Peggy Levitt

Every September, music luminaries from around the world gather in New York City's Central Park for the Global Citizen Festival. Attended by a capacity crowd of over 60,000, the festival addresses a single, stubborn mission: the end of extreme poverty worldwide. It is an informal summit and a demonstration of public concern, designed to coincide with the opening of the United Nations General Assembly. Consciousness-raising is mixed with rock and roll by the likes of Elvis Costello, Stevie Wonder, and Alicia Keys. Concertgoers earn rather than buy their tickets, becoming concerned global citizens while accruing points online by completing a series of awareness building tasks.

Down the street on Madison Avenue, at the high-end luggage store, TUMI, this year's latest suitcase model is displayed side-by-side with a large sign, 'Global Citizen.' In this case, a simple purchase makes one a cosmopolitan. The old adage, 'you are what you eat,' should now read 'you are what you buy.'

These two examples speak to the central concerns of this chapter—the relationship between migrating people and migrating culture. In the contemporary world on the move, how does the movement of people contribute to and transform the movement of culture? How, in turn, does cultural circulation enable the movement of bodies and the social relations and processes that are unleashed as a result? This is a big question—too large to answer fully here. This essay contains selective thoughts that try to bring previously isolated strands of the discussion into conversation with each other.

One challenge making this task so difficult is that much work on global culture or cultural globalization asks questions at different levels, about different types of traveling ideas and institutions, and does not always link its findings to other sites and scales. Neo-institutionalists and World Polity Theorists, for example, assert the existence of global culture, but do not generally explain how these norms and institutional arrangements came into being or why they get used on the ground (or not) as they do.[1] Researchers studying how global cultural products actually

---

1 For more recent work which discusses these questions more fully, see Barrie Axford, *Theories of Globalization*, Polity, 2013; G. Drori et al. eds., *Global Themes and Local Variations in Organization and Management: Perspectives on Glocalization*, Blackwell, 2014; and F. Lechner and J. Boli, *World Culture*, Blackwell, Oxford. Also see the special volume of Poetics 40.2 on Cultures of Circulation (published in Spring 2012) in which editors Melissa Aronczyk and Ailsa Craig and their collaborators ask how cultures

circulate and are appropriated frequently sidestep how these dynamics are shaped by and speak back to larger processes of cultural production and dissemination. They take the spaces of global cultural production as given, failing to recognize the interaction between their constantly changing layers and the networks of networks and specific sites in which cultural producers and consumers are embedded.

Analytical Framing

Culture is context: the discourses, regimes and assumptions embedded in institutions, and the repertoires of meanings that are marshaled to respond to dilemmas and opportunities (Alexander and Smith, 2010). It makes certain actions possible by providing the building blocks with which to enact them, and by marking them as socially appropriate, while restricting others by rendering them unacceptable. Research on culture often assumes that it lives in contained spaces—be they communities, organizations, congregations, or nations—and that it is static and bounded. But in today's highly mobile world, culture is more likely a contingent clustering of diverse elements that is often on the move rather than a packageable, stable set of beliefs and practices rooted in a particular place. Ong calls this working within an 'analytics of assemblage' as opposed to an 'analytics of structure.' By that she means focusing 'on the emerging milieus over the stabilization of a new global order—not a fixed set of attributes with predetermined outcomes but as a logic of governing that migrates and is selectively taken up in diverse political contexts' (Ong, 2007, p. 3).

Moreover, we need to understand cultural circulation as taking place within social fields whose breadth and depth extend far beyond the boundaries of the nation-state—interlocking, multi-layered, unequal networks of individuals, institutions, and governance regimes that connect cultural producers and consumers to multiple people and places on the basis of multiple identities. Unfortunately, many of the ways we talk about cultural circulation are still plagued by methodological nationalism. We assume something that is hybridized was initially pure, or that ethnicity or nationality is the primary pathway through which people are incorporated into fields (Schiller and Meinhof, 2011).

Using a transnational gaze, or optic, brings these dynamics more clearly into view (Khagram and Levitt, 2007b). In contrast to traditional perspectives, which treat the transnational as belonging somewhere between the national and the global, this view starts somewhere different. What are assumed to be bounded and bordered social units or identities are actually understood to be transnationally constituted, embedded and influenced social arenas that interact with one another. The world consists of multiple sets of dynamically overlapping and interacting transnational social fields that create and shape seemingly bordered and bounded

---

of circulation inform critical scholarship and relations between academic work and public engagement in globalized settings http://ipk.nyu.edu/news/12-poetics-40-2-spring-2012.

structures, actors, and processes. Assemblages come together and travel within these transnational spaces.

A transnational gaze begins with a world without borders, empirically examines the boundaries and borders that emerge at particular historical moments, and explores their relationship to unbounded arenas and processes. It does not take the appropriate spatial unit of analysis for granted, but interrogates the territorial breadth and scope of any social phenomena without prior assumptions. Nor does it privilege the global or the local, but tries to hold these layers of social experience, and all others in between, in dialogue with each other by paying close attention to how these multiple sites and layers interact with and inform one another.

Any study, therefore, whether of norms, practices, institutions, or policies would begin by ascertaining the level and intensity of connection to actors and institutions located at other sites and levels of the social field. It would not treat these dynamics as closed, isolated containers nested automatically in local, regional, or national scales, but see them instead as potential sites of clustering and convergence, which, once constituted, circulate and re-circulate, constantly changing as they move. The logical next question is to ask how these contingent clusters take shape, and what explains how they travel? Elsewhere, I proposed four conceptual hooks with which to answer these questions that I briefly summarize here (Levitt and Rajaram, 2013).

Individuals are the key *carriers* of culture in motion, but because they move for different amounts of time across varying distances, the encounter between what is moving and what is in place varies. Culture carried by the pilgrim, tourist, or temporary worker does not have the same impact as when it is carried by a permanent settler. Material objects, practices, policies, and institutions are also carriers of culture, as are saints, spirits and deities, their value and meaning changing as they move (Durand and Massey, 1995; Oleszkiewicz-Peralba, 2007; Lambek, 1993; Meyer and Moors, 2006; Hewelmeier and Krause, 2009).

How and why these concrete, imagined, and embodied cultural carriers circulate depends upon the geography and boundaries of the transnational social fields within which they travel. Some terrains are more settled than others. The social fields connecting Mexico and the United States or Germany and Turkey have relatively long and stable histories, while the economic uncertainty, civil unrest, or climactic disasters plaguing other social fields make them more difficult to navigate.

In addition, the geographies through which culture travels are not virgin territories. Places are transformed into spaces by their history, politics, and demography (LeFebvre, 1991; Knott, 2005). They are deeply rutted. Just as new eruptions of lava must find their way through crevices that previous eruptions laid down, so new cultural infusions must accommodate themselves to the twists and turns of existing terrains. The geographies of social fields are multi-layered and multi-scalar, influenced by discourses, regimes, and circuits of power that intersect, span, and jump its many levels. Neoliberalism and global economic restructuring disrupt the traditional nested hierarchies between the local, regional, national, and global by distributing resources and power unevenly between cities and regions. As a result, institutions and circuits of power on seemingly lower scales can trump what are assumed to be their higher counterparts (Glick, Schiller and Caglar, 2009).

Many kinds of global cultural packages circulate through these spaces. How they are framed strongly influences their journey and use. Bob studied social movements among India's Dalits, who succeeded by abandoning their long-standing focus on caste-based discrimination in favor of a broader, internationally-accepted framing of discrimination based on 'work and descent' (Bob, 2005). The Ogoni in Nigeria and the Zapatistas in Chiapas succeeded because they deployed 'master frames' that their potential partners could understand. Anna Tsing (2005) described 'activist packages'—stories about environmental heroes, which detach from their original contexts as they travel and are reframed to attract different audiences.

Ong, Collier and their colleagues expand the focus beyond discourse to ideational and material packages of people, objects, technologies, laws and policies that circulate widely as assemblages (Ong and Collier, 2005). My own work on how social remittances affect the health sector in Gujarat, India revealed three types of assemblages used differently by providers and patients on the ground (Levitt and Rajaram, 2013; Levitt, 2001). The first was a *neo-liberal assemblage* that favored privatization or public-private partnerships and emphasized economic efficiency and the logic of the market over equity. A second, *welfare state assemblage*, still focused on curative rather than preventive care but emphasized the role of the state in providing for vulnerable populations. A third *integrated health* assemblage stressed the relationship between health and other aspects of development, favoring more public health oriented and preventive approaches provided by low-cost, low-tech, low-skilled providers. The neo-liberal assemblage 'reigned supreme,' however, because Western foundations and international organizations supported it so strongly, despite widespread reservations among some adopters about its appropriateness for the Indian context.

How global assemblages actually circulate and get used also depends on the institutional arrangements, normative regimes, and pathways they encounter as they travel. For analytical purposes, we might think of the layers of the social fields as discrete, but the boundaries between them can be quite porous, and they blend into each other. The most overarching is the global. In our study about how global ideas about women's rights actually get used by local activists, Sally Merry and I identified a range of global institutions and regimes that influenced appropriation (Levitt and Merry, 2009). International laws and practices, such as the Convention on the Elimination of all Forms of Discrimination against Women (CEDAW) and the Universal Declaration of Human Rights (UDHR), constituted and spread these assemblages. The World Conferences on Women, convened by the United Nations; annual celebrations of International Women's Day; and international associations like the Association for Women's Rights in Development were sites where these assemblages took shape and were disseminated. Women's and Feminist studies programs at universities around the world also drove assemblage production and consumption forward.

But national institutions and regimes strongly affect global cultural circulation as well. The gendering of national labor, health, and social welfare policies influence what is appropriated and what gets ignored (Yuval-Davis, 1997). In our project about global women's rights, elements of global assemblages combined with similar national policy frames and social movements to produce very different results on the ground. In China, they blended with social work ideologies; in Peru, with Liberation Theology; in India, with Gandhian thought and socialism; and in the United States, with LGBT and people of color activism. The global rights assemblage also connected to different organizational forms and technologies, including communal soup kitchens and Catholic base communities in Peru, the 'government's' Women's Federation and universities in China, the US battered women's movement, and caste and village *panchayats* in India.

In each case, NGOs and activists, connected to various networks of partners near and far, then drew selectively on different pieces of the circulating assemblages. Ideas about women's human rights and strategies for protecting women from violence adopted by elite women lawyers in China, for example, lead to the creation of a legal aid center that prosecuted a small number of 'model' or 'impact' cases designed to change policies. The same ideas adopted by a women's center in India committed to grassroots, Gandhian, and Marxist ideologies gave rise to a project that paid poor women to make kites printed with messages that warned against sex selection policies.

Sites of Encounter

How can we better understand these 'sites of encounter' where traveling words, objects, and strategies from different contexts, with different meanings, come into contact with those already on the ground? Here again, there is no shortage of metaphors from different disciplines to capture aspects of these 'meetings.' Some scholars, primarily concerned with circulation and the transfer of state structures, management approaches, and policies, speak of glocalization (Featherstone et al., 1995), translation (Czarniawska and Sevon, 2005), and hybridization (Pieterse, 2003). Others talk of mimesis as a way to bring into focus the relationship between the imperial source, or the colonizer, and the impersonator who is being colonized, thereby bringing power centrally into these discussions (Ashcroft, 1998).

Pratt (1992) wrote of contact zones where multiple cultures bump up against and mix with each other. Ortiz (1995) wrote of transculturation—cultural encounters that resulted not in assimilation or deculturation, but in the production of something new. Tsing (2005) wrote of the 'frictional' encounters globalization engenders that produce conflict and movement, action and effect. According to Canclini (2001), globalization results in cultural 'deterritorialization,' or its uncoupling from the places where it is generated, and a 'reterritorialization' when it is relocalized, mixed, and comes into contact with modern and postmodern discourse and practices. The end results are *tiempos y espacios mixtos e híbridos*, or new spatio-temporal hybrid configurations that transform culture and the public arena. In their work on circulating popular culture, Cohen and Sheringham (2013) found that incoming cultures are creolized and, in the process, they are 'nationalized, officialized or commercialized' and subject to mechanisms of 'destructive tolerance.' At the same time, the desire for authenticity and creativity makes actors draw on original (or imagined original) and emergent diasporic practices and identities—'diasporic echoes,' which influence circulation and appropriation anew.

Whatever the terminology, these encounters are multi-directional, involve multiple actors and scales of social experience, and take shape in particular places whose geopolitical position influences their impact. They do not originate from some pure idea, identity, or product that is then somehow compromised. We need to put aside false, unproductive binaries such as native versus foreigner, familiar versus strange, or national versus global. Instead, we need to see the world as multiple, overlapping yet uneven networks of power, resources, and goods within which cultural producers and consumers are differently positioned and therefore hybridize, transculturalize or mimic culture differently. Still, many questions remain. Why are some things appropriated while others are ignored? Why are some things discussed while others are silenced?

One broad set of factors that explains appropriation and vernacularization is the *social status of the carriers and the receivers*, be they individuals, organizations, or nations. 'Marginal' individuals or institutions are more likely to take risks because they care less about social norms (Rogers, 2003; Strang and Stroule, 1998; Wejnert, 2002). More powerful individuals and organizations are in a better position to pressure others to adopt innovations. Groups who want to be perceived as equal to their peers may also mimic their behavior (DiMaggio and Powell 1983; Dobbin, Simmons and Garret, 2007; McAdam, Tarrow and Tilly, 2001). They want to 'keep up with the Jones' whether the unit of comparison be a colleague, neighboring community, or comparable institution.

Ideas and practices acquired and applied in one setting can scale up to other levels of social organization, and scale out to other domains of practice. When people come to expect transparent budgeting in a health project, they may come to expect it in an education project (Levitt and Lamba-Nieves, 2011). When they come to expect accountability from their local government, they may also come to expect it from its provincial and regional counterpart. Snow and Benford (2005) use the term 'diffusion' to describe information transfers along established relational lines, while 'brokerage' involves transfers linking two or more previously unconnected social sites, thus making shifts in scale more likely. When actors 'accommodate,' or frame claims and identities so they are more familiar and easy to understand and rally behind, more changes in scale are likely to occur.

Kaufman and Patterson (2005), for example, blame high status gatekeepers for keeping cricket on the margins of the North American sports scene. Mears (2011) emphasizes the importance of agents in hiring practices in the global fashion world.

Because they function in an environment of uncertainty, two different aesthetics guide the commercial and high-end fashion markets. Racial inclusiveness, sex appeal, and attainable beauty drive the former, while distinction, sexual unavailability, and rarified beauty reign supreme in the latter, which perpetuates the organization of femininity along race and class lines.

A cultural product's symbolic values, and what users signal about themselves and their social status by engaging with it, also influences circulation. Kaufman and Patterson (2005) also blame the failure of cricket in the United States and Canada on elites because they did not use it to draw symbolic boundaries between themselves and others while their peers in the rest of the British Empire did. Sylvanus' (2013) research is a fascinating account of how textiles' meaning and value change through their exchange. Wax fabrics were first produced in Indonesia in the nineteenth century, and then traveled to Europe, India, and Africa over established trade routes. Perfectly imitated copies, adjusted for quality and aesthetics to meet local tastes, eventually became part of African consumption structures and are now considered African. What became even more important than the fabric itself, however, is how it is used to position owners and wearers in relation to each other.

A second broad set of factors influencing circulation is the *difference between the objects or rituals in motion and those that are already in place*—not only how easy something is to package, communicate, and transmit, but also how different it is from what is currently being done. Some rituals and objects are clearly more portable than others, and some messages more readily applicable to new settings. Voting and campaigning are easy to replicate almost anywhere, while defining democratic practice is not nearly so straightforward. Boundaries can be high when adoption requires a major change, or they can be low when what comes to ground has a lot in common with what is already there. Boundaries can be thick, creating tight data packets that travel easily and efficiently, or they can be thin, creating leaky packages that move with greater difficulty because they are more likely to spill. Written traditions travel in packages that are literally bounded, while stories transmitted orally are more likely to change when they are translated and retold over time.

For example, television programming is said to travel easily when the media rituals featured in the series connect to wider belief structures and resonate with shared structures of meaning (Couldry, 2007, p. 248). Viewers in Canada adopted the program *Deal or no Deal* because its generic structure could be readily customized to feel national. Producers made it 'Canadian' by featuring Canadian contestants and stars, including Canadian-inspired prizes, and filling its sets with Canadian iconography. In contrast, Gutiérrez-Zuñiga (2013) found limits to the malleability of the Conchero-Azteca dance she studied. This popular Catholic tradition from Mexico could only be refashioned so far into a therapeutic act by new age seekers, despite its pretensions to universality and cosmopolitanism.

The outcome of the circulatory encounter also depends on the *presence of exogenous elements* that stimulate, enhance, or cancel out their effects. Certain ideas and practices travel together in a kind of partnership, producing an interaction effect. Sometimes their relationship is parasitic: what is introduced piggybacks onto a host that it decimates as it travels. Other flows cancel each other out. Finally, other ideas and practices depend on each other symbiotically for survival (Levitt, 2012a). For instance, the idea that women can be political leaders is unlikely to take root if it does not circulate in tandem with the idea that women can work outside their homes.

The *frequency and strength of contact* between what circulates and what is in place also influences the nature of the encounter. Think of the allergy sufferer who rubs medicine onto her skin as opposed to the person who uses an inhaler. The drug's effect is greater when it is introduced directly into the bloodstream. Kuiper and colleagues' (2014) work on the global fashion industry not only highlights the importance of the intensity of contact, but also the *importance of position within the transnational cultural field.* They argue that the Dutch, Chinese, and US versions of Vogue magazine differed over how much healthy body types were featured because of each nation's different status. While the American media embraced the importance of healthy body types and went on to globally champion the cause, the Dutch and Chinese responses were far more lukewarm. In Dutch media, *Vogue* was portrayed as an outside force, which automatically limited its moral relevance. In China, *Vogue*'s Health Initiative initially lacked relevance because this had not been a central issue in earlier public debates.

Similarly, Kiwan and Meinhof (2011) found stark differences in the ease with which musicians from Madagascar could circulate, as well as deep divisions over what it means to be a 'Malagasy musician.' Markovits and Hellerman (2001) argued that soccer only recently became popular in the United States because it was previously crowded out of the 'sports space' by football from above and baseball from below. American sports exceptionalism, they wrote, is part and parcel of American exceptionalism in general, including American hegemony and its legacy as the 'first new nation.' Meisch (2002), following the circulation of yarn, shows how Otavalan traders from Ecuador went from being spinners and weavers to become middlemen and even independent merchants through their integration in the world economy. When competition in the craft trade became too steep and borders too difficult to cross, music became their new form of transnational entrepreneurship (see also Kyle 2000).

The *characteristics of the pathways or channels* that culture traverses, whether real or mediated, also affect sites of encounter. How tightly structured these networks are, the hierarchies of control within them, and how much they overlap and intersect with each other strongly influences the ease, directness, and level of protection with which culture travels.

The Catholic Church is an archetypical example of a transnational religious network—a transnational religious corporation with its headquarters in the Vatican and its CEO, the Pope. When new migrants settle in new places, the network simply broadens and deepens, but in ways that maintain brand integrity. New parishes, or new congregations within them, cannot deviate too much from the prescribed ways of doing things or the central script. Other migrating religions and traveling faiths,[2] be they Christian, Muslim, or Hindu, have similar hierarchical, centralized religious architectures (Levitt, 2007). In contrast, there are national religious networks that operate transnationally; they are based in a single country with clear national roots, but are structured, financed, and run transnationally. Still other religious groups are structured like flexible specialization models of economic production—horizontally managed, loosely coupled, changing sets of partnerships designed to respond quickly and easily to the shifting market. How formalized, protected, centrally controlled, and far-reaching each network is strongly influences the ease and rhythm with which things circulate within it.

Transnational cultural fields arise from and reinforce deep cultural structures, which also influence how cultural artifacts circulate (Levitt, 2012). Contemporary Hinduism, for example, travels primarily within a British post-colonial space. Its carriers, whether they move between Europe, the United States, the Caribbean, South Asia, or Africa, enact their religious lives against a common meta-cultural frame that is still influenced in subtle and not-so-subtle ways by British colonial assumptions about law, governance, and social cohesion. A common ethos and set of social dynamics characterizes life in South Asia, Trinidad, and East Africa, although it bumps up against very different local backdrops. Circulating religious elements and actors land in terrains that are similar but different, familiar yet strange. The BBC World Service created what Baumann and his colleagues (2011) called a 'diasporic contact zone' by uniting listeners in remote villages in Tanzania with their counterparts in London, evoking a sense of belonging each time they heard the opening notes of the overture to the news. The Brazilian sociologist Gilberto Freyre (1959) used the term 'Lusotropicalism' to describe a comparable Portuguese colonial space characterized by what he argued was a more humane imperial footprint within which racial mixing was more accepted. Though many criticized his benevolent view of Portugal, the interconnected cultural space he described, although now reconstituted in new ways, still influences how ideas about race and human rights circulate within its ambit.

When cultural products circulate, they also create new social spaces. As the Anáhuaz-Aztlán dance circulated among migrants and non-migrants in Mexico and the United States, a community that was rooted in the old empire of Aztlán broadened into a seamless territory on both sides of the border. An 'electric chord' or 'placenta,' according to De la Torre and Gutiérrez Zúñiga (2012), connects people in Taos, New Mexico with their counterparts in Ixcateopan, although the religious practices they engage in and how they imagine the spiritual, racial and territorial nation to which they all belong differs significantly.

---

2   Migrant religions travel *within* the local ethnic confines of the migrant (and home) population, even as they re-territorialize and adapt to new contexts. Travelling faiths are religious movements with universal claims around which a religious community is formed—de-territorialized religions—which travel in order to proselytize (Wong and Levitt, 2014).

Vernacularization

Moving from the site of encounter to actual use involves some kind of communication and translation—the actual work of hybridization, mimicry, or glocalization. Levitt and Merry's (2009) global women's rights project revealed three types of vernacularization. The first type relied on the imaginative space created by women's human rights rather than the discourse of rights itself. Staff did not talk about rights directly in their work, but used the momentum and power inherent in these global discourses to advance their cause. The second type vernacularized ideas. It stretched the boundary of issues taken up by women's groups by using the language of human rights to tackle new problems. In India, for example, staff linked English words to local narratives and symbols as a way to apply the human rights framework to the issue of sexuality rights. They appealed to the magic and allure of the West while stressing that these ideas also had deep Indian roots. The third type of vernacularization involved using the core concepts of women's human rights, articulating them in locally appropriate ways, and specifying pragmatic ways to put them into practice. Staff explicitly referenced women's human rights to encourage their clients to shift their understandings of self and then to put these into practice.

Vernacularization involves the disentangling of global universals so that they are applicable to a wide variety of ideas and technologies for communicating reforms and helping with problems. It is a fragmentary and dialogic process. Because they are differentially positioned geopolitically, localities differ significantly with respect to their exposure to global assemblages over time. As actors and organizations move across local, national, and international fields of power and meaning, they forge moral and instrumental strategies to promote their organizational goals given the constraints of funding, community support, and North/South power relations.

Cultural Institutions and Policies

In this section, I shift away from my discussion of studying and explaining culture in motion to thinking about how and where culture provides the backdrop for creating successful diverse societies and communities that transcend national boundaries. First, I look at how cultural policy and institutions are used to drive globalization forward by creating global cities and then global citizens. Then I look at the cultures of knowledge production that shape if and how we see and talk about these dynamics.

At least some of the cultural products I describe get anointed in informal and formal global cultural canons—indexes or packages of objects, places, and ideas that come to be considered what all good global citizens should know. UNESCO's 1972 World Heritage Convention, which began as an exercise in shared responsibility for humanity's most prized sites, is now a sort of 'go-to' list for the global cultural connoisseur (Rausch, 2013). The curriculum taught at International Baccalaureate programs, initially created to enable the children of transnational executives to move seamlessly between one international school and another, is also a statement about what the next globalized generation must master. The new branch campuses created by American and English universities, in partnership or not with their local hosts throughout the Gulf and Asia, are the college level version of the same exercise. Less formal, but also canonizers in their own right, are media outlets like Al Jazeera in English, CNN in Español, and the BBC World Service whose programming distinguishes the places and events that worldly people should be familiar with.

Of course, agreeing upon and disseminating any kind of 'sanctified knowledge package' is ridden with self-interest and unequal power. This is what Post-Colonial Studies and Critical Theory is all about. Some see cosmopolitanism as beyond redemption, precisely because the requisite grand tour only included European cultural production. National interests are always jockeying for their place. Because The World Heritage List is such a powerful catalyst for tourism, nation building, and economic development, the national interests behind the desire to be included on it often overshadow concerns about global patrimony (Baumann, 2014). At Education City in Qatar, where over eight US universities have established branch campuses, there is a seeming paradox between Qatarization, an employment policy that structurally favors citizens, and an American-style university system designed to create cosmopolitan 'global citizens' who embrace individualism, meritocracy, and multiculturalism. In fact, as Vora (2014) argues, Qatari non-liberal state policies and American liberal higher education have long been intertwined in ways that mutually benefit these seemingly opposing logics of governance and belonging.

Cities also use cultural policy to further globalization. Using Singapore as an example, Kong (2012) identified three ways culture has been deployed to promote urban development. In the early 1960s and 1970s, the newly independent city-state used arts and culture as nation-building tools. However, once the new nation was established, the government looked to arts and culture, first, to attract tourists, and later to attract the transnational capitalists who could drive economic development forward. In a recent twist, Singapore is using its 'cultural social policy' to convince citizens of the important role that art and culture play in their daily lives. For Singapore to be a truly global city, it not only needs a lively cultural scene, but also culturally literate residents who can participate actively in the global cultural world.

Numerous theorists highlight how cultural industries and cultural policies are harnessed as tools for 'regenerating' and 'renewing' cities like Singapore—or they critique the practical and intellectual consequences of city leaders' attempts to use art and culture in this way (Montgomery, 2005; Barnes et al., 2006; Bontje and Musterd, 2009; Evans, 2003; McGuigan, 2009; Peck, 2005). At the same time, local immigrant communities, and the cultural diversity and multiculturalism they bring with them, are also deployed in service of similar goals by attracting tourists, driving economic development, and rebranding urban centers. In fact, Glick Schiller and Caglar (2009) argue that cultural diversity has become an important factor in the competitive struggle between cities. Immigrants can be marketable assets in the places where they settle, even enabling some cities to reposition themselves within the geopolitical hierarchy.

The extent to which cities can use diversity as a developmental tool depends upon their cultural endowments. Brettell (2005, p. 247) stresses the importance of a dominant set of values or an urban ethos in shaping immigrant incorporation. My colleagues and I call this the urban cultural armature: a combination of each city's (1) history and cultural geography, (2) urban self-presentation, (3) cultural responses to demography, and (4) prevailing ethos toward immigrants (Jaworsky et al., 2012). Nations are also endowed with cultural assets that strongly influence their location in the global cultural field (Bandelj and Werry, 2011).

Cities can fuel the multiculturalism that drives rescaling by attracting diverse businesses and people. They can also change what they do in response to more diverse communities they serve, thereby supplying some of the cultural building blocks needed to create successful diverse societies. Again, Singapore provides a good example. The government strategically used the museum sector to catapult the city to global economic prominence and create the kinds of citizens it believes the country needs to attain and sustain its position (Levitt, 2015).

Conclusion

Circulation, as Lee and LiPuma (2002) argue, should be an object of sociological scrutiny that evolves in 'culturally' structured ways. We need better tools for explaining culture in motion and what happens at the sites of encounter where what is traveling comes into contact with what is already on the ground. Using a transnational optic and thinking of culture as assemblages brings into sharp focus what is often obscured by methodological nationalism and a view of culture as a static, rooted whole. Rather, producers and consumers of cultural goods, be they ideas, practice, institutions, or policies, are embedded in multiple, unequal networks of power and resources that constitute and are constituted by transnational social fields. Such a view (1) challenges false dichotomies such as pure/hybrid, native/ stranger or national/global; (2) means that even the most seemingly local actor or institution is connected in multiple ways, with varying degrees of strength and impact, to actors and institutions far away; and (3) understands that these multiple, interlocking connections locate cultural producers and consumers very differently within the global geopolitical hierarchy, and strongly influence their ability to create, transform, or appropriate cultural assemblages.

A next step, but a road not often taken, is to study cultural circulation comparatively. This is a challenging task that, so far, is more aspirational than empirical. Again, there is no shortage of work examining how particular types of culture travel. Tsing and her colleagues looked at 'words in motion,' following the histories of important and powerful words and phrases to understand how political cultures take shape within and beyond the nation (Tsing, 2005). Kearney and Besserer (2003) urged us to 'follow the tomato' as a way to better understand the transnational migration experience. The next step is to ask if all cultural artifacts circulate in a similar manner. What difference does it make when what is traveling is a note, word, icon, or institutional model? If we tried to bring these various studies of circulation together, what would we learn about how the characteristics of the cultural artifact, the networks, and the geopolitical backdrop against which things move add up? Here, I have only begun to lay the groundwork for this analytic task that I hope inspires and models productive ways forward.

References

Alexander, J.C. and P. Smith. 2010. 'The Strong Program: Origins, Achievements and Prospects.' In *The Handbook of Cultural Sociology*, edited by J.R. Hall, L. Grindstaff, and M. Lo, 13–24. New York: Routledge.

Anthias, F. 2006. 'Belongings in a Globalising and Unequal World: Rethinking Translocations.' In *The Situated Politics of Belonging*, edited by N. Yuval-Davis, K. Kannabiran, and U. Vieten, 17–32. London: Sage.

Aronczyk, M., and A. Craig. 2012. 'Introduction: Cultures of Circulation.' *Poetics* 40(2): 93–100.

Ashcroft, B. 1998. *Key Concepts in Post-Colonial Studies*. London: Routledge.

Associated Press. 2013. 'Swedish Cinemas Launch Feminist Movie Rating.' *Times Union.* http://www.timesunion.com/entertainment/article/Swedish-cinemas-launch-feminist-movie-rating-4961718.php#src=fb.

Axford, B. 2013. *Theories of Globalization*. Malden and Cambridge: Polity.

Bandelj, N., and F.F. Wherry. 2011. *The Cultural Wealth of Nations*. Stanford, CA: Stanford University Press.

Barnes, K., G. Waitt, N. Gill, and C. Gibson. 2006. 'Community and Nostalgia in Urban Revitalisation: A Critique of Urban Village and Creative Class Strategies as Remedies for Social "Problems".' *Australian Geographer* 37(3): 335–54.

Baumann, G, M. Gillespie, and A. Sreberny. 'Epilogue: Transcultural Journalism: Translation, Transmissions, and Transformation.' *Journalism* 12(2): 235–8.

Bob, C. 2005. *The Marketing of Rebellion: Insurgents, Media and International Activism*. New York: Cambridge University Press.

Bontje, M., and S. Musterd. 2009. 'Creative Industries, Creative Class and Competitiveness: Expert Opinions Critically Appraised.' *Geoforum* 40(5): 843–52.

Boyle, E.H. 2002. *Female Genital Cutting: Cultural Conflict in the Global Community*. Baltimore, MD: Johns Hopkins University Press.

Brettell, C.B. 2005. 'The Spatial, Social, and Political Incorporation of Asian Indian Immigrants in Dallas, Texas.' *Urban Anthropology* 34(2/3): 247–80.

Castles, S., and R. Delgado Wise (eds). 2007. *Migration and Development: Perspectives from the South*. Geneva: International Organization on Migration.http://www.imi.ox.ac.uk/pdfs/migration-and-development-perspectives-from-the-south.

Couldry, N. 2007. 'Researching Media Internationalism: Comparative Media Research as if We Really Mean It.' *Global Media and Communication* 3(3): 247–50.

Czarniawska, B., and G. Sevón (eds). 2005. *Global Ideas: How Ideas, Objects and Practices Travel in a Global Economy*, Vol. 13. Copenhagen: Copenhagen Business School Press.

De Haas, H. 2010. 'Migration and Development: A Theoretical Perspective.' *International Migration Review* 44(1): 227–64.

De la Torre, R., and C. Gutiérrez Zúñiga. 2012. 'Atravesados por la Frontera. Anáhuac-Aztlán: danza y construcción de una nación imaginada [Crossing the Border: Anáhuac-Aztlán dance and the construction of an imagined nation. In the Opposite Direction].' In *En Sentido Contrario: Transnationalizacíon de Religiones Africanas Latinoamericanas* [The Transnationalization of Afro and Latin American Religions], edited by K. Argyriadis, S. Capone, R de la Torre, and A. Mary, 145–75. Guadalajara: Ciesas, Belgium: Editorial Academia, and Mexico, DF: IRD.

Delgado Wise, R., and H.M. Covarrubias. 2009. 'Understanding the Relationship between Migration and Development: Toward a New Theoretical Approach.' *Social Analysis* 53(3): 85–105.

DiMaggio, P., and W. Powell. 1983. 'The Iron Cage Revisited.' *American Sociological Review* 48(2): 147–60.

Dobbin, F., B. Simmons, and G. Garrett. 2007. 'The Global Diffusion of Public Policies: Social Construction, Coercion, Competition, or Learning?.' *Annual Review of Sociology* 33(1): 449–72.

Drori, G.S., M.A. Hollerer, and P. Walgenbach. 2014. *Global Themes and Local Variations in Organization and Management: Perspectives on Glocalization*. New York and London: Blackwell.

Durand, J., and D. Massey. 1995. *Miracles on the Border*. Tucson: University of Arizona Press.

Dwyer, C., and K. Jackson. 2003. 'Commidifying Difference: Selling Eastern Fashion.' *Environment and Planning D. Society and Space* 21(1): 269–91.

Ebaugh, H.R.F., and J.S. Chafetz. 2002. *Religion across Borders: Transnational Immigrant Networks*. Walnut Creek, CA and Oxford: Altamira, division of Rowman & Littlefield Press.

Euben, R.L. 2006. *Journeys to the Other Shore: Muslim and Western Travelers in Search of Knowledge*. Princeton: Princeton University Press.

Evans, G. 2003. 'Hard-branding the cultural city—from Prado to Prada.' *International Journal of Urban and Regional Research* 27(2): 417–40.

Faist, T., F. Margit, and E. Reisenhauer. 2013. *Transnational Migration*. Cambridge: Polity.

Favell, A. 2001. *Philosophies of Integration: Immigration and the Idea of Citizenship in France and Britain*, 2nd edn. New York, NY: Palgrave.
Featherston, M., S. Lash, and R. Robertson. 1995. *Global Modernities*. London and Thousand Oaks, CA: Sage.
Freyre, G. 1959. *New World in the Tropics: The Culture of Modern Brazil*. New York: Knopf.
Garcia Canclini, N. 2001. *Consumers and Citizens: Globalization and Multicultural Conflicts*. Minneapolis: University of Minnesota Press.
Glick Schiller, N., and A. Caglar. 2009. 'Towards a Comparative Theory of Locality in Migration Studies: Migrant Incorporation and City Scale.' *Journal of Ethnic and Migration Studies* 35(2): 177–202.
Glick Schiller, N., and T. Faist. 2013. *Migration, Development, and Transnationalization: A Critical Stance*. New York: Berghahn Books.
Glick Schiller, N., A. Çaglar, and T.C. Guldbrandsen. 2006. 'Beyond the Ethnic Lens: Locality, Globality, and Born-Again Incorporation.' *American Ethnologist* 33(4): 612–33.
Gutiérrez Zúñiga, C. 2013. 'Narrativas poscoloniales: la resignificacíon de la danza conchero-azteca como práctica terapéutica new age in México y España [Postcolonial Narratives: the resignification of conchera-aztec dance as a therapeutic practice in new age Mexico and Spain].' In *Variaciones y apropiaciones latinoamericanas del new age* [Latin American New Age Variations and Approriations], edited by R. de la Torre, C. Gutiérrez Zúñiga, and N. Juárez Huet, 227–55. Guadalajara: CIESAS y El Colegio de Jalisco.
Hagan, J.M. 2008. *Migration Miracle*. Cambridge, MA: Harvard University Press.
Hall, S. 2003. 'Créolité and Creolization: Creolization, Diaspora, and Hybridity in the Context of Globalization.' In *Créolité and Creolization: Documenta 11 Platform 3*, edited by O. Enwezor. Ostfidern-Ruit: Hatje-Cantz.
Hervieu-Léger, D. 2000. *Religion as a Chain of Memory*. Cambridge: Polity.
Hewelmeier, G., and K. Krause. 2009. *Traveling Spirits: Migrants, Markets and Mobilities*. New York: Routledge.
Jaworsky, N., W. Cadge, P. Levitt, and S. Curran. 2012. 'Rethinking Immigrant Context of Reception: The Cultural Armature of Cities.' *Nordic Journal of Migration and Ethnicity* 2(1): 78–88.
Johnson, P. 2007. *Diaspora Conversions*. Los Angeles, Berkeley, CA: University of California Press.
Keck, M., and K. Sikkink. 1988. *Activists beyond Borders: Advocacy Networks in International Politics*. Ithaca, New York: Cornell University Press.
Kaufman, J., and O. Patterson. 2005. 'Cross-National Cultural Diffusion: The Global Spread of Cricket.' *American Sociological Review* 70(1): 82–110.
Khagram, S., and P. Levitt. 2007a. *The Transnational Studies Reader*. New York: Routledge.
Khagram, S., and P. Levitt. 2007b. 'Constructing Transnational Studies.' In *The Transnational Studies Reader*, 1–18. New York and London: Routledge.

Kiwan, N., and U.H. Meinhof. 2011. *Cultural Globalisation and Music: African Artists in Transnational Networks*, Basingstoke: Palgrave Macmillan.

Knott, K. 2005. *The Location of Religion: A Spatial Analysis*. London: Oakville.

Kong, L. 2012. 'Ambitions of a Global City: Arts, Culture and Creative Economy in 'Post-Crisis' Singapore.' *International Journal of Cultural Policy* 18(3): 279–94.

Kurien, P. 2007. *A Place at the Multicultural Table: The Development of American Hinduism*. New Brunswick, NJ.: Rutgers University Press.

Kyle, D. 2000. *Transnational Peasants: Migrations, Networks, and Ethnicity in Andean Ecuador*. Baltimore, MD and London: Johns Hopkins University Press.

Lambek, M. 1993. *Knowledge and Practice in Mayotte: Local Discourses of Islam, Sorcery and Spirit Possession*. Toronto: University of Toronto Press.

Lee, B., and E. LiPuma. 2002. 'Cultures of circulation: The imaginations of modernity.' *Public Culture* 14(1): 191–213.

Lechner, F.J., and J. Boli. 2008. *World Culture: Origins and Consequences*. Hoboken: John Wiley & Sons.

LeFebvre, H. 1991. *The Production of Space*. Oxford: Basil Blackwell.

Legg, S. 2010. 'Transnationalism and the Scalar Politics of Imperialism.' *New Global Studies* 4(1). ISSN (Online) 1940–0004, DOI: 10.2202/1940–0004.1103, August 2010.

Levitt, P. 2001. *The Transnational Villagers*. Berkeley: University of California Press.

Levitt, P. 2007. *God Needs No Passport: Immigrants and the Changing American Religious Landscape*. New York: The New Press.

Levitt, P. 2012a. 'What's Wrong with Migration Studies: A Critique and Way Forward.' *Identities* 1(1): 1–8.

Levitt, P. 2012b. 'Religion on the Move.' In *Religion on the Edge: De-Centering and Re-Centering the Sociology of Religion*, edited by C. Bender, W. Cadge, P. Levitt and D. Smilde, Chapter 7. New York: Oxford University Press.

Levitt, P. 2015. *Artifacts and Allegiances: How Museums Put the Nation and the World on Display*. Berkeley and Los Angeles: University of California Press.

Levitt, P., and N. Glick Schiller. 2004. 'Transnational Perspectives on Migration: Conceptualizing Simultaneity.' *International Migration Review* 34(145): 1002–40.

Levitt, P., and D. Lamba-Nieves. 2011. 'Social Remittances Revisited.' *Journal of Ethnic and Migration Studies* 37(1): 1–22.

Levitt, P., and S. Merry. 2009. 'Vernacularization on the Ground: Local Uses of Global Women's Rights in Peru, China, India and the United States.' *Global Networks* 9(4): 441–61.

Levitt, P., and N. Rajaram. 2013. 'Reform through Mobility? Migration, Health, and Development in Gujarat, India.' *Migration Studies* 1(3): 328–62.

McAdam, D., S. Tarrow, and C. Tilly. 2001. *Dynamics of Contention*. New York: Cambridge University Press.

McGuigan, J. 2009. 'Doing a Florida Thing: The Creative Class Thesis and Cultural Policy.' *International Journal of Cultural Policy* 15(3): 291–300.

Mandaville, P.G., 2002. *Transnational Muslim Politics: Reimagining the Umma*. London: Routledge.

Marcus, G.E., and E. Saka. 2006. 'Assemblage.' *Theory, Culture & Society* 23(2–3): 101–6.

Markovits, A.S., and S.L. Hellerman. 2001. *Offside: Soccer and American Exceptionalism*. Princeton, NJ: Princeton University Press.

Masuzawa, T. 2005. *The Invention of World Religions: Or, How European Universalism Was Preserved in the Language of Pluralism*. Chicago, IL: University of Chicago Press.

Mears, A. 2011. *Pricing Beauty: The Making of a Fashion Model*. Berkeley: University of California Press.

Meisch, L. 2002. *Andean Entrepreneurs: Otavalo Merchants and Musicians in the Global Arena*. Austin: University of Texas Press.

Meyer, B., and A. Moors. 2006. *Religion, Media, and the Public Sphere*. Bloomington: Indiana University Press.

Montgomery, J. 2005. 'Beware 'the Creative Class': Creativity and Wealth Creation Revisited.' *Local Economy* 20(4): 337–43.

Mooney, M. 2009. *Faith Makes Us Live*: Surviving and Thriving in the Haitian Diaspora. Berkeley: California University Press.

Oleszkiewicz-Peralba, M. 2007. *The Black Madonna in Latin America and Europe: Tradition and Transformation*. Albequerque: University of New Mexico Press.

Ong, A. 2007. 'Neoliberalism as a Mobile Technology.' *Transactions of the Institute of British Geographers* 32(1): 3–8.

Ong, A., and S.J. Collier (eds). 2005. *Global Assemblages: Technology, Politics, and Ethics as Anthropological Problems*. Malden, MA: Blackwell Publishing.

Ortiz, F. 1995. *Cuban Counterpoint, Tobacco and Sugar*. Durham, NC: Duke University Press.

Peck, J. 2005. 'Struggling with the Creative Class.' *International Journal of Urban and Regional Research* 29(4): 740–70.

Pieterse J.N. 2003. 'Social Capital and Migration: Beyond Ethnic Economies.' *Ethnicities* 3(1): 29–58.

Pratt, M.L. 1992. *Imperial eyes: Travel writing and Transculturation*. London: Routledge Press.

Revilla López, U. 2000. 'La chilena mixteca transnacional [The Transnational Chilena Mixteca].' Unpublished thesis, The Autonomous Metropolitan University, Iztapalapa Campus, México.

Richman, K. 2005. *Migration and Voodoo*. Gainesville: University of Florida Press.

Rogers, E.M. 2003. *Diffusion of Innovations*, 5th edn. New York: Free Press.

Roy, O. 2006. *Globalized Islam: The Search for a New Muslim Ummah*. Paris: CERL.

Sheringham, O., and R. Cohen. 2013. 'Quotidian creolization and diasporic echoes: Resistance and co-optation in Cape Verde and Louisiana.' International

Migration Institute (IMI) Working Papers Series, 72, pp. 1–30. www.migration.ox.ac.uk/odp/pdfs/WP72-Quotidian%20creolization%20and%20diaporic%20echoes.pdf.

Simon, H.A. 1982. *Models of Bounded Rationality: Empirically Grounded Economic Reason*. MIT Press.

Sinha, V. 2005. *A New God in the Diaspora?*. Copenhagen, Denmark: NIAS Press.

Snow, D.A. 2007. 'Framing Processes, Ideology, and Discursive Fields.' In *The Blackwell Companion to Social Movements*, edited by D.A. Snow, S.A. Soule, and H. Kriesi, 380–412. Oxford: Blackwell.

Snow, D.A., and R.D. Benford. 2005. 'Clarifying the Relationship between Framing and Ideology.' In *Frames of Protest: Social Movements and the Framing Perspective*, edited by H. Johnston and J.A. Noakes, 205–12. Lanham: Rowman & Littlefield.

Starkloff, C. 2002. *A Theology of the In-Between*. Milwaukee, WI: Marquette University Press.

Strang, D., and S.A. Stroule. 1998. 'Diffusion in Organizations and Social Movements: From Hybrid Corn to Poison Pills.' *Annual Review of Sociology* 24(1): 265–90.

Sylvanus, N. 2013. 'Chinese Devils, the Global Market and the Declining Power of Togos Nana-Benzes.' *African Studies Review* 56(1): 65–80.

Tsing, A.L. 2005. *Friction: An Ethnography of Global Connection*, Princeton, NJ: Princeton University Press.

Wejnert, B. 2002. 'Integrating Models of Diffusion of Innovations: A Conceptual Framework.' *Annual Review of Sociology* 28(1): 297–326.

Werbner, P. 2005. *Pilgrims of Love*. Bloomington: Indiana University Press.

Wong, D., and P. Levitt. 2014. 'Traveling Faiths and Migrant Religions: The Case of Circulating Models of Da'wa among the Tablighi Jamaat and Foguangshan in Malaysia.' *Global Networks* 14(3): 348–62.

Yue, Q.L. 1990. *Family and State in China*. Shenyang: Liaoning People's Press.

Chapter 10
China in the Process of Globalization: A Primarily Cultural Perspective

Wang Ning

Dramatic changes in world economy and politics have undoubtedly proved that China is one of the countries in the world which have benefited most from globalization. This has manifested itself with increasing clarity over time. People may well think that globalization makes the cultures of different countries or nations increasingly homogenous; but in recognizing this homogenizing tendency we should also note the other important factor that is—at least superficially—opposed to globalization namely: (cultural) localization. In fact, cultural diversity is more and more conspicuous in the present era. It could well be argued that this is especially true of China where Chinese traditions are so strong that everything is susceptible to being localized. It would be better to say that globalization in the Chinese context might well be called 'glocalization,' or global in the local.

Although in many places globalization is often viewed as synonymous with Westernization, or more specifically, Americanization, humanities scholars seem ideologically more ambivalent about Westernization—though arguably, less so about globalization. A much neglected aspect of globalization is the frantic search for ways of embracing modernity on cultural and political terms. Although modernity in the Chinese context is largely an 'imported' or 'translated' concept from the West, it has at the same time, with many indigenous elements, seriously undermined the myth of singular 'modernity,' paving the way for an alternative modernity or modernities with Chinese characteristics.

Thus, the globalization of culture also means prompting localization, or—as previously stated—'glocalization,' which in turn redefines and reconfigures this hidden 'empire' in a local context. The present chapter aims to let 'the outside world' know how China is moving closer to it by absorbing more and more foreign cultural elements, and nevertheless how Chinese culture still maintains its sense of uniqueness. Apart from discussing Chinese modernity as an alternative modernity, the chapter will also deal with the popularization of the Chinese language and the Chinese version of world literature which has certainly helped the remapping of the world language system and also pluralized the concept of world literature; with Chinese literature increasingly characterized by cosmopolitanism and transnationalism.

A Rising China in the Eye of Western Academia

About the rise of China, especially in economy, politics and society, international scholarship and mass media have been paying more and more attention to it and have published extensively on this issue. They have constructed various versions of 'Chinese myth' or 'Chinese fantasy' as if China were really the most prosperous country in the world. But what is the real picture about China? There is no doubt that China, together with the United States, has 'triumphed' the most in contemporary globalization. However, Western scholars and the Western mass media view rising China from a number of different angles. Some, such as Doug Guthrie, in associating China with globalization, offer their description on how China, over the last 25 years, has shifted from communism to capitalism, and has transformed from a desperately poor nation into a country possessing one of the fastest-growing and largest economies in the world, which is certainly 'a story of the forces of globalization.'(Guthrie, 2012, p. 3). After a vivid description of the very impressive development in China's major cities like Shanghai, Beijing, Chengdu and Chongqing, Guthrie points out:

> All of these facts and images are, by now, well known. Indeed, the headlines announcing 'China's Century,' 'The China Challenge,' 'The China Syndrome,' 'Buying up the World,' 'America's Fear of China,' 'China Goes Shopping,' 'Can China be Fixed?' and many others, have thundered across the covers of such magazines as *Business Week*, the *Economist*, *Forbes*, *Newsweek*, *U.S. News and World Report*, and many other major publications. (Guthrie, 2012, p. 2)

Although this is largely true of the current Chinese situation, it is only one side of the Chinese situation since the country has been developing in an uneven way in recent decades. In his popular and influential book, he also raises such questions as: Will China become more democratic? Will the government become more serious about protecting human rights and creating a transparent legal system? How will China's explosive growth impact upon East Asia and the larger global economy? It should be recognized that Guthrie's description is relatively precise and fair; not least because it is largely based on his personal experience in China and his long meticulous observation from the outside. After analyzing some of its problems, he still believes that a 'form of democracy' with Chinese characteristics 'will emerge in China, but for reasons that are not well understood by Western politicians and pundits' (Guthrie, 2012, p. 19).

Others, for example, Daniel Vukovich, who grew up in the United States and who is now teaching at the University of Hong Kong, have a great appreciation of China and are therefore very optimistic about China's rapid development:

> Why China, then? Let us begin by assuming the antagonisms and epistemological challenges—such as orientalism—that have subtended the China-West relationship for, say, three hundred years ... .So, too, let us recall that 'our'

relationship to China is overwhelmingly an economic (and political) one. China's rise, its status as the 'next' superpower, the manufacturer of the world, the new Asian hegemon, the world-historical consumer market, the buyer of last resort for U.S. dollars, the second largest economy—and so forth. (Vukovich, 2012, p. 142)

Frankly speaking, in recognizing China's fast growth and prosperity, such authors tend to overlook the fact that China as such a large country has striking contrasts between the rich and the poor, between urban and rural areas and between coastal and interior cities. China on the whole is still a developing country, moving toward being an affluent society.

Still others while recognizing that, although it is miraculous that China, 'one of the globe's poorest countries' before its reforms, has 'become a booming economy—second biggest in the world' in the present century, nevertheless point out that it has problems which form severe 'challenges' (Perry, 2014, p. 5):

> While major cities boast gleaming new infrastructures and attendant urban amenities that equal or surpass those of the advanced industrial world, much of the rural interior remains mired in grinding poverty. The affluence of new urban middle and upper classes, flush with the proceeds from lucrative real estate deals, is offset by the indigence of the millions of migrants who labor in their midst. (Perry, 2014, pp. 5–6)

Thus, to such authors, since China is unique in many aspects, they 'would be foolhardy to disregard or discount China's efforts to resolve global problems' simply because they 'predict that its political system is some day destined to disappear' (Perry, 2014, p. 13).

Whether or not we agree with the above different views of China such authors have offered their impression and expectation of China from their own perspectives—mostly economic, political and social. Also, these different opinions at least represent the fact that China in the present era is increasingly like an awaking lion, and may well help transform the world as a whole. As a Chinese humanities scholar specializing in literary and cultural studies, I will now add and incorporate my view on China in the process of globalization, from a cultural perspective.

Reconstructing Chinese Modernity as an Alternative Modernity

In this section, I will deal mostly with the issue of modernity, viewing it as a sort of 'translated' modernity. But translation here by no means refers to its traditional sense, linguistic rendition, but rather to a kind of cultural translation or transformation in the process of which different cultures will most probably be relocated. Although modernity is by no means a new topic in the Western context, it has always been attractive to Chinese literary and cultural studies scholars during the past century. Following some of my Western colleagues such as Fredric Jameson, Terry Eagleton and Matei Calinescu,[1] I will chiefly deal with the issue from the perspectives of literature and culture. But unlike them, I rely mainly on the Chinese experiences and examples taken from Chinese literature and culture.[2] In other words, in dealing with the above theoretical and cultural topics I will start from the angle of modern Chinese literature and culture, which has largely been influenced by Western literature and culture and therefore is usually viewed by Western scholars distant from China's long literary and cultural tradition, and closer to global culture and world literature. We could probably recognize that modern Chinese literature, which is now close to the mainstream of world literature, is thereby an inseparable part of it. But for a long period of time, the study of this phenomenon was largely confined to sinological circles in the West. Seldom does a non-sinologist touch upon Chinese literature and culture in her/his discussion of world literature and global culture.[3] As compared with the enthusiastic translation and critical and creative reception of Western literature and cultural theories in China, modern Chinese literature is little known to scholars and ordinary readers in the West; although in recent years it has been increasingly attractive to the non-Chinese audience after Mo Yan won the Nobel Prize in 2012.[4] This unbalanced cultural translation is, indeed, surprising in an age of globalization.

---

1   All these Western scholars or theorists are well known and frequently quoted and discussed in the Chinese context: Jameson is best known for his lecture tour to China in 1985 and his work on postmodernism; Eagleton is best known for his critique of postmodernism and cultural theory from a Marxist perspective; Calinescu is best known for his book *Five Faces of Modernity*. The former two theorists have been to China several times and maintain contact with some Chinese scholars, including myself.

2   As for detailed discussion on how translation plays the unique role in reconstructing Chinese and world literature, see Ning Wang (2012a), 'Translating Modernity and Reconstructing World Literature,' *Minnesota Review* 2012 (79): 101–12.

3   In this aspect, David Damrosch may be one of the very few exceptions. In his *What Is World Literature?*, he spends some space discussing Chinese diasporic poet Bei Dao's poetry and the metamorphosis caused by the English translation. See 'Introduction' of the book, pp. 19–24, Princeton, NJ, and Oxford: Princeton University Press, 2003. Before him, Earl Miner, an American comparatist and Japanologist, also did research on Chinese literature from a comparative and intercultural perspective. See Earl Miner (1990), *Comparative Poetics: An Intercultural Essay on Theories of Literature*, Princeton, NJ: Princeton University Press.

4   I wish to emphasize that I seldom found Mo Yan's books in English in any book stores before 2012. It was his winning of a Nobel Prize that made him suddenly well known in the world. Subsequently I found quite a few of his recent works in English in many big book stores during my visit to Oregon, USA, in November 2012, immediately after the news of his prize winning.

Since globalization is also a concept 'translated' or 'imported' from the West to China, it is undoubtedly marked by its strong West-centric hegemonic sense. When discussing this in China it is often heard that globalization is nothing but Westernization, and that, moreover, Westernization means Americanization as the West is the richest part of the world and the United States stands at the forefront of the Western world. This is partly correct, but those holding this opinion usually overlook another remarkable fact: in the process of globalization, imperial hegemonic cultural notions and values quickly penetrate into non-Western societies; yet some non-Western cultural notions and values are also steadily moving to the imperial center, thereby increasingly hybridizing it. Modern Chinese culture and literature are inevitably influenced by Western culture and literature, but they are also attempting to dialogue with mainstream global culture and world literature. In this respect, translation has played a vital role in the former, but it appears rather feeble in the latter. Consequently, modern Chinese literature and culture are little known to the outside world and are consequently 'marginalized.'

It is true that because of its long-standing isolation from the world as a whole and its conservative attitude to foreign influences, classical Chinese literature developed almost cut off from Western influence. In contrast, the new tradition of modern Chinese literature was forged directly under the Western influence. One cannot avoid mentioning its existence when dealing with global modernity and world literature; for modern Chinese literature widely participates in the metamorphosed and 'glocalized' practice of global modernity. As a result, different versions of modernity have been produced in China: economic, political, cultural, literary and aesthetic. These together constitute a sort of alternative modernity or modernities that have deconstructed the 'grand narrative' of a 'singular' modernity dominated by Western culture and ideology.

As in political and theoretical discourse, the different versions of modernity that exist in China also assume its different faces geographically: on mainland China, modernity is often viewed as an open, developing and democratic concept closely related to China's economic, political, cultural and literary modernization and post-modernization. However, because of their past colonial experiences, Hong Kong and Taiwan modernities are usually related to the decolonization practice of their culture, while among overseas Chinese, modernity is often associated with their diasporic status and indeterminate identities in the age of globalization. Modernity here is undoubtedly associated with various factors of postmodernity. Hence, Chinese modernity is not similar to the West's, for China is such a big country that there is striking contrast between different regions and people. Therefore, China's alternative modernity is characterized by three different coexisting conditions: premodern, modern and postmodern. Its various versions are naturally represented differently in literature and culture. In this way, the appearance of Chinese modernity, as an alternative modernity or modernities, has no doubt deconstructed the myth of a singular modernity in the West-centric sense.

In recent years, with China's closer involvement in the international community, major Western humanities scholars have increasingly become interested both in the Chinese language and classical and modern Chinese literature and culture.[5] Since literature in a global era has gone far beyond fixed national and linguistic boundaries, it is necessary to re-examine modern Chinese literature that has been under the Western influence from a cross-cultural and global perspective. If put in a broader context of global culture and world literature, modern Chinese literature is actually a process moving toward the world that is attempting to identify with world literature within the process of cultural globalization. In this respect, translation has indeed played an important and dynamic but different role in pushing China closer to the world, Chinese culture closer to global culture, and Chinese literature closer to world literature (Wang, 2010a, pp. 1–14). In the past, when China was poor and backward, it was necessary to modernize itself by largely translating all the advanced sciences and cultural thoughts from the West. But now, due to the unbalanced import and export of knowledge and culture, Chinese culture and literature are far from known to the outside world except to a few sinologists. It is therefore all the more necessary for us Chinese scholars to translate China, including its literature and culture, into the world, or more specifically, into the major Western languages.

It is well known that Chinese literature once had a long tradition and a splendid cultural and literary heritage. But along with the swift development of European countries after the Renaissance, Chinese culture and literature were 'marginalized' for a long period of time, due largely to the corruption and inefficient government of feudal and totalitarian regimes isolating the country from the outside world. Upon entering the twentieth century, Chinese literary scholars and humanities intellectuals increasingly acknowledged the 'marginalized' position of its literature in the broad context of world literature. To regain its past grandeur it had to move from the periphery to the center by identifying with a prior dominant force, i.e. Western cultural modernity or modern Western literature. That is why these scholars strongly supported the large-scale translation of Western literary works, along with cultural and academic reflections on this practice, as the best way for China to emerge from its state of isolation. Undoubtedly, this effort to translate Western literature promoted the internationalization or globalization of modern Chinese literature and culture, giving it a different cast of its own. Although some domestic Chinese scholars accuse translation of promoting foreign literature and culture and giving it an 'overall Westernized' or even 'colonized' orientation, I still believe that translation has played a dual role: both of 'colonization' (if there were one) and 'decolonization,' the latter becoming increasingly conspicuous (Wang, 2002).

It is widely known that Western discourse has shaped the orientation of literary and cultural studies in a context of global culture and world literature, consequently

---

5 Apart from Fredric Jameson, who has been to China many times, J. Hillis Miller has become more and more interested in Chinese literature. He has not only read excerpts of Chinese literature from antiquity to the present time in English, but also written something about it. See J. Hillis Miller (2008), 'Reading (about) Modern Chinese Literature in a Time of Globalization,' *Modern Language Quarterly* 69(1): 187–94.

the process of Chinese literature and culture opening up to the world is actually one of Westernization. Yet in this process, in its interaction with globalization, or we could say a sort of 'glocalization,' national culture waxes and wanes. If the entire objective phenomenon is not taken into account and the action of any one aspect is over-emphasized while the others are overlooked, the orientation of contemporary world culture and literature cannot be clearly grasped, nor can modern Chinese literature be relevantly periodized.

Globalization has indeed impacted upon all of aspects of contemporary Chinese people's life and work. The rapid development of Chinese economy has enabled the government to set up hundreds of 'Confucius Institutes' and more 'Confucius Classrooms' worldwide for the purpose of promoting Chinese language and culture. China is now in a post-revolutionary and post-socialist state; experiencing a 'depovertization' (tuo pinkunhua) and 'de-third-worldization' (qu disan shijie hua), and transforming itself from a 'theory consuming' country into a 'theory producing' one (Wang, 2012b). In any event, to describe a comprehensive picture of cultural globalization without taking into account its practice in China is at least incomplete. Similarly, to be considered either objectively or comprehensively, any comparative history of world literature must include the achievements of modern Chinese literary creation, theory and criticism. Since cultural dissemination cannot be realized without the intermediary of language, I will consider the blossoming of Chinese language worldwide as a direct consequence of cultural globalization.

The Popularization of Chinese and the Relocation of Chinese Culture in the Global Context

The popularization of English has of course both positive and negative sides (Wang, 2010b). In this respect, as the most frequently used language in the current world next to English, how has Chinese confronted the strong impact of globalization? Since we cannot deny that in the present era, cultural globalization has given rise to cultural plurality and diversity, where does this manifest itself specifically? It lies in the fact that peripheral cultures are moving toward the center in an attempt to deconstruct the sense of center. It could be said that the future development of global culture depends on the tension and interaction between globalization and localization. It is therefore very appropriate to use the term 'glocalization' to describe this sort of tension.

In speaking of language, we could find more evidence in such a 'glocalized' cultural situation. Take English for example. On the one hand, English has largely influenced world-people's communication and cultural life; but on the other hand it has long been undergoing a sort of 'splitting': from one standard English into many postcolonial 'Englishes' of indigenous dialects and grammatical rules. We can even predict that in the future, along with such a 'splitting,' we may well need translation when we speak different kinds of 'English.' Thus as the process of globalization of culture has 'ruthlessly' deconstructed English as merely a national language, only pushing it to the state of *lingua franca* in the world, then, as the second most frequently used language next to English, what is the present state and future orientation of Chinese? What role will the latter play in the global context? This is what I will deal with in this section.

Globalization has involved virtually all countries and nations. Therefore it is China, pursuing swift development, and in a comprehensive way, that is inevitably involved in this process. Politically speaking, China has established an image of a newly emergent very large country, which has an equal say as much as the great powers in international affairs. At the same time China is building its cultural image by promoting its literature and culture worldwide. In this respect, language plays a very important role.

Globalization has certainly brought to China very precious opportunities of development. It has enabled the country to develop itself swiftly on a vast ground on which it could compete with those Western countries and have dialogues with the latter in an equal manner. As far as its economic development is concerned, China has made remarkable achievements with its steady increase of GDP in the past decade. However, it has still needed a long time to catch up with those developed countries as a result of China developing in an uneven way at the expense of exhausting many of its natural resources; although in the field of cultural production, this has not necessarily been the case. Undoubtedly, China as a vast country with the biggest population in the world was once called the 'Middle Kingdom.' However, it was not long after the Opium Wars broke out in 1840 that a series of shameful treaties were signed between its weak rulers and those of the Western powers and Russia and Japan; in terms of which large parts of land were either lost to or 'colonized' by these empires. The former 'Middle Kingdom' was thus dissolved and gradually marginalized. In order to resume its old splendor and power, China had to identify itself with economically developed countries. Due to its overall Westernizing practice, Chinese culture almost became a marginalized 'colonial' culture. The Chinese language was thus 'Europeanized' or 'colonized' as a result of the large-scale translation of Western literary works and cultural and academic trends at the turn of the twentieth century.

Although large-scale emigration has taken Chinese culture abroad, the Chinese language did not at first have much influence. Having migrated to foreign countries, many overseas Chinese had, first of all, to think of how they could be involved in mainstream cultures and societies. But if they really wanted to be involved in mainstream cultures, they had to be proficient in one or more of their languages. And if they wanted to master the spirit of the language of their country of residence they had to express their ideas in the language at the expense of 'forgetting' their own mother tongue. These are the bitter experiences that many of the Chinese American writers and intellectuals underwent.[6] Some of them are

---

6   It is true that many of the Chinese American writers, such as Maxine Hong Kingston, have even forgotten how to speak and write in Chinese for the purpose of identifying themselves with those mainstream writers.

often in a contradictory state: on the one hand, they try to express their ideas out of their Chinese experience in the English language, but on the other hand, in order to obtain favor with the mainstream cultural taste, they have to describe Chinese cultural conventions in a critical and sometimes distorted way. Another group, especially those new immigrants coming to American society after China's reform and opening up to the outside world, such as Ha Jin and Qiu Xiaolong, become active in mainstream cultural circles and write with their unique Chinese experience in English to accommodate to the American book market.[7] Yet others such as Yan Geling, who writes and publishes both in English and Chinese, and Beila, who mainly writes in Chinese, are both popular in China and North America with their works more attractive to ordinary readers. Whether these authors write in English or in Chinese, their writing practice has already come into the scope of research of scholars of both comparative literature and cultural studies as the phenomenon of 'diasporic writing' in the Chinese or global cultural context. The rapid development of diasporic writing by overseas Chinese has undoubtedly promoted the popularization of Chinese culture in the non-Chinese speaking world.[8] Although their efforts are slowly proving effective in face of the advent of globalization, from a long term point of view, they will apparently manifest themselves more with the swift development of China's economy and the strengthening of its comprehensive power.

It is indeed a fact that Chinese has grown to become another major world language, which is of certain significance to the popularization of Chinese culture worldwide. Perhaps we have merely noticed the positive aspect of the expansion of the boundary of Chinese, while overlooking the other aspect of such expansion. In expanding its boundary, Chinese national and cultural identity has been blurred, becoming more inclusive and hybridized like English. A significant number of scholars are greatly concerned about this phenomenon. However, it could readily achieve the effect of being inclusive and hybridized like English. In other words, Chinese would become the second major world language next to English and could play a unique role that English cannot play. In other respects, it could function as a major means of communication in an interactive and complementary way with English. This promising prospect has already manifested itself in the following

---

7 Frankly speaking, writers like these two coming from mainland China are very rare, but their successes are indeed remarkable: Ha Jin (Jin Xuefei) was elected a fellow of the American Academy of Arts and Sciences in 2006, which indicates that his literary creation has been recognized by American literary scholarship; Qiu Xiaolong's detective and mystery novels have so far been translated into 18 languages, which proves his popularity among ordinary readers of different languages.

8 Along with the increasing popularization of Chinese, some international conference organizers also try to use Chinese as the working language, especially in discussing issues of Chinese culture and literature. For instance, at the International Conference on National Boundaries and Cultural Configurations on June 23–25, 2004 in Singapore, Chinese was exclusively the working language.

respects: (1) the large-scale emigration of Chinese people overseas has maintained the language in a dynamic state; (2) the economic growth of China has made it possible for the language to become increasingly popular and taught in more and more countries; (3) the popularization of the Internet and other means of electronic communication has enabled China to become the largest user of computers and cellphones. This will in turn contribute to promoting Chinese culture and literature (Wang, 2010b).

Apart from the above reasons there is another important factor: namely, the powerful intervention of the Chinese government which has invested a huge amount of money in order to promote Chinese globally. Since the beginning of the present century, the Chinese Hanban (State Office for Teaching Chinese as the Foreign Language) has set up over 400 Confucius Institutes and more than 2000 Confucius' Classrooms throughout the world. One of the major tasks for these is to promote Chinese language and culture. In this way, we could reach a tentative conclusion: the process of cultural globalization has broken through the fixed nation-state boundary and expanded the boundaries of the major world languages. In this process, some of the minor languages have become victims of cultural globalization while the new phenomenon of global languages has come into being.

In the years to come, it is not only English but also Chinese that will benefit greatly from globalization. So we can expect that in the future a new framework of world culture will gradually come into being. It will not only have the nation-state as its boundary, but the language as its boundary as well. There will not merely be one English or Chinese culture, but rather multiple cultures in English or Chinese. In the new framework of different coexisting cultures, Chinese culture will play a more and more important role along with the increasing 'Chinese fever' in the world.

World Literature and the Construction of its Chinese Version

Although the rise of China economically and politically is an undeniable fact, its literature and culture are not so influential in the current world. Just as Guthrie points out, 'It is no longer a question of whether China is going to play a major role in world economic and political arenas, it is only a question of what role China will play' (Guthrie, 2012, p. 5; see also Shambaugh 2013). In the present postmodern society, elite literature and art are severely challenged by popular culture and even consumer culture, especially in the age of globalization in which Internet literature has also threatened print literature. But on the other hand, world literature, an old topic which was not attractive for a long time during those years when nationalism was rising, has once again become a cutting edge theoretical topic.

When we say that China is one of the biggest winners in the process of globalization, it does not necessarily mean that it merely benefits from economic globalization. As I have already indicated above, China also benefits from cultural globalization, which has been proved by the rise of world literature in the country during the past few years.[9] Although for a long period of time, China was isolated from the outside world, and Chinese literature before the nineteenth century was seldom influenced by literatures of other countries, it still has had close relations with the outside world. Ancient China developed very quickly and during the Tang Dynasty it even became one of the most powerful and prosperous countries in the world, not only politically and economically but also culturally. As Chinese people at the time viewed their country as the 'Middle Kingdom,' the country was also called a 'kingdom of poetry,' as Tang poetry was the most flourishing in the history of Chinese literature. In contrast, Europe was still in the 'dark' Middle Ages. And the United States had not yet been founded. Such eminent Chinese poets of different dynasties like Qu Yuan, Tao Yuanming, Li Bai, Du Fu, Li Shangyin, Bai Juyi and Su Shi all appeared much earlier than such prominent European writers as Dante, Shakespeare and Goethe. But unfortunately, due to corruption and the later rulers' inability to govern the country well, it was not long after that China became a second-class feudal and totalitarian country. Even so, Chinese literature still inspired Goethe, and the concept 'Weltliteratur' was first elaborated by this great European writer and thinker with the help of his critical reading and dynamic understanding of Chinese and other Asian literatures. Goethe, after reading some Chinese literary works of minor importance, put forward his utopian conjecture of 'Weltliteratur':

> I am more and more convinced that poetry is the universal possession of mankind, revealing itself everywhere and at all times in hundreds and hundreds of men ... .I therefore like to look about me in foreign nations, and advise everyone to do the same. National literature is now a rather unmeaning term; the epoch of world literature is at hand, and everyone must strive to hasten its approach. (cited in Damrosch, 2003, p. 1)

It should be said that Goethe himself benefited from translation, which even helped him enlarge his European and international reputation, moving from Germany to Europe as a whole and then to most of the entire world. In the age of Eurocentric dominance, to be a famous European writer also involved being a world renowned writer. In addition, his interest in Oriental literature and the translation and reception of his works in China and other Oriental countries, meant that Goethe has indeed become one of the most famous writers in the world.

Despite the above facts, Chinese literature has long been marginalized on the map of world literature since the late Qing Dynasty. In order to change this situation and bring China closer to the world, Chinese intellectuals launched large-scale translation of Western cultural and literary works into Chinese. Due to this

---

9   As for the rise of world literature in China, I should mention two international conferences on world literature: one held in Shanghai in August 2010 organized by myself at Shanghai Jiao Tong University, and the other held in Beijing in July 2011, organized by Zhao Baisheng at Peking University.

overall Westernization, literary translation in China is rather imbalanced even today, with numerous Western literary works available in Chinese, while very few excellent Chinese works translated into other languages, partly due to the absence of excellent translation and partly due to the bias of Orientalism prevailing in Western literary scholarship as well as in mass media. In the age of globalization, Chinese literature, like literatures elsewhere, is severely challenged by the rise of popular culture and consumer culture. Literature and literary studies are severely challenged, often being reported to be 'dead.' But on the other hand, we should realize that globalization has, in homogenizing national cultures, also offered China a precious opportunity to bring its culture and literature to the world. In order for Chinese literature to be part of world literature in the shortest possible time, some Chinese scholars and translators, including myself, once thought it merely a matter of translation. That is, we have seldom translated our own literature into the major world languages, especially English. This is only one of the reasons that may account for the current marginal position of Chinese literature in the world.

Frankly speaking, the current situation of book marketing is far from satisfactory. If we go to any British or American book store, we can seldom find many books written by Chinese writers even in the English translation, let alone those written directly in the Chinese language. In sharp contrast, if one goes to any book store in China, it is easy to find many foreign literary works translated into Chinese. There are quite a few publishing houses, such as Shanghai yiwen chubanshe (Shanghai Translation Press), Yilin chubanshe (Yilin Press), and Waiguo wenxue chubanshe (Foreign Literature Press), which devote almost all their efforts to the publishing of translated foreign literary works, among which Western literary works occupy the most part of their entire titles. Such leading publishers in Beijing as Shangwu yinshuguan (Commercial Press) and Sanlian shudian (Sanlian Press) make the most profits by publishing translated books, of which contemporary Western literary works and those of humanities sell extremely well. In contrast, books with similar titles authored by Chinese scholars can hardly be circulated smoothly even in China. Some young scholars have to pay quite large sums of money for the costs of publishing their academic monographs or dissertations. So it is not strange that today's young people do admire Western thinkers and writers much more than their Chinese counterparts. We cannot but be puzzled: Why does such a phenomenon appear in today's China? Does it mean that China has not produced excellent literary works, or China does not have its own literary masters? The answer is obviously negative if we have some knowledge of modern Chinese literature and culture. And Mo Yan's Nobel Prize winning in 2012 has further proved that Chinese literature is now moving toward the world, and China will play a more and more prominent role in global culture and world literature.[10] Since

---

10 According to the Swedish Academy, Chinese novelist Mo Yan was awarded the Nobel Prize in Literature in 2012 largely due to his work as a writer 'who with hallucinatory realism merges folk tales, history and the contemporary.' In this respect, the English and Swedish translations of his major works offered great help.

simple answers to the above questions cannot convince us, we should make some investigations and find the reasons behind this. In my preliminary observations, I think there are at least the following.

First of all, due to the prevalence and ideological intervention of Orientalism, Western audience has some long-lasting bias against the Orient and Oriental people, including China and Chinese people. To many who have never been to China, the country is still poor and backward. Chinese people are uncivilized far from the elegance of Western people. Thus they can hardly produce excellent literary works. It is true that through my own observation there is a sharp contrast between the image of the West in the eye of Chinese people and that of China in the eye of Western people. It is a shame for a Chinese high school student not to know about such Western intellectual giants as Plato, Aristotle, Shakespeare, Goethe, Mark Twain, Joyce, Eliot, Faulkner, Einstein, and Hemingway. Their books have sold extremely well in China. But in contrast, it is quite natural for a Western literary scholar not to know about Qu Yuan, Tao Yuanming, Li Bai, Du Fu, Su Shi, Wang Yangming, Lu Xun and Qian Zhongshu, let alone ordinary readers. I suppose that the above literary masters' works, even if English translations are available, hardly sell well in the English speaking world, let alone in other languages. Due to such an unbalanced situation of translation and reception, Chinese literature still has a significant distance from world literature although it has been trying to move toward the mainstream of world literature.

The second reason for this is the absence of excellent translation. As is well known, foreign language teaching in China has been a big educational enterprise out of which great profits are made by quite a few publishing houses. In recent years, along with the booming of Chinese in the world, this enterprise has gradually been on the decline.[11] However, even in large cities, great importance has always been attached to English language teaching in China's high schools, colleges and universities which is almost compulsory for the majority of university students in China. However, the fact is that most of the Chinese college students and teachers, including those with English majors, can only read English books or newspapers and have simple daily communications with native English speakers. They can hardly discuss academic issues with their international colleagues in correct and idiomatic English. Although a lot of Chinese scholars have the ability to translate literary or theoretic works from foreign languages into Chinese, very few of them can translate Chinese works into excellent and publishable foreign languages, let alone write and publish directly in foreign languages. Sometimes, even when they have translated great Chinese literary works into English or other major foreign languages, their versions are either not appreciated by native speakers because of the foreignizing elements, or are unable to be circulated in the target book market. The different circulations and receptions of the two different English translations

---

11 One of the typical examples for English teaching and learning in China on the decline is the partial exclusion of the English test from the national entrance examinations for study at the institutions of high learning.

of the Chinese classic *Hong Loumeng* translated by David Hawkes et al. (as *The Story of the Stone*) and the Yang couple (as *A Dream of Red Mansions*) in the English speaking world has proved this: the former is extremely popular in the English speaking world, but the latter is largely circulated domestically and seldom read in the libraries (Wang, 2011, p. 304).

In this sense, I would say that Mo Yan's Nobel Prize winning for Literature in 2012 was largely due to the excellent English translation accomplished by Howard Goldblatt, who actually retold the stories written by Mo Yan in perfect and readable English and sometimes even improved upon the narrative language. Without Goldblatt's superb English translation, plus the equally excellent Swedish translation done by Anna Chen, of his major works, Mo Yan's prize winning would have, at least, been postponed or he would most probably have missed this great honor.

The third reason might be a paradox. Nowadays, we live in a postmodern consumer society, in which serious literature and other high cultural products are severely challenged by the rise of popular, consumer culture. Since classical Chinese literary works of high aesthetic quality are far from the reality of the current consumer society, they may not be attractive to contemporary readers even if English translations are available. If faithfully translated into English or other major foreign languages, they can hardly be appreciated by the broad reading public, let alone be commercially successful like many of the Western literary or theoretic works in China. As far as modern Chinese literature is concerned, since it has largely been developed under the Western influence, it naturally cannot be compared to its Western counterpart even when translated into English or other major foreign languages. We Chinese literary critics and scholars often complain that we do not have our own literary masters like T.S. Eliot, William Faulkner, Marcel Proust, James Joyce, Ernest Hemingway, V.S. Naipaul, Garcia Marquez and Milan Kundera. So ours is an age of lacking literary and theoretic masters. So, for many people, what we should do is only translate as many literary and theoretic masters and their masterpieces from the Western languages into Chinese. Thus the current unbalanced situation of translation appears in China's literary and critical circles. If we do not solve this problem we cannot expect the real age of world literature to come about.

Apart from the above three major reasons, there is one further reason which is of vital importance: Chinese scholars' self-isolation which has certainly helped prevent Chinese literature from being part of world literature. As we know, world literature is an imported Western theoretical concept which, through translation, came to China and was transformed. During the past decades, it has always appeared in the name of 'foreign literature,' far from the mainstream discourse of Chinese literature studies. Even in the years after the Cultural Revolution, it was called world literature, and was still placed under the comprehensive discipline of Chinese language and literature, whose major task of teaching and research does not include Chinese literature. It was even separated from comparative literature until 1998, when China's Ministry of Education readjusted academic disciplines and had these two disciplines merged into one, i.e. comparative and world literature under the umbrella of Chinese language and literature. So today's Chinese scholars of comparative and world literature are enthusiastically promoting world literature in the context of which they could re-examine Chinese literature.

Globalization has offered China very precious opportunities to promote its culture and literature in the world. Since at present English is the lingua franca most frequently used in the world, to push Chinese literature and culture toward the world we should make full use of this hegemonic language and translate as many Chinese literary and theoretical works as possible into English so that Chinese culture and literature will contribute significantly to the relocation of global cultures and the remapping of world literatures.

Toward a 'Glocalized' Orientation in the Process of Globalization

Although China is one of the biggest winners in the process of globalization, from a cultural perspective, I would rather argue that it is the 'glocalized' orientation that enables China to relocate itself in the broader context of global cultures. In this sense, we would say that China benefits most from glocalization, which is especially true of Chinese culture. Just as Roland Robertson, one of the most influential and frequently quoted Western scholars in globalization studies, especially in China, pointed out many years ago,

> the notion of glocalisation actually conveys much of what I have in fact been writing in recent years about globalisation. From my standpoint the concept of glocalisation has involved the simultaneity and the interpenetration of what are conventionally called the global and the local, or---in more general vein---the universal and the particular. Talking strictly of my own position in the current debate about and the discourse of globalisation, it may even become necessary for me (and others) to substitute occasionally the term 'glocalisation' for the contested term 'globalization,' in order to make my, or our, argument more precise. (Robertson, 1994, pp. 38–9; see also Robertson in general)

It goes without saying that the publication of Robertson's book *Globalization: Social Theory and Global Culture* in Chinese in 2000 in Shanghai[12] did help globalization come to China; and it is even truer that the publication of the *Encyclopedia of Globalization* in Chinese in 2011 in Nanjing has certainly popularized this concept and enabled more people to know about this contemporary phenomenon.[13] In respect to this, I should say that Robertson made a tremendous

---

12 Published in China as *Quanqiuhua: shehui lilun he quanqiu wenhua*, trans. Liang Guangyan. Shanghai: Shanghai renmin chubanshe, 2000.
13 Published in China as *Quanqiuhua baikequanshu*, trans. Wang et al. Nanjng: Fenghuang chuban chuanmei jituan, Yilin chubanshe, 2011. (Roland Robertson and Jan Aart Scholte, eds, *Encyclopedia of Globalization*. New York and London: Routledge,

contribution to helping to introduce this concept to China. If we re-examine what I have analyzed the above three different versions of cultural globalization in the Chinese context, this would be proven particularly true. Although Chinese scholarship has welcomed the advent of globalization by quoting Robertson's description and discussion of globalization, they seem to have neglected that Robertson is among the first to conceptualize the term 'glocalization' and apply it to describing cultural globalization in the world. The practice of globalization in China, especially in Chinese culture and literature, has undoubtedly proved that globalization cannot be realized in those countries where there is a long cultural history and strong cultural mechanism unless it is 'localized' thus going toward a 'glocalized' orientation. No doubt China will continue to benefit from globalization, but most probably from a sort of glocalization as its practice of modernity is also an alternative modernity with Chinese characteristics.

References

Damrosch, D. 2003. *What Is World Literature?*. Princeton and Oxford: Princeton University Press.
Guthrie, D. 2012. *China and Globalization: the Social, Economic, and Political Transformation of Chinese Society*, 3rd edn. New York: Routledge.
Miller, J.H. 2008. 'Reading (about) Modern Chinese Literature in a Time of Globalization.' *Modern Language Quarterly* 69(1): 187–94.
Miner, E. 1990. *Comparative Poetics: An Intercultural Essay on Theories of Literature*. Princeton, NJ: Princeton University Press.
Perry, E.J. 2014. 'Growing Pains: Challenges for a Rising China.' *Daedalus* 143(2): 5–13.
Robertson, R. 1992. *Globalization: Social Theory and Global Culture*. London: SAGE.
Robertson, R. 1994. 'Globalisation or Glocalisation?.' *Journal of International Communication* 1(1): 33–52.
Robertson, R. 1995. 'Glocalization: Time-Space and Homogeneity-Heterogeneity.' In *Global Modernities*, edited by M. Featherstone, S. Lash, and R. Robertson, 25–44. London: Sage.
Robertson, R. 2014. 'Situating Glocalization: A Relatively Autobiographical Intervention.' In *Global Themes and Local Variations in Organization and Management: Perspectives on Glocalization*, edited by G.S. Drori, M.A. Höllerer, and P. Walgenbach, 25–36. London: Routledge.
Robertson, R., and J.A. Scholte (eds). 2007. *Encyclopedia of Globalization*. New York and London: Routledge,

---

2007.) See also Roland Robertson, 'Situating Glocalization: A Relatively Autobiographical Intervention,' in G. Drori et al., eds, *Global Themes and Local Variations in Organization and Management: Perspectives on Glocalization.* London: Routledge, 2014: 25–36.

Shambaugh, D. 2013. *China Goes Global: The Partial Power*. Oxford: Oxford University Press.

Vukovich, D.F. 2012. *China and Orientalism: Western Knowledge Production and the P.R.C.* London and New York: Routledge.

Wang, N. 2002. 'Translation as Cultural "(De)Colonization."' *Perspectives: Studies in Translatology* 10(4): 283–92.

Wang, N. 2010a. 'World Literature and the Dynamic Function of Translation.' *Modern Language Quarterly* 71(1): 1–14.

Wang, N. 2010b. 'Global English(es) and Global Chinese(s): Toward Rewriting a New Literary History in Chinese.' *Journal of Contemporary China* 19(63): 159–74.

Wang, N. 2011. '"Weltliteratur": from a Utopian Imagination to Diversified Forms of World Literatures.' *Neohelicon* 38(2): 295–306.

Wang, N. 2012a. 'Translating Modernity and Reconstructing World Literature.' *Minnesota Review* 2012(79): 101–12.

Wang, N. 2012b. 'Chinese Literary and Cultural Trends in a Postrevolutionary Era.' *Comparative Literature Studies* 49(4): 505–20.

Chapter 11
'America' in Global Culture

Frank J. Lechner

'America' and the Americanization of the World

In the title of his 1901 bestseller, *The Americanization of the World*, the prolific British journalist W.T. Stead put a common European perception into a ringing phrase. The perception stemmed from the transatlantic 'American invasion' of the preceding decades: American food and technology, for example, had brought home to Britons that they no longer lived in a world of their own making (Stead, 1901, p. 342). The United States (US), Stead said, had 'arrived at such a pitch of power and prosperity as to have a right to claim the leading place among the English-speaking nations' (Stead, 1901, p. 4)—high praise, of course, coming from the old country. Trying to put patriotic minds at ease, Stead described the creation of the Americans as 'the greatest achievement of our race'; just as Jewish monotheism had conquered the world through Christianity, English ideals expressed in English would make the 'tour of the planet' thanks to the growing US influence (Stead, 1901, pp. 2–3). Yet the Americans had already given their own twist to those ideals, putting their distinctive stamp on religion, by creating a 'great Christian community' without state support (Stead, 1901, pp. 262–3), and on sports, by performing exceptionally well in international competition (Stead, 1901, p. 334). Spreading the ideals had given the Americans a sense of their white man's burden, as years of warfare had 'not yet induced the Filipinos to recognize the brotherly love and benevolent intentions of the invaders' (Stead, 1901, p. 202). For Great Britain, America's inexorable rise left only a choice between merging the empire into a new union of English-speaking peoples or simply supersession by the US (Stead, 1901, p. 396). Against the Americanization of the world, Stead implied, resistance would be futile. Among the British, the sentiment was widely shared: around the time of Queen Victoria's Diamond Jubilee in 1898, they were 'ready to defer to American power,' says John Lukacs, and in the years leading up to World War I a 'full revolution' took place in British attitudes toward Americans (Lukacs, 2004, pp. 202, 209). Whether in 1898 or 1901, we may infer, British views of world order or global consciousness changed as perceptions of America's merit and place in the world changed.

The change would seem to confirm that in globalization connectivity drives consciousness. In the last decades of the nineteenth century, after all, the world had become more fully and deeply connected. In that 'takeoff phase' of globalization (Robertson, 1992, p. 59), the world was becoming a single place thanks to more rapid communication, transportation, and travel. It was a busy period for connecting more places and people in more different ways, as telegraph cables crossed oceans, World's Fairs and international sporting events were staged, international organizations began to address common problems, and imperially-minded states kept or extended their control abroad. The US was in the thick of it, as a magnet for migrants and investment, a source of new inventions and consumer products, and a military force to be reckoned with, surprisingly engaged in its own imperial venture after defeating Spain. For many Europeans, but not only for them, the US was concretely present in a way it had not been before—in Bologna and many other venues, for example, Buffalo Bill gave audiences a new taste of American life (Rydell and Kroes, 2010). Already by the 1870s, Eric Hobsbawm argued, citing much evidence of international economic activity, all parts of the globe had been drawn in to a single world, a 'world unified' (1975, pp. 64, 82–3). Around the turn of the century, that sense of connectivity was even more obvious. The global consciousness of all involved, particularly on both sides of the North Atlantic Ocean, shifted accordingly. New visions of world order evolved to meet new facts of world order.

For the takeoff period in globalization, then, the connectivity-to-consciousness sequence seems to work well. Yet as a well-known student of culture and consciousness once remarked, people make their own history but with the tradition of dead generations always weighing on their brains. Ideological superstructure, he implied, has some life of its own. So it does in this case. Though we need not fully adopt the conceptual apparatus that famous scholar might impress upon us, his insight helps to bolster the notion that even in a period when turbulent change and imperial-capitalist expansion are afoot in the political-economic base, definitions of the global situation will depend in part on the independent legacy of past imaginations. In this case, the Americanization that figured so prominently in the globalization discourse of Stead's day derived in part from long-standing visions of 'America.' Dead generations had a voice in the new constructions of world order and America's role in it. 'America' hemmed in America. To explain the 'secrets' to American success, for example, Stead invoked familiar clichés of the United States as an exceptionally dynamic and youthful country, inspired by the religious motivation of some early settlers, committed to a particular vision of liberty. At the same time, as his comments on American imperialism indicate, the exemplary offspring became embroiled in the ways of the world as it confronted the great responsibility that comes with great power. Nonetheless, as a country with exceptional endowments, the US was bound to have a transformative impact. Stead thus cheerfully paid his respects to the tradition of dead generations that had already attributed such special qualities to the US That does not mean that he and others in his day simply carried forward a cultural burden; the brains of the living brought about some change as well—Stead's estimation of American influence is a case in point, and his later advocacy of Esperanto, among other causes, suggests that his own global consciousness was not just handed down. Though 'America' shaped diagnoses of what he and others called the 'Americanization of the world,' its content and role were also unstable, a global trope always locally renegotiated and reinterpreted. The positive rendering of Stead's time and place contrasted with the perhaps more common critical European view.

Viewed positively or negatively, 'America' had long figured in European global consciousness: once discovered, the New World obviously had to be fit into old conceptions of world order. Columbus himself initiated one way of coming to terms with it, by giving 'those strange lands the form of our own' (Pérez de Oliva, cited in Greene, 1993, p. 15). From the outset, of course, the new was also inferior, as American savages, even if recognized as human, could not live up to civilized standards. But more than just a site of distorted projection, America also soon became the locus for many 'imaginary ... utopian constructions' (Echeverria, cited in Greene, 1993, p. 26). Even when the prospect of finding utopias ready-made receded, 'America' became the place where the old world could renew itself, seeking a more abundant and purified life, as illustrated in Richard Hakluyt's late-1500s justifications for settlement in North America (Greene, 1993, p. 36). Before many actual connections with the northern part of the hemisphere evolved, it was already part of a discourse veering between 'eulogy and slander, the panegyric and vituperation' (Gerbi, 1973, p. xi). Many scholars have enjoyed discussing the eighteenth-century contributions to the discourse by Buffon and de Pauw, who were eager to deride the stunted animals, flaccid sexuality, and enervating climate of the degenerate new world, at least in de Pauw's case to argue that 'the conquest of the new world ... has been the greatest of miseries that humanity has suffered'—against which Europe should protect itself (Ceaser, 1997, p. 40; see also Gerbi, 1973). Alexander von Humboldt, among others, joined the 'dispute of the New World' on the opposing side by collecting evidence of its natural wonders.

In later decades, the dispute turned from the natural to the social world, to focus on the northern settlers and their institutions, but the pattern of argumentation, Gerbi (1973) and Woodward (1991, pp. 9–11) suggest, provided parameters for later debate about 'America' as model, mirage, or menace. Of course, one important discursive shift occurred when the United States of America gained independence. On both sides of the Atlantic, 'America' turned into shorthand for that new entity. Henceforth, it was the country, as imaginatively rendered by foreign observers, which had to find a place in their global consciousness. Whatever world they were creating, it had to make room for 'America' in it. European visitors delighted in reporting the bad manners of the uncouth Americans, and European racists oddly lamented the American threat to proper racial hierarchies; with subtly formulated ambivalence Tocqueville treated the US as a model democracy while questioning its racial exclusions; occasional enthusiasts thought America stood for things missing at home; but for much of the European intellectual elite 'America' became the symbol representing 'worlds with which they found themselves at odds' (Woodward, 1991, pp. 16, 28, 33).

In the late nineteenth century, James Ceaser has argued, 'America was entering the realm of the spirit' (1997, p. 163). That makes sense as a way to capture the renewed European obsession with palpable American influence across the Atlantic, due to which uncouth manners threatened to contaminate the old continent. Yet 'America,' the symbolic America that Ceaser himself and others have charted, had entered the 'realm of the spirit' long before, helping to define European global consciousness in advance of the tangible industrial-age connections that triggered concern about the 'Americanization of the world.' As the case of 'America' suggests, at least in certain instances forms of global consciousness precede and transcend the evolution of global connectivity.

'America' in American Global Consciousness

Like the world as a whole, America itself was being Americanized around the time Stead wrote his book. One of the chief protagonists in the effort was, of course, Theodore Roosevelt, who would ascend to the presidency in the year the book appeared. In his thinking, at least, the meaning of 'America' as symbol was closely tied both to domestic Americanization and to a more prominent American role in the world. For him, as for many of his compatriots, global consciousness revolved around 'America.' America could not fully be 'America' without asserting itself as a global power.

Roosevelt helped to turn America into an –ism. True Americanism, he argued in 1894, stood for a distinctly national patriotism, wholly opposed both to the 'noxious element' of the undesirable Europeanized citizen and the 'flaccid habit of mind its possessors style cosmopolitanism' (Roosevelt, 1894). It was particularly important, he thought, to instill it in newcomers, to 'Americanize' them so that they would fully adopt true American speech and principles and ideas about Church and State. But Americanism, he insisted, was 'a question of spirit, conviction, and purpose, not of creed or birthplace.' He returned to the topic some 20 years later, in a 1915 Columbus Day speech to the Knights of Columbus. 'We of the United States,' he reminded his audience, may be kin to European nations but are 'also separate from each of them,' 'developing our own distinctive culture and civilization' on a 'virgin' continent (Roosevelt, 1921 [1915]). The US was a nation 'founded to perpetuate democratic principles,' specifically, that 'each man is to be treated on his worth as a man' and that all have the right to hold religious views that meet their own souls' needs. Even more emphatically than before, he declared that '[t]here is no room in this country for hyphenated Americanism'; allowing such room would turn the country into a 'tangle of squabbling nationalities.' Military strength and preparedness for war required singular commitment: 'complete Americanization' was necessary for self-defense. In a united America, even race prejudice would have to be challenged. As war continued overseas, he called on each man to do his duty 'to the great nation whose flag must symbolize in the future as it has symbolized in the past the highest hopes of all mankind.' The flag had already become an object of Francis Bellamy's campaign for a national salute meant to promote Americanism and to Americanize the 'alien child' (Ellis, 2005, pp. 24–37), one of many efforts to boost American national identity in that era of high immigration. Roosevelt's nationalist rhetoric was distinctly his own, linking manly vigor to moral character and the principle of equality in a suitable 'myth' of America (Dorsey, 2007), and it obviously served specific political purposes at various stages in his career, in 1915 as a means of promoting entry into war, but his reworking of America-as-ism resonated widely.

For Roosevelt and many others, Americanism also had global implications. In one strand of his particular global consciousness, a rising power committed to democratic principles should both defend its interests and assist others in sharing America's blessings. Whatever new world order emerged in the twentieth century, it would have to grant a greater voice to the US As an active participant in the Spanish-American War, he promoted US assistance for Cuban independence; as president, he defended US control in the Philippines as benevolent preparation for future autonomy; for his mediation between Russia and Japan he earned the Nobel Peace Prize; a relentless promoter of the Isthmus Canal, he took forceful action to bring the project to fruition; and as a believer in naval power, he famously sent the White Fleet on a public relations tour. By his assertive stance in foreign policy, he advanced the Americanization of international relations. To be sure, many of his actions were controversial at home and abroad, not least America's imperial entanglements. But in their own way, his domestic opponents, less enamored of ocean-crossing mission creep, also affirmed that American identity and Americanized world order were bound to be intertwined.

The Rooseveltian reworking of American global consciousness would appear to be another case of connectivity-first: the arrival of immigrants had created new ties that demanded affirmation of distinction, and growth in wealth and power had created new foreign relations that demanded affirmation of responsibility. Such a reading has much support in the historical literature that treats the fin-de-siècle as a break in American traditions. For example, according to Walter McDougall (1997), this is the era in which the US turned from pursuit of its own 'promised land' to becoming a 'crusader state.' Until that fateful year of 1898, he argues, the US focused on protecting its liberty and expanding the space in which to exercise it, unilaterally following its Manifest Destiny; later it was tempted first by 'progressive imperialism' and then by Wilsonian 'liberal internationalism' to intervene more aggressively abroad, as a crusader in search of monsters to destroy. Already more entangled than before, the US also deliberately valued those entanglements as a way to project its own identity. Real world order, as the aftermath of World War I showed, proved a little more resistant than expected to American ministrations. But the intellectual construction of 'America' through foreign policy, in tandem with American views of desirable world order, nonetheless changed.

As in the case of outsiders' attempts at defining America, the insiders' process may owe more to long-standing tradition than the McDougall thesis allows. The meaning of power for Americans shows some continuity: from the start many thought of the country as a vessel of world-historical change. 'The cause of America,' said Thomas Paine with characteristic immodesty, 'is in a great measure the cause of all mankind' (LaFeber, 1994, p. 20). Though often cited as counseling against seeking foreign monsters to destroy, even John Quincy Adams was motivated by a belief in the US as agent of God's work on earth (Weeks, 2002, p. 17). The country's development, Secretary of State William Seward added in his funeral oration for Adams, was 'the most important secular event in the history of the human race' (Seward, 1849, p. 362). The US, its leaders typically thought, had a 'providentially assigned role' to better the world; beyond territorial expansion, that was its true 'manifest destiny' (Stephanson, 1995). They argued over precisely how to realize that destiny, of course, but both 'exemplarists' and 'vindicationists' (Brands, 1998) were committed to maximizing American power as intrinsically good for Americans and for humanity. Far from involving a break in tradition, nation-building in America, 'liberty's surest guardian,' naturally segued into global nation-building (Suri, 2011, p. 8). Exceptionally ambitious, Americans were always bound to worry about 'what America owes the world' (Brands, 1998). Well before 1898, such partial evidence indicates, at least American elites already developed a distinctive kind of global consciousness that assigned a global role to their own country. In light of such evidence, it seems plausible to view the American imagined community as both a continuous and a world-historical project, with early generations providing ample symbolic resources to the likes of Roosevelt and Wilson as they brought new American power to bear on new global problems. New entanglements acquired meaning when framed by old ideas.

None of this is meant to deny the rather drastic policy departures or intellectual creativity represented by leaders like Roosevelt or Wilson. Nor can this brief discussion try to settle the dispute among US foreign policy scholars about continuities in an exceptional foreign policy tradition. But regardless of whether Americans on the whole really changed their minds and at some point threw off a tradition handed down by dead generations, different sides in the dispute appear to affirm that across the generations an exceptional, even exceptionalist, version of 'America' has had a dynamic of its own, providing terms on which Americans connected to the world at large.

'America' and Global Anti-Capitalism

When Werner Sombart visited the US during Roosevelt's presidency, he was surprised, or professed to be surprised, that the most highly developed capitalist country lacked a large, radical workers' party that could agitate for socialist reform. There was a radical Socialist Party, but it had no power; there was a growing labor movement, notably the American Federation of Labor, but it was not socialist. Hence his classic question: 'Why is there no socialism in the United States?' In answering it, he and fellow leftists constructed their own 'America,' integral to future socialist or communist visions of world order, if only as the power that obstructed the path to the proletarian paradise.

Sombart himself focused on features that might make the US exceptionally resistant to socialism. Citing many statistics, he tried to prove that American workers were indeed better off than their European peers, typically consuming three times as much meat and four times as much sugar (1976, p. 63). With more money to spend on cheaper goods, they were better housed and better dressed. A bit reluctantly, Sombart conceded that, 'this prosperity was not in spite of capitalism but because of it' (Sombart, 1976, p. 105). Comfort and progress hampered revolutionary fervor: 'All Socialist utopias came to nothing on roast beef and apple pie' (Sombart, 1976, p. 106). American workers did not feel such fervor to begin with. 'I believe,' said Sombart, 'that emotionally the American worker has a share in capitalism: I believe that he loves it' (Sombart, 1976, p. 20). For lack of 'oppositional consciousness' among members, trade unions adopted a 'business approach' to advancing worker interests, focusing on better working conditions rather than large-scale change (Sombart, 1976, pp. 21–2). Politics took any remaining sting out of worker activism. America's democratic from of government, Sombart thought, induced workers to try and reach their goals by electing officials rather than working outside the system (Sombart, 1976, p. 38). Two parties and their machines controlled politics, always able to buy off potential troublemakers; apart from the Republicans, third parties had proved unable to break the duopoly (Sombart, 1976, pp. 41–4). More than defend principles, both parties wanted to get or keep power, which gave both a reason to appeal to workers—further complicating any radical challenge (Sombart, 1976, pp. 44–51). As citizens of a democratic republic, workers had no great incentive to take that route anyway, since they were part of the People and could make their influence felt through public opinion (Sombart, 1976, p. 56). In fact, Sombart implied, it was more difficult for American workers to think of themselves as a class. Educated and comfortable, they did not need to bow and scrape before their betters; social distance between classes was small (Sombart, 1976, p. 110). Free land was America's safety valve, since any class radicalism that might bubble up could be siphoned off by workers moving west to 'escape into freedom' (Sombart, 1976, pp. 115–17). And yet, like many leftists before and after, Sombart could not quite give up hope: the factors obstructing socialism would disappear, he thought, and 'in the next generation Socialism in America will probably experience the greatest possible expansion of its appeal' (Sombart, 1976, p. 119).

From the outset, America presented a problem for the kind of global consciousness transnational Marxism or socialism intended to promote. Marx and Engels had already grappled with the issue. In theory, of course, capitalism would fuel crises, crises would fuel class conflict, and the highest stage of capitalism would heighten its contradictions. If anywhere, therefore, capitalism's gravediggers should have been getting their shovels ready in the US Yet Marx himself had already noted American exceptions: workers had it better, and they could more easily seek land, which shielded them against the worst exploitation (Lipset and Marks, 2000, pp. 24–5). Engels added that in a country that was 'bourgeois' from the start, Americans would be 'born conservatives' and capitalist ideas become 'strongly rooted' in the working class (Lipset and Marks, 2000, p. 21). Both recognized that if American workers had a decent standard of living and could hope to do better, revolution might not be a priority (Lipset and Marks, 2000, p. 25). The partners in theory also worried—with good reason, it turned out—that 'sectarian' and 'dogmatic' 'Yankee socialists' might take their doctrine too seriously, isolating themselves from the mainstream working class by insisting on ideological purity (Lipset and Marks, 2000, pp. 32–3). In short, Marx and Engels realistically recognized the US as a potential exception to the presumed revolutionary rule, though they did not draw the full implications from that recognition. 'America' became a specter haunting anti-capitalist radicals everywhere.

After the Russian Revolution, that was a problem for members of the newly formed Communist Party USA. The Russians had shown what was possible. In theory, the more advanced Americans should follow their lead. But in the Roaring Twenties the demise of capitalism seemed far off. Communist Party USA leader Jay Lovestone explained to his comrades that the US was bound to frustrate them. American communists would have a harder time defeating the merely reformist, backsliding socialists because of the 'peculiar specific conditions in which the labor movement as a whole is very weak and, especially, politically backward' and in which '[t]he overwhelming majority of our working class still follows the parties which are openly the political expression of the big bourgeoisie' (Lovestone, 1928, p. 660). In the party newspaper, two comrades complained a few months later that, 'This American "exceptionalism" applies to [the Lovestone group's] whole tactical line ... as applied to America' (cited in Zimmer, 2013). Unfortunately for Lovestone, a more powerful orthodox communist, Joseph Stalin, also disagreed. When Lovestone appeared in Moscow to explain himself, Stalin objected that Lovestone and his faction 'exaggerate the significance of specific features of American capitalism and thereby overlook the basic features of world capitalism as a whole'—and any Communist Party obviously had to base its policy on those 'basic features' (Draper, 1977, p. 409). Impervious to being mugged by reality, American communists toed the Soviet party line, expelling Lovestone and ridiculing the heresy they named 'exceptionalism.'

The expulsion did not solve the problem. As world revolution failed to materialize, even Stalinists had to reconsider the merits of American exceptionalism. The very existence of deviant America meant their global vision fell short. '[I]f only the impediments interfering with the natural course of history could be identified and removed,' so most leftists had assumed, 'all would be well' (Katznelson, 1997, p. 37). As the main such impediment, 'America' entered the realm of the anti-capitalist spirit early on, a necessary element in the ideological processing of expanding capitalist connections. Stalin's dismissal notwithstanding, viewed from the left, 'America' became more menace than model. Speaking in 1951, prodded by the Soviets in the early phase of the Cold War, a British Communist Party official nicely combined what were becoming familiar anti-American clichés, as he denounced America's 'synthetic, imperialist culture ... [that is] coldly and cynically devised for the debasement of man' (Chiddick, 2007, p. 179). Imperialism and debasement: during the 'American century' those features of 'America' became reference points against which more than a few progressives defined their global vision.

'Global America'

While W.T. Stead caught the tenor of the times in the Britain with his fairly sunny rendering of Americanization, across the Channel prevalent attitudes were less favorable. After the US attacked Spain in Cuba in 1898—that year again—French critics opposed its growing power. For example, *The Conspiracy of Billionaires*, a story serialized for a large popular audience by Gustave le Rouge, depicted Americans as brutal and uncultivated 'Yankees' pursuing the 'enslavement of the Old World,' all the more grating due to America's 'double offense' of being racist and multiracial, oppressing blacks while creating the 'mud of all the races,' as Le Rouge put it (Roger 2005, pp. 149–52, 178, 204). Though American 'mud' may not provoke such objections anymore, the other elements of European anti-Americanism persist: the 'uncouth nation' that contaminates through dangerous 'Americanization,' Markovits (2007) has shown, remains a discursive staple. For him, as for other students of anti-Americanism, the crudely portrayed American other serves mainly to bolster imagined European or other national communities. In that reading, Europe positions itself, politically and culturally, with reference to 'America.' Both procedure and content have spilled over to other continents.

Partly because those crude portrayals seeped into scholarship as well, one group of scholars proposed, a century after Stead and his contemporaries had taken on the issue, to pursue a more nuanced approach to America and its global cultural impact, under the heading 'global America' (Beck et al., 2003). For example, drawing on ideas of Arjun Appadurai, Natan Sznaider and Rainer Winter (2003, p. 5) suggest that:

> Americanization does not run uniformly and is not imposed from above. It leads to heterogeneous answers and different accentuation. Even the capacity of making a personal image of America and taking over its imagery has become a global phenomenon. By means of plural constructions, the picture of America has also become reflexive.

Ulrich Beck ostensibly encouraged such 'plural constructions' by rejecting the concept of 'Americanization' because it is based on an outdated national understanding of globalization; by contrast, 'cosmopolitanization' promises to capture the complexity of globalization more adequately because it avoids the kind of 'methodological nationalism' that treats nations as the prime active units and naively opposes a national 'We' to an alien 'Them' (2003, pp. 16–17). In keeping with other trends in globalization studies, Rainer Winter (2003, pp. 206–7) questions the stereotype of a stereotyped mass culture made in America, proposing instead that popular culture displays far more 'difference, syncretism and hybridity,' evident in the way even seemingly 'imperialistic texts' such as the movie *Rambo* acquire various meanings in different contexts. Roland Robertson (2003) adds a plea for a more complex analysis of Americanization, one that distinguishes different dimensions, recognizes variations, adjudicates contrasting orientations, and treats the US itself as an increasingly heterogeneous, globalized place.

In view of the nuance, reflexivity, and complexity recommended in this twenty-first-century approach to Americanization, it is surprising, then, that in the immediate aftermath of the 9/11 attacks two of the authors diagnose the US response as a 'not very global politics in which the USA is affirming its hegemonic aspirations' (Sznaider and Winter, 2003, p. 10). In spite of his critique of methodological nationalism, Beck himself appeared to credit critical claims about 'American hegemony' and laments the US tendency to 'feel comfortable presenting itself as if it were a missionary to the heathens' (Beck, 2003, pp. 15–16). Other authors in the same group go even further down well-trodden paths, for example by treating Americanization as 'a powerful one-directional process that tends to overwhelm local processes' and includes various forms of 'imperialism' (Ritzer and Stillmann, 2003, p. 35). In a paper that acknowledges the multivocal literature on 'America' and disclaims any interest in rehashing 'boring' anti-Americanism, Jan Nederveen Pieterse nonetheless belabors old refrains: America is the 'bottleneck' preventing properly progressive global reform, a 'self-absorbed country engrossed in collective narcissism,' exporter of its 'brand' of capitalism comprising Taylorism, Fordism, and the like (though it also remains an 'anomaly'), instigator of a Washington consensus that 'matches the core profile' of American exceptionalism, and a country inclined to 'transpose' its 'domestic inequality and war on the poor to a world scale' (Nederveen Pieterse, 2003, pp. 67, 74, 81, 84, 86). For all its global impact, he argues, American exceptionalism is a self-caricature (whether in that regard it is exceptional among imagined communities he does not explain); like many other versions of 'America' offered by progressive critics distressed at American power and impact for more than a century, the response risks caricaturing the self-caricature. Perhaps that is to be expected from an author who attributes a 'strident conservatism' to CNN (Nederveen Pieterse, 2003, p. 89). In this effort, as in other strands of global analysis, dead generations still have their say.

Conclusion

With examples drawn from discourse about 'America' as symbol in modern thought, this paper has sketched some ways that global consciousness preceded and framed global connectivity, in support of Roland Robertson's (2011) argument to that effect. At least in some instances, a global vision centered on or derived from preexisting constructions of 'America' shaped the representation of new global relations. More broadly, going slightly beyond the evidence described here, one could argue that 'America' has long served to articulate various global visions, not least those produced by Americans themselves of course, that defined the units in world order and the relations among them, as well as the nature of individuals and indeed the claims of humanity as a whole (Robertson, 1992).

At the end of *The Protestant Ethic and the Spirit of Capitalism*, Max Weber famously denied that he intended to replace materialist accounts of the rise of capitalism with an idealist alternative. In the same vein, the argument in this paper highlights only one thrust in links between connectivity and consciousness as aspects of globalization, but it does not entail any large assertion about the primacy of culture in globalization. I have a stake in debates on the subject (Lechner and Boli, 2004), but this is not the place to revisit the pertinent points. In a Weberian vein, an appreciation of historical contingency in the entwinement of global processes might facilitate a productive modus vivendi among contending perspectives. After all, much ink has been spilled and many pixels have been activated to resolve old antinomies in social thought. Figurational, multidimensional, system, action, structuration, and process theories have variously tried to overcome base and superstructure, structure and agency, rational choice and normative constraint, and so on. Unfortunately, both in general and in globalization theory, the absolute spirit has yet to achieve full transcendence. My purpose is not to complicate its task by turning potentially fruitful questions—How are relations represented? How do we become conscious of connections?—into another needless antinomy.

As the case of 'America' illustrates, in global identity formation imagined other communities play an important role. That in global analysis, scholarly or otherwise, 'America' is treated as the near-universal imagined Other suggests that habits of methodological nationalism are hard to shake. It raises the larger question how, in interpersonal interaction or intercommunal imagination, one really can take the perspective of others, as George H. Mead and his successors posited, perhaps more optimistic about movement toward what he called the human social ideal than is warranted today. Without answering that question directly, this paper has tried to promote a more 'reflexive' understanding of the United States' place in world society by lifting the weight of traditions handed down by dead generations just a bit. That may not change how 'America' will work in fact to define global situations. But it would be unfortunate if the study of America and Americanization continued to be constrained by a century of dashed leftist hopes.

References

Beck, U. 2003. 'Rooted Cosmopolitanism: Emerging from a Rivalry of Distinctions.' In *Global America?*, edited by U. Beck, N. Sznaider, And R. Winter, 15–30. Liverpool: Liverpool University Press.

Beck, U., N. Sznaider, and R. Winter (eds). 2003. *Global America? The Cultural Consequences of Globalization.* Liverpool: Liverpool University Press.

Brands, H.W. 1998. *What America owes the World: The struggle for the Soul of Foreign Policy.* Cambridge: Cambridge University Press.

Ceaser, J.W. 1997. *Reconstructing America: The symbol of America in Modern Thought.* New Haven, CT: Yale University Press.

Chiddick, J. 2007. 'The Cold War and anti-Americanism.' In *Anti-Americanism, Vol. 2: Historical Perspectives*, edited by B. O'Connor, 151–75. Oxford: Greenwood World.

Dorsey, L.G. 2007. *We are all Americans, Pure and Simple: Theodore Roosevelt and the Myth of Americanism*. Tuscaloosa: The University of Alabama Press.

Draper, T. 1977 [1960]. *American Communism and Soviet Russia: The Formative Period*. New York: Octagon Books.

Ellis, R. 2005. *To the Flag: The Unlikely History of the Pledge of Allegiance*. Lawrence: The University of Kansas Press.

Gerbi, A. 1973. *The Dispute of the New World: The History of a Polemic, 1750–1900*. Pittsburgh: University of Pittsburgh Press.

Greene, J.P. 1993. *The Intellectual Construction of America: Exceptionalism and Identity from 1492 to 1800*. Chapel Hill: University of North Carolina Press.

Hobsbawm, E.J. 1975. *The Age of Capital, 1848–1875*. London: Weidenfeld and Nicolson.

Katznelson, I. 1997. 'Working-class Formation and American Exceptionalism, Yet Again.' In *American Exceptionalism? US Working-Class Formation in an International Context*, edited by R. Halpern and J. Morris, 36–41. Houndmills: Macmillan.

Lafeber, W. 1994. *The American Age: United States foreign policy at home and abroad: 1750 to the present*. New York: W.W. Norton.

Lechner, F.J., and J. Boli. 2004. *World Culture: Origins and Consequences*. Malden, MA, Blackwell.

Lipset, S.M., and G. Marks. 2000. *It Didn't Happen Here: Why Socialism Failed in the United States*. New York: W.W. Norton.

Lovestone, J. 1928. 'The Sixth World Congress of the Communist International.' *The Communist* VII: 659–75.

Lukacs, J. 2004. *A New Republic: A History of the United States in the Twentieth Century*. New Haven, CT: Yale University Press.

McDougall, W.A. 1997. *Promised Land, Crusader State: The American Encounter with the World since 1776*. New York: Houghton Mifflin.

Markovits, A.S. 2007. *Uncouth Nation: Why Europe Dislikes America*. Princeton, NJ: Princeton University Press.

Nederveen Pieterse, J. 2003. 'Hyperpower Exceptionalism: Globalization the American Way.' In *Global America?*, edited by U. Beck, N. Sznaider, and R. Winter, 67–95. Liverpool: Liverpool University Press.

Ritzer, G., and T. Stillman. 2003. 'Assessing McDonaldization, Americanization and globalization.' In *Global America?*, edited by U. Beck, N. Sznaider, and R. Winter, 30–49. Liverpool: Liverpool University Press.

Robertson, R. 1992. *Globalization: Social Theory and Global Culture*, London, SAGE.

Robertson, R. 2003. 'Rethinking Americanization.' In *Global America?*, edited by U. Beck, N. Sznaider, and R. Winter, 257–70. Liverpool: Liverpool University Press.

Robertson, R. 2011. 'Global Connectivity and Global Consciousness.' *American Behavioral Scientist* 55(1): 1336–45.

Roger, P. 2005. *The American Enemy: A Story of French Anti-Americanism.* Chicago, IL: University of Chicago Press.

Roosevelt, T. 1894. 'What 'Americanism' Means.' *The Forum*, April, 196–206.

Roosevelt, T. 1921 [1915]. 'Americanism.' In *Immigration and Americanization: Selected Readings*, edited by P. Davis. Boston: Ginn.

Rydell, R.W., and R. Kroes. 2010. *Buffalo Bill in Bologna: the Americanization of the world, 1869–1922.* Chicago, IL: University of Chicago Press.

Seward, W.H. 1849. *Life and Public Services of John Quincy Adams, Sixth President of the United States with the Eulogy Delivered before the Legislature of New York.* Auburn, Derby: Miller.

Sombart, W. 1976. *Why is There No Socialism in the United States?.* White Plains, NY: International Arts and Sciences Press.

Stead, W.T. 1901. *The Americanization of the World; Or, the Trend of the Twentieth century.* New York and London: H. Markley.

Stephanson, A. 1995. *Manifest Destiny: American Expansionism and the Empire of Right.* New York: Hill and Wang.

Suri, J. 2011. *Liberty's Surest Guardian: American Nation-Building from the Founders to Obama.* New York: Free Press.

Sznaider, N., and R. Winter. 2003. 'Introduction.' In *Global America?*, edited by U. Beck, N. Sznaider, and R. Winter, 1–15. Liverpool: Liverpool University Press.

Weeks, W.E. 2002. *John Quincy Adams and American Global Empire.* Frankfort: The University Press of Kentucky.

Winter, R. 2003. 'Global Media, Cultural Change and the Transformation of the Local: The Contribution of Cultural Studies to a Sociology of the Local.' In *Global America?*, edited by U. Beck, N. Sznaider, and R. Winter, 206–22. Liverpool: Liverpool University Press.

Woodward, C.V. 1991. *The Old World's New World.* New York: Oxford University Press.

Zimmer, B. 2013. 'Did Stalin Really Coin 'American Exceptionalism'?.' Blog entry, Language and Politics. http://languagelog.ldc.upenn.edu/nll/?p=7225 [accessed August 2014].

Chapter 12
Taking Japan Seriously Again: The Cultural Economy of Glocalization and Self-Orientalization

Koji Kobayashi

More than two decades ago, Roland Robertson (1992) published his seminal work emphasizing the importance of culture, individuals and non-Western perspectives to the study of the multidimensionality and complexity of globalization. In particular, Robertson (1992) views Japan as a good example of a society that has incorporated ideas, cultures and systems of 'dominant' Others—including early medieval China and modern Western nations—to eventually contribute to the formation of global consciousness and interdependency. Thus, according to Robertson (1992):

> Japan is of great sociological interest not because it is 'unique' and 'successful,' but because it fulfills the function in the contemporary world of the society from which 'leaders' of other societies can learn how to learn about many societies. *That* is what makes Japan a global society, in spite of claims to the contrary. (p. 86, emphasis in original)

This point of view effectively challenged a general tendency of globalization theories in reproducing discourses of economic determinism, cultural homogenization and Western superiority (Dirlik, 2003; Hardt and Negri, 2000; Harvey, 2003; Ritzer, 2003). In other words, globalization has been predominantly discussed in relation to the deregulation of international trade, investment and financial flows and the associated expansion of economic power of transnational corporations (TNCs) while significantly reducing the importance of *local* and *non-Western* forms of agency, culture and particularity (Nederveen Pieterse, 2009; Ong, 1999, 2006; Tomlinson, 1999).

Despite Robertson's insistence and some notable exceptions (e.g. Allison, 2006; Condry, 2006; Iwabuchi, 2002; Miyoshi and Harootunian, 1993), the cultural dynamics of Japanese interactions and negotiations with the West remains on the margins of scholarly theorizing of globalization. From a reductionist view, Japan's economy, technology and TNCs are often subsumed under the convergence of the global economy whereas Japanese culture, identity and particularity are somehow separately viewed as victims, or passive recipients, of Western capitalist modernity

(Iwabuchi, 2002; Robertson, 1992, 1995). Indeed, this polarization of economy and culture runs counter to Robertson's (1992) earlier insistence that 'both the economics and the culture of the global scene should be analytically connected to the general structural and actional features of the global field' (p. 51).

As such, this chapter aims to reassert Robertson's (1992) focus on globalization by: (a) (re-)locating the roles of culture, language and identity within the globalization of Japanese corporations; and (b) revealing how Japanese corporations and their practices are constitutive of, and constituting, the structuring forces and changing dynamics of the global cultural economy. In contrast to the economic-centered analysis of globalization, my focus is the intersection of cultural-economic processes—'glocalization' and 'self-Orientalization'—that were pioneered and disseminated by Japanese TNCs. In doing so, I argue that Japanese corporate globalization in alliance with Western creative/marketing institutions and individuals has played a pivotal role in reinvigorating hitherto Western-centric—thus geographically, ethnically and culturally limited—capitalism. In particular, the 'strategic creative alliance' between Japanese TNCs and Western advertising agencies facilitated the shift in the mode of corporate dominance to be more sensitive to, and reflexive of, local culture and consumer differentiation during the late twentieth century. In what follows, I illustrate how the strategic creative alliance was forged as a key part of Japanese corporate globalization and functioned as scaffolding for the commercial processes of glocalization and self-Orientalization. My understandings and contentions were derived from the comparative and empirical analysis of two global sport brands and their practices: Nike (American-based) and Asics (Japanese-based).[1]

The chapter begins by explaining a wider context of global cultural economy to which Japanese TNCs made a significant contribution in terms of how dominant corporate strategies and ideologies were shifted from global standardization/

---

1 The case studies were conducted as part of a larger project on globalization and advertising production of sport brands. The project focused on particular advertising campaigns and examined: (a) the contexts in which they were produced and consumed; (b) the representations of culture and identity within the advertisements; and, (c) the conditions of production and the perspectives of the key producers and workers. The campaigns of the focus were: Nike's 'Where is the Next?' (released in 2007) that was produced across the national markets in Asia and the Pacific; and Asics' 'Made of Japan' (released from 2007 to 2010) that was developed as a series of global campaigns for its Onitsuka Tiger brand. These two campaigns offer interesting contrasts because they represent opposite directions of cultural flows—from the West to Japan/Asia and from Japan to the West. The insight in this chapter was largely drawn on the contextual analysis of global and glocal advertising production and interviews with marketing and advertising experts involved in the production. The interviews were conducted with six workers from Nike Asia Pacific Headquarters, Nike Japan, Wieden+Kennedy Tokyo and Daiko for the Nike case and another six workers from Asics Headquarters, Asics Europe, Amsterdam World Wide and Panda Panther for the Asics case (for more information about the methodologies and methods of this project, see Kobayashi, 2012a, 2012b).

economic rationalism to local adaptation/cultural differentiation. Next, I explicate how the transnational creative collaboration was formed out of Japanese TNCs' struggles to compete against Western rivals due to their lack of competency in English language as the de facto lingua franca and Western-centered culture of global business. This is then followed by explanations of how glocalization and self-Orientalization have been reinforced by the development of the strategic creative alliances. In particular, these sections identify the essential principles of the cultural-economic processes and discuss how a legacy of pioneering practices remains relevant to contemporary business of TNCs as exemplified by Asics. Finally, the conclusion highlights the key points of discussion and calls for more research on cultural-economic contributions of East Asian or non-Western business actors and institutions to the formation of global consciousness, connectivity and interdependence.

The Cultural Economy of Japanese Corporate Globalization

Whereas the acceleration of interconnectivity and interdependency has altered, and is altering, our sense of identity and belonging, they do not seem to guarantee the formation of a homogeneous 'global society' or 'global culture.' One of the most hegemonic forms of global convergence is promotional/consumer culture that has been disseminated through and beyond Western society. Nevertheless, less is known about how this Western-originated promotional/consumer culture has been embraced, negotiated and even altered by non-Western actors, institutions and practices. Notably, Nederveen Pieterse (2009) claims:

> In the course of the twentieth century, the 'orientalization of the world' and easternization, in contrast to westernization, resumed with the growing influence of Japan. Japan's 'Toyotism,' or lean production, has become a world standard (and Toyota the world's leading automaker), and Japanese management techniques such as quality control circles have been widely adopted. This was followed by the rise of the Asian Tiger economics and Southeast Asia, which spawned the (controversial) ideas of an 'Asian model' and of the twenty-first century as an 'Asian century.' (p. 138)

Although the comment may overstate the global impact of Easternization and Japanization, Nederveen Pieterse's point is well-taken in that Japan has made a considerable impact on management of transnational production and distribution. As such, it comes as no surprise that the characteristics of Japanese management styles and production systems have been widely discussed among both Western/Asian managers and scholars (e.g. Abegglen and Stalk, 1985; Dore, 1987). In these managerial discourses, the success of Japanese TNCs has often been credited to their flexible production systems, networks of subcontractors and cultural influences on the mode of organization and operation—though the latter is now considered to be a hindrance to Japanese TNCs' adaptation to the world best practices for economic success in the twenty-first century (Whitley, 1999).[2] However, as a point of departure for this chapter, fewer scholars have attended to the pioneering role of Japanese corporations in developing and disseminating the model of strategic creative alliance as a key cultural-economic contribution to the global capitalist expansion.

Initially, as advocated by Levitt (1983), when Western—and particularly American—TNCs expanded their business beyond national borders in the 1970s and 1980s, they predominantly employed the strategy of global standardization. This strategy was considered as the most *rational* and *efficient* in maximizing the scale and speed of capital gain through the production of the same products and services all over the world. The dominance of corporate standardization and convergence during the era led some to conceptualize such concepts as Fordism, Taylorism and other equivalents of the global homogenization thesis including 'cultural imperialism' (Tomlinson, 1991) and 'McDonaldization' (Ritzer, 1993). Nevertheless, a range of standardization strategies were severely criticized in the 1990s for their tendency in reducing human creativity into mathematic calculations in the form of what Boltanski and Chiapello (2005) call 'artistic critique.' According to Boltanski and Chiapello (2005), the artistic critique eventually entailed reforming the mode of capitalist domination to enable more flexibility and differentiation based on consumer choices, tastes and lifestyles. Indeed, this shift of managerial focus to flexibility and differentiation is best epitomized by Toyota's transformation of the global automobile industry through 'the displacement of mass production techniques by a system of *lean production*' (Dicken, 2011, p. 339, emphasis in original; see also Edwards and Ferner, 2004).

In contrast to American TNCs' standardization strategies with an emphasis on American lifestyle and values, Japanese corporations had to construct an alternative approach due to the lack of capacities and resources for mass production at a time of deprivation after the Second World War. By neutralizing Japanese cultural attributes of their brands and exported goods due to the negative image associated with the war, Japanese goods were deliberately promoted through local languages of various international markets (Iwabuchi, 2002). This approach was later referred to as 'glocalization'—also known as 'global localization' or 'flexible specialization.' In this context, Japanese corporations built an economic model in which their quality products—particularly for automobiles and electronics—were produced domestically by flexible production systems and then marketed and distributed by their overseas local partners in conjunction with local needs, tastes and distribution channels during the era of Japan's so-called 'economic miracle' (Morgan et al., 2003).

---

2 For instance, Dore's (1987) account, *Taking Japan Seriously*, suggested British (and Western) corporations to learn from the Japanese practices of industrial arrangement, quality control technique, life-time employment and long-term thinking.

By learning from Japanese TNCs, Western corporations recognized the limits of the global standardization strategy and the need to take into account 'irreducible' local particularities for successful global operations and marketing (Amis and Silk, 2010; Andrews and Ritzer, 2007; Cho, 2009; Cho, Leary and Jackson, 2012; Jackson, Batty and Scherer, 2001; Scherer and Jackson, 2010). Since the 1990s onward, Western TNCs thus have deployed the glocalization strategy to respond to the 'artistic critique' of standardization. As a result of nimble learning and adoption by Western and Asian rivals, Japanese TNCs eventually lost their first-mover advantage for the pioneering practice. In the next section, further attention is given to the context in which Japanese corporations pioneered a glocalization strategy and its implication for the constitution of the global (and glocal) cultural economy.

The Strategic Creative Alliance in the Making of the Glocal Cultural Economy

When Japanese corporations globalized their distribution of goods and services, they invariably faced difficulty in communicating their ideas and values to Western consumers. Limited by the particularity of Japanese language, culture and business orientation, Japanese TNCs soon realized that it would be best to collaborate with Western marketers and advertising agencies. Clearly, this contrasts with American TNCs who partnered with American advertising agencies as part of an international management strategy. Even though the giants of Japanese advertising agencies such as Dentsu and Hakuhodo have to date been highly profitable, even in comparison with other world-top agencies, they remained national-market-driven and their international status has been far behind their Western rivals. Given that Japanese advertising agencies were reluctant, or unable, to 'go global' due to linguistic and other cultural-economic barriers to enter overseas markets, it can be argued that the Japanese corporate globalization of business and communication was *only possible* through collaboration with Western marketers and advertising agencies (Johansson and Nonaka, 1996; Takada, Mizuno and Bith-Hong, 2012). This pattern of strategic alliance between Japanese/Asian TNCs and Western advertising agencies has been widely adopted by East Asian TNCs, some of which are now more successful in making the best out of such collaboration than Japanese TNCs.

In contrast to a range of homogenization theses of globalization, the difference in hiring marketers/advertising agencies from the same or different nations at the dawn of corporate globalization marked a significant change in the ways in which commodities and cultures are communicated. To apply a view of the spread of American products and images as cultural imperialism, it can be said that the American mode of 'imperialistic' communication—based on the 'intra-national' alliance—was challenged by the Japanese mode of 'glocal' communication through which local marketers and advertising agencies were positioned central to their promotional activities in respective local markets (see Takada, Mizuno and

Bith-Hong, 2012). In fact, in most cases when Japanese brands were recognized for their excellence in creative communication at prestigious advertising contests such as Cannes Lions International Festival of Creativity, it was Western advertising agencies that were primarily in charge of production and distribution. For examples, the top awards, 'Grand Prix,' were presented to Toyota's 'IQ Font' in 2010 (with Happiness Brussels in Belgium), Honda's 'Grrr' in 2005 (with Wieden+Kennedy (W+K) in the UK) and Sony's 'Mountain' in 2004 (with TBWA in the UK).

Given the vast gaps in language, identity and culture between Japanese corporations and Western marketers/advertising agencies, it is imperative to examine the dynamics of cultural interactions and negotiations within the processes of transnational cultural production. Below, I focus on two sport brands, Nike and Asics, that exemplify the contrasting ways in which American and Japanese corporations form strategic alliances with advertising agencies.

Cases: Nike and Asics in the Sport Industry

One of the most emblematic industries that represent the forging of the economic and the cultural is the sport industry (Goldman and Papson, 1998). Also, sport brands along with other companies in the clothing industry were 'the first to take on a global dimension because of the low barriers to entry to clothing production; in the 1970s, they epitomized that so-called "new international division of labour"' (Dicken, 2011, p. 302). In particular, Nike has been a prominent figure as it received considerable public criticism towards its management of Asian factories which began to be referred to as 'sweatshops' in the late 1990s (Sage, 1999). Despite often being underplayed in the literature, outsourcing as a form of strategic alliance is undertaken across a range of sections in Nike's production management including: (a) 'goods production' with subcontracted manufacturers in Asia; (b) 'advertising production' with advertising agencies, film directors and production companies; and, (c) 'distribution' by retailers such as Foot Locker and Finish Line.

Given this chapter's focus on transnational collaboration/alliance between corporations and overseas marketers/advertising agencies, specific attention is given to the outsourcing of, or strategic alliance for, 'creative' functions such as marketing and advertising. Nike has globalized its marketing operation through establishment of its overseas subsidiaries and a strong partnership with American advertising agency W+K. W+K is primarily a so-called 'creative agency' whose work is mainly associated with production of advertisements through coordination of resources, organizations and specialists. This form of 'intra-national' collaboration between Nike and W+K (both headquartered in Oregon, the USA) is situated at the global center of creative operation which then delegates to their overseas subsidiaries. Its strength lies in enforcing a clear hierarchical order of commands and generating consistent organizational values and brand messages including, for instance, the most widely known corporate slogan 'Just Do It.' Thus, core creative direction and guidance for advertising production are communicated rather hierarchically—from creative directors and brand managers at headquarters to marketers, art directors, copywriters and account managers at subsidiaries.

In contrast, Asics has never had any partnership with Japanese advertising agencies for its global operation of marketing and advertising campaign production. Rather, during the early years of its global sales operation, it chose to almost fully delegate local marketing initiatives to overseas subsidiaries. However, in 2010, Asics changed its decentralizing strategy of local delegation and appointed its global agencies of record for its two main brands: American advertising agency Vitro Robertson for its Asics (Performance) brand and Dutch advertising agency Amsterdam Worldwide for its Onitsuka Tiger brand. The purpose of the change in strategic direction to coordinate global advertising campaigns was to raise its brand values based on consistent promotional messages and images across various international markets. The change brought many challenges to Asics because a strategic alliance with overseas advertising agencies in the making of a global brand was more complex involving greater dynamics of cross-cultural communication and negotiation than an intra-national alliance—like the one between Nike and W+K. As overseas subsidiaries were positioned to mediate and translate language, culture and business styles between the Japanese headquarters and overseas advertising agencies, diverse groups of workers were involved in decision-making processes through multiple points of negotiation, accommodation and (mis)communication. To clarify such an important distinction, I characterize Asics' model of creative collaboration as relatively 'polycentric' in contrast to Nike's 'monocentric' model (see Figure 12.1).

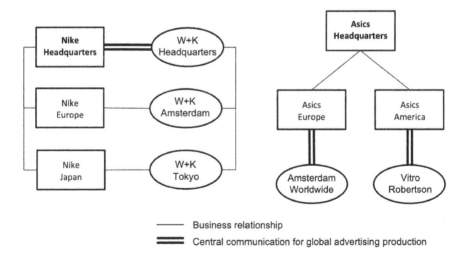

Figure 12.1 Nike and Asics' models of strategic creative alliances in 2010

Asics' model of strategic creative alliance is polycentric because the Japanese headquarters is not in a definite position to determine an entire creative direction and process; rather, multiple points of communication between its overseas subsidiaries and advertising agencies are central to its creative production of global branding and advertising campaigns. In what follows, the section for glocalization outlines how this model of strategic creative alliance was rooted in the cultural-historical context of Japan and practice of glocalization while the section for self-Orientalization discusses both positive and negative consequences of the alliance.

Glocalization: 'Relative' Autonomy to the Local and Reverse Diffusion to the Global

Glocalization was originally coined from a Japanese word, *dochakuka* or indigenization that referred to agricultural practice to domesticate food production and was later applied to business practice. The term was then deployed and developed by Roland Robertson (1995) as a theoretical concept for socio-cultural analysis of globalization. As part of an analytical framework, Robertson (1992, p. 100, emphasis in original) conceptualizes glocalization as one manifestation of what he calls '*the particularization of universalism*'—that constitutes, together with '*the universalization of particularism*,' the twofold process of globalization. To put it very simply from this analytical standpoint, globalization can be considered as a process of dialectical interactions between the 'globalization of the local' and 'localization of the global.' The rise of Japanese corporate glocalization in the 1970s and 1980s brought to the fore discussions about the underplayed process of glocalization, or 'localization of the global.'

The pioneering role of Japanese TNCs needs to be located within the historical context of Japanese cultural hybridization and incorporation of Others' knowledge, languages and systems. For instance, Robertson (1992) points out Japan's history of selective learning from overseas in relation to the universalism-particularism continuum:

> Japan's crystallization of a form of 'universalistic particularism' since its first encounter with China has resulted in its acquiring paradigmatic, global significance with respect to the handling of the universalism-particularism issue. Specifically, its paradigmatic status is inherent in its very long and successful history of selective incorporation and syncretization of ideas from other cultures in such a way as to particularize the universal and, so to say, return the product of that process to the world as a uniquely Japanese contribution to the universal. (p. 102)

Briefly tracing Japan's history of cultural hybridization, one can easily find an enormous volume of learning and adoption of cultural practices and institutions from China in the pre-modern era—particularly from the Tang Dynasty (618–907),

Europe in the era of modernization or the Meiji Restoration (1868–1912) and the USA in the post-war era. As Giulianotti and Robertson (2007) assert, the principle philosophy of Japanese modernization was 'encapsulated in the implicitly glocalist aphorism, *wakon yōsai* ("Japanese spirit, Western learning")' (p. 180, emphasis and macron added). Through these interactive and interpenetrative processes with both the West and the East, foreign influences have been translated, adapted and indigenized within Japanese society to produce new articulations of forms, practices and cultures. It is within this historical context that we can make sense that Japanese TNCs were geopolitically and cultural-economically well-positioned to pioneer a glocalization strategy even in the era of global standardization or cultural imperialism as a dominant ideology.

Although it must have been shaped collectively rather than achieved by a single person, the idea of corporate glocalization can be symbolically traced back, and is often credited, to a co-founder of Sony, Akio Morita (du Gay et al., 1997; Morley and Robins, 1995; Ohmae, 2005).[3] For instance, du Gay et al. (1997) discuss Akio Morita's idea about glocalization:

> Akio Morita has often referred to these various dynamics of the 'global-local nexus' as a process of 'global-localization.' This he has presented rather benignly as a policy in which the company makes use of local talent whilst being sensitive to local cultural differences ... In addition to 'caring for the community,' Sony has frequently presented 'global-localization' as involving '*decentralized management*'—a practice of devolving 'investment decisions, research and development, product planning and marketing' to enable local people to do things 'on the spot' ... . (p. 80, emphasis added)

Thus, from the viewpoint of Japanese corporations, or at least of Sony, corporate glocalization represents less of a promotional tactic to superficially decorate overseas marketing and advertising with local symbols than a transnational practice of decentralized management that delegates decision making for local matters to local subsidiaries and managers. However, Western TNCs including Coca-Cola, Nike and McDonald's, as early adopters of the glocalization strategy, applied the concept mainly for strategic promotional purposes to customize their products and services to meet local tastes and needs (Silk and Andrews, 2001). These different embodiments of glocalization between Japanese and American (or Western) corporations are indicative of the above-mentioned contrast between Asics' polycentric and Nike's monocentric models of creative production and communication. Therefore, when Japanese corporate glocalization was adopted and altered (or glocalized) by American/Western TNCs, the central discourse of corporate glocalization was

---

3 According to Ohmae (2005), Akio Morita 'famously advised companies to "Think Globally, Act Locally." This philosophy was christened *glocal* by the Japanese magazine *Nikkei Business* and led to the coining of a new word, *glocalization*' (p. xxi, emphasis in original).

largely shifted from *decentralization of management* to *customization of products and services*. Nevertheless, notwithstanding such a difference, it is possible to identify a consistent principle of glocalization that has been inherited through American/Western appropriation of Japanese corporate glocalization.

Essential Principle of Glocalization

An essential principle of glocalization that is drawn from my analysis is that a glocalization process grants *'relative' autonomy to the local* and generates *reverse diffusion to the global*—much like a rip in an ocean current.[4] First, glocalization allows a substantial room for the local—or the particular—to interpret, adjust and make use of the global—or universalism—for its own economic, political or social benefits. The degree of autonomy given to the local nonetheless varies from organization to organization, from context to context. For instance, it is fair to say that Asics' polycentric model of transnational creative alliance provides less restrictions on autonomous/creative activities of overseas subsidiaries and advertising agencies than Nike's monocentric model. A downside of this however is that there are likely to be more points of key negotiations away from the global headquarters, thereby rendering the decision-making processes more confusing, complicated or fragmented. Second, glocalization more subtly generates 'reverse diffusion'—or what Giulianotti and Robertson (2012) call 'reverse glocalization'—that ultimately changes the structure and dynamics of the global by returning the localized element of the global into a renewed form of the global. To apply Robertson's (1992, 1995) analytical framework, it can be argued that reverse diffusion produced by glocalization represents a form of 'universalization of particularized universalism' or 'globalization of the glocal.' As this is the process largely overlooked in the studies of globalization/glocalization, this section offers one brief example from Asics' corporate glocalization.

Onitsuka Tiger, one of the two main brands of Asics, was an original brand of Onitsuka Corporation, the forerunner of Asics, established in 1949. This brand was once terminated in 1977 when Onitsuka Corporation as an athletic shoe company merged with two athletic wear companies to become a general sporting goods company under the uniform brand, Asics. The revival of the Onitsuka Tiger brand was prompted around 2002 when the booms of retro goods and Japanese popular culture stimulated European fashion buyers and consumers to demand the original models of Onitsuka Tiger shoes (Kobayashi et al., 2010). As the Japanese headquarters was located geographically and culturally distant from the center of the surge in demand for Onitsuka Tiger originals, European subsidiaries and advertising agencies—especially, Asics Europe and Amsterdam Worldwide both of which were located in Amsterdam—played a central role in the brand's remarkable

---

4   The term 'reverse diffusion' was borrowed from Edwards and Ferner (2004) who used it to refer to the diffusion of human resource practices from foreign subsidiaries to headquarters in the country of origin.

growth over the decade through the re-fashioning of the Onitsuka Tiger brand and production of regionally- and globally-wide campaigns. Therefore, it was *local/* European subsidiaries—*not* the *global/*Japanese headquarters—that capitalized on these booms and led the transformation, or re-positioning, of an athletic shoe brand into a fashion and lifestyle brand.

Consequently, the reverse diffusion from the *local*/European subsidiaries has fundamentally challenged and then changed the brand management of Asics at the global level in at least two substantial ways. First, the company moved away from strict compliance with the founder's original aspiration to provide sporting goods only for 'serious athletes' to a more relaxed stance to accommodate areas of fashion and lifestyle as part of its business. Second, the revival of Onitsuka Tiger brought the company to the realization that strategic coordination of global marketing and advertising was necessary to promote the consistent values and messages in branding across various overseas markets. This eventually led to the appointment of global agencies of record from 2010. Furthermore, this example confirms the contention that when host markets—in this case Europe—are large and distinctive from the home market, subsidiaries tend to possess relatively stronger bargaining power against the headquarters and this may entail a higher degree of local autonomy and reverse diffusion (Birkinshaw and Hood, 1998; Geppert and Williams, 2006). The next section elaborates on how this collaboration between Japanese TNCs and Western marketers/advertising agencies has resulted in another process called self-Orientalization.

Self-Orientalization: Self-Stereotyping for Economic Success

This section first overviews wider discussions about the West-East binary with respect to the discourse of Orientalism and then explores the key contributions of self-Orientalization, exemplified by Japanese TNCs and Asics in particular, to this debate. By building on Edward Said's (1978) theorizing of Orientalism, the concepts of self-Orientalism and self-Orientalization are deployed and developed extensively by Dirlik (1996) and Iwabuchi (1994). For instance, Iwabuchi (1994) contends that '[w]hile Orientalism enjoys the mysterious exoticism of the Other, self-Orientalism exploits the Orientalist gaze to turn itself into an Other' (p. 70). Accordingly, self-Orientalization can be understood as a process of strategic self-stereotyping for the purpose of being accepted by dominant groups and cultivating its own position within the dominant structure.

For Said (1978), Orientalism was constructed on 'the idea of European identity as a superior one in comparison with all the non-European peoples and cultures' and stabilized as 'the result of cultural hegemony at work' (p. 7). In his theorizing, the Orient is a subject shaped solely by Occident's interests and ideology and therefore characterized by an absolute lack of agency, power and capacity for resistance or creation. While the thesis of Orientalism offers us a valuable approach to problematize the normalization of Western domination, such a deterministic, one-way view of the power relation has drawn a backlash from those who insist the Orient's central role in the development of world's economy and technology in the pre-modern era and capacity to resist, negotiate and even change certain aspects of the currently dominant Western forces (Dirlik, 1996; Frank, 1998; Iwabuchi, 1994, 2002; Irwin, 2006; Macfie, 2000; Nederveen Pieterse, 2009; Varisco, 2007). Indeed, several scholars argue that there is a need to take account of Orient's construction of worldview through demonizing of the West or Occidentalism 'which centred upon claims as to the selfish individualism, materialism, decadence and arrogance of westerners' (Robertson, 1990, p. 192; see also Buruma and Margalit, 2004; Chen, 1995).

Japan is a great example of how Western forces are negotiated and appropriated, as opposed to being resisted all together, to produce the changing dynamics and counter-force towards, and perhaps *within*, the dominant structuring of 'Westernization.'[5] With the major slogan *datsua nyūo* (leave Asia, enter Europe or the West) in the late nineteenth century, Japan desperately attempted to join the West as one of the leaders of the world's economy and politics by appropriating Westernization in a way that constituted political autonomy against the forces of Western colonialism and its own version of military-industrial imperialism. As the first 'modernized Orient,' Japan adopted and reproduced an Orientalist view towards other East Asian nations as uncivilized, backward and underdeveloped—constructing them as ideal subjects for Japanese colonial rules—within a discourse of what some scholars call 'Oriental Orientalism' (Iwabuchi 1994, 2002; Robertson 1998).

Despite the massive development of economy, technology and science, Japan has remained vastly different from the West in its culture and identity. Although education and cultural practices and customs have been significantly influenced by Western styles, Japan's core belief systems, morality and spirituality have continued to be underpinned by non-Western forms—such as Confucianism, Buddhism and Shintoism—and served as sources of nationalism and Occidentalism. As Robertson (1990) contends, 'Japanese identity largely rests on a form of occidentalism, since in functional terms China was the original "Occident" for Japan and the concern with the west since the sixteenth century has been constituted by a generalization of "China" so as to encompass the Western world, particularly since the 1850s' (p. 193). Since Japan has never been colonized by foreign states, its engagement with Sinicization and Westernization can be distinguished from cultural (ex) changes forced by colonization and thus characterized by 'voluntary acceptance and acculturation of foreign cultures' (Kozakai, 1996), or perhaps more radically '*self*-colonization of culture' (Yoshioka, 1995, emphasis in original).

As a part of the process of accepting and internalizing the Western worldview and world order, self-Orientalization is considered as a foundational base for the

---

5 According to Hall (1992), '[b]y "western" we mean the type of society discussed in this sense: a society that is developed, industrialized, urbanized, capitalist, secular, and modern' (p. 277).

epistemological shift into the modern, military-industrial mode of development in Japan—and East Asia more generally. In the context of global cultural economy, self-Orientalization is emblematically manifested in creative collaboration between Japanese/East Asian TNCs and Western marketers/advertising agencies. While the strategic creative alliance with Western advertising agencies helped Japanese corporations to 'go global,' it simultaneously rendered Japanese TNCs prone to Orientalization of their national culture, identity and values through advertising and marketing overseas. Through this strategy, Japanese TNCs prioritized an economic imperative of exporting goods and generating sales in Western markets by allowing and even encouraging the West's representations of Japanese goods, brands and cultural distinctions.

Essential Principle of Self-Orientalization

An essential principle of self-Orientalization drawn from my analyses is that it enhances the Orient's own economic, political or social benefits and therefore strategic position within the dominant structure by appropriating and internalizing dominant representations, or stereotypes, of the Orient itself. The principle of self-Orientalization is evidenced by the case study of Asics that used its own national culture and identity for global marketing and advertising. For example, Onitsuka Tiger's series of campaigns called 'Made of Japan' were produced mainly by the European partners from 2007 to 2010 to promote the brand in association with fun and stylish aspects of Japanese popular culture. The central promotional objects used for the campaigns were shoe-shaped dioramas that symbolized: Japanese toys in 2007; Tokyo urban illumination in 2008; the Zodiac Race in 2009; and *tansu* (Japanese drawers) in 2010. Up until 2010, the central ideas, themes and processes of campaign production were primarily managed and coordinated by Asics Europe and Amsterdam Worldwide whereas the Japanese headquarters acted only to approve or disapprove their ideas and proposals. Because 'Made of Japan' campaigns were initially launched for European markets and later upgraded to the global level, they were designed to stimulate interests and imaginations of European consumers who wanted to attain Japanese cultural symbols as signs of distinction, exoticism and coolness.

The 2009 'Cycle of Life' (as part of 'Made of Japan') campaign featuring a web film of an animated version of the Zodiac Race is an illustrative case for such a gap in understanding of 'authentic' representation of Japan. The aim of the campaign was to celebrate the 60th anniversary of the Onitsuka Tiger brand by appreciating and representing the Japanese traditions of *kanreki* (60th birthday that is traditionally celebrated as the year of 'rebirth' according to the lunar calendar). As a source of visual attraction and entertainment, the European partners chose to use the legend of the Zodiac Race that has a close historical link with the Zodiac and lunar calendar. However, this celebration of Japanese culture and brand was apparently contradicted by the fact that the Zodiac, Race and lunar calendar were all brought from medieval China and thus not the 'original products' of Japan.

Although *kanreki* traditions were largely regarded as a product of indigenization and animation was an integral part of Japanese popular culture, it may be confusing for consumers to understand what 'authentic' representations of Japanese identity and traditions are from the animated version of the Chinese Zodiac and the legend of the Zodiac Race. To their credit, the European marketers and creatives were considerate of cultural sensitivity and spent several weeks of learning the subject matter. Yet, given their European cultural backgrounds and limited time allowed for the production, it was an onerous task to satisfy the needs both for creative ideas to attract European consumers' interests and for authentic representations of which the Japanese headquarters was more concerned. Regardless of the different views towards authenticity of cultural representation between the European partners and the Japanese headquarters, the Japanese brand was able to cultivate Western markets of fashion and lifestyle in this context of corporate self-Orientalization—through collaboration with European marketers/creatives who took charge of representing Japanese culture and identity at the global level.

Conclusion

The chapter examined the pioneering role of Japanese TNCs in developing and disseminating the commercial processes of glocalization and self-Orientalization that have impacted the ways in which the cultural economy has been constituted globally and glocally. As demonstrated throughout this chapter, the historically interactive location of Japan between the global and the local and between the West and the East has shaped its ambivalent position in both complementing and challenging Western cultural-economic hegemony. By using case studies of sport brands Nike and Asics, the chapter was able to identify and analyze the essential principles of glocalization and self-Orientalization beyond commercial practice of advertising production. Both processes infer that dominant structuring forces (e.g., globalization and Orientalization) can be affected and even altered by their internal changes resulting from the incorporation of 'the particular' (e.g., the local and the Other).

Moreover, the chapter discussed how the commercial processes of glocalization and self-Orientalization were underpinned by the different models of strategic creative alliance that were developed by Japanese and American/Western TNCs. While such an analytical distinction is useful in avoiding the pitfalls of treating empirically different processes and contexts as the same, it is important to note that the different models of strategic creative alliance by Nike and Asics offered here *do not* predetermine: (a) that the American model *only* reinforces a discourse of cultural imperialism based on the intra-national partnership between American TNCs and advertising agencies at the global center of creative production; *nor* (b) that the Japanese model *only* enhances a decentralization of key creative decision making in a way resonant with overseas cultures and conditions. The overall picture is much more complicated requiring further research and analysis. In fact, some parts of Nike's overseas marketing operation have been transformed into highly glocal institutions and processes in which its local subsidiaries and workers play major roles in the creative activities for local campaigns—especially when authenticity of local representations and complexity of local negotiation are concerned (Kobayashi, 2012a, 2012b). On the other hand, Asics, once a provider of a large amount of creative autonomy to overseas subsidiaries, is now concentrating its focus on the production of globally consistent promotional messages and streamlining of global advertising production.

What is important therefore is that there is a need for thorough attention to, and in-depth analysis of, a range of collaborations, negotiations and struggles that may lead, or may have led, to key changes in institutions, processes and relations within/from the context of transnational advertising/cultural production—the point utterly absent in a discourse of neoliberal globalization and equivalents of cultural homogenization thesis. Lastly, this account should not be regarded as a celebration of Japanese cultural practices and economic achievement; rather, its intention is to insist on the need for taking non-Western—of which Japan is a part—subjectivities, cultures and practices seriously. Arguably, this will help us understand how cultural-economic struggles, contestations and negotiations in everyday business activities—for instance, through transnationally coordinated creative production—matter to the making of global connectivity and interdependence.

Acknowledgements

I would like to thank Roland Robertson, Steve Jackson and John Amis for their helpful comments on the earlier drafts of this chapter.

References

Abegglen, J.C., and G. Stalk. 1985. *Kaisha, the Japanese Corporation.* New York: Basic Books.
Allison, A. 2006. *Millennial Monsters: Japanese Toys and the Global Imagination.* Berkeley: University of California Press.
Amis, J., and M.L. Silk. 2010. 'Transnational Organization and Symbolic Production: Creating and Managing a Global Brand.' *Consumption Markets & Culture* 13(2): 159–79.
Andrews, D.L., and G. Ritzer. 2007. 'The Global in the Sporting Glocal.' *Global Networks: A Journal of Transnational Affairs* 7(2): 135–53.
Birkinshaw, J., and N. Hood. 1998. 'Multinational Subsidiary Evolution: Capability and Charter Change in Foreign-Owned Subsidiary Companies.' *The Academy of Management Review* 23(4): 773–95.

Boltanski, L., and È. Chiapello. 2005. *The New Spirit of Capitalism*. Translated by G. Elliott. London: Verso.

Buruma, I., and A. Margalit. 2004. *Occidentalism: The West in the Eyes of its Enemies*. New York: Penguin Press.

Chen, X. 1995. *Occidentalism: A Theory of Counter-Discourse in Post-Mao China*. New York: Oxford University Press.

Cho, Y. 2009. 'The Glocalization of U.S. Sports in South Korea.' *Sociology of Sport Journal* 26(2): 320–34.

Cho, Y., C. Leary, and S.J. Jackson. 2012. 'Glocalization and Sports in Asia.' *Sociology of Sport Journal* 29(4): 421–32.

Condry, I. 2006. *Hip-hop Japan: Rap and the Paths of Cultural Globalization*. Durham, NC: Duke University Press.

Dicken, P. 2011. *Global shift: mapping the changing contours of the world economy*, 6th edn. Los Angeles: Sage.

Dirlik, A. 1996. 'Chinese History and the Question of Orientalism.' *History and Theory* 35(4): 96–118.

Dirlik, A. 2003. 'Global Modernity?: Modernity in an Age of Global Capitalism.' *European Journal of Social Theory* 6(3): 275–92.

Dore, R. 1987. *Taking Japan Seriously: A Confucian Perspective on Leading Economic Issues*. London: Athlone Press.

du Gay, P., S. Hall, L. Janes, H. Mackay, and K. Negus. 1997. *Doing Cultural Studies: The Story of the Sony Walkman*. London: Sage.

Edwards, T., and A. Ferner. 2004. 'Multinationals, Reverse Diffusion and National Business Systems.' *MIR: Management International Review* 44(1): 49–79.

Frank, A.G. 1998. *ReOrient: Global Economy in the Asian Age*. Berkeley: University of California Press.

Geppert, M., and K. Williams. 2006. 'Global, National and Local Practices in Multinational Corporations: Towards a Sociopolitical Framework.' *The International Journal of Human Resource Management* 17(1): 49–69.

Giulianotti, R., and R. Robertson. 2007. 'Recovering the Social: Globalization, Football and Transnationalism.' *Global Networks* 7(2): 166–86.

Giulianotti, R., and R. Robertson. 2012. 'Glocalization and Sport in Asia: Diverse Perspectives and Future.' *Sociology of Sport Journal* 29(4): 433–54.

Goldman, R., and S. Papson. 1998. *Nike Culture: The Sign of the Swoosh*. London: Sage.

Hall, S. 1992. 'The West and the Rest: Discourse and Power.' In *Formations of Modernity*, edited by S. Hall and B. Gieben, 275–331. Cambridge: Polity Press.

Hardt, M., and A. Negri. 2000. *Empire*. Cambridge, MA: Harvard University Press.

Harvey, D. 2003. *The New Imperialism*. Oxford: Oxford University Press.

Iwabuchi, K. 1994. 'Complicit Exoticism: Japan and its Other.' *Continuum: An Australian Journal of the Media* 8(2): 49–82.

Iwabuchi, K. 2002. *Recentering Globalization: Popular Culture and Japanese Transnationalism*. Durham, NC: Duke University Press.

Irwin, R. 2006. *For Lust of Knowing: The Orientalists and their Enemies*. London: Allen Lane.
Jackson, S.J., R. Batty, and J. Scherer. 2001. 'Transnational Sport Marketing at the Global/Local Nexus: The Adidasification of the New Zealand All Blacks.' *International Journal of Sports Marketing & Sponsorship* 3(2): 185–201.
Johansson, J.K., and I. Nonaka. 1996. *Relentless: The Japanese Way of Marketing*. New York: HarperCollins.
Kobayashi, K. 2012a. 'Corporate Nationalism and Glocalization of Nike Advertising in "Asia": Production and Representation Practices of Cultural Intermediaries.' *Sociology of Sport Journal* 29(1): 42–61.
Kobayashi, K. 2012b. 'Glocalization, Corporate Nationalism and Japanese Cultural Intermediaries: Representation of *Bukatsu* through Nike Advertising at the Global-Local Nexus.' *International Review for the Sociology of Sport* 47(6): 724–42.
Kobayashi, K., J. Amis, R. Irwin, and R. Southall. 2010. 'Japanese Post-Industrial Management: The Cases of Asics and Mizuno.' *Sport in Society* 13(9): 1334–55.
Kozakai, T. 1996. *Ibunka juyō no paradokkusu* [Paradox of accepting foreign cultures]. Tokyo: Asahi Shinbunsha.
Levitt, T. 1983. 'The Globalization of Markets.' *Harvard Business Review* (May-June): 92–102.
Macfie, A.L. (ed.). 2000. *Orientalism: a Reader*. New York: New York University Press.
Miyoshi, M., and H.D. Harootunian. 1993. *Japan in the World*. Durham, NC: Duke University Press.
Morgan, G., B. Kelly, D. Sharpe, and R. Whitley. 2003. 'Global Managers and Japanese Multinationals: Internationalization and Management in Japanese Financial Institutions.' *The International Journal of Human Resource Management* 14(3): 389–407.
Morley, D., and K. Robins. 1995. *Spaces of Identity: Global Media, Electronic Landscapes and Cultural Boundaries*. London: Routledge.
Nederveen Pieterse, J. 2009. *Globalization and Culture: Global Melange*, 2nd edn. Lanham, MD: Rowman & Littlefield Publishers.
Ohmae, K. 2005. *The Next Global Stage: Challenges and Opportunities in our Borderless World*. London: Pearson/Prentice Hall.
Ong, A. 1999. *Flexible Citizenship: The Cultural Logics of Transnationality*. Durham, NC: Duke University Press.
Ong, A. 2006. *Neoliberalism as Exception: Mutations in Citizenship and Sovereignty*. Durham, NC: Duke University Press.
Ritzer, G. 1993. *The McDonaldization of Society: An Investigation into the Changing Character of Contemporary Social Life*. Newbury Park, CA: Pine Forge Press.
Ritzer, G. 2003. *The Globalization of Nothing*. Thousand Oaks, CA: Pine Forge Press.

Robertson, J. 1998. *Takarazuka: Sexual Politics and Popular Culture in Modern Japan.* Berkeley: University of California Press.

Robertson, R. 1990. 'Japan and the USA: the Interpenetration of National Identities and the Debate about Orientalism.' In *Dominant Ideologies*, edited by N. Abercrombie, S. Hill and B.S. Turner, 182–98. London: Unwin Hyman.

Robertson, R. 1992. *Globalization: Social Theory and Global Culture.* London: Sage.

Robertson, R. 1995. 'Glocalization: Time-Space and Homogeneity-Heterogeneity.' In *Global modernities*, edited by M. Featherstone, S. Lash and R. Robertson, 25–44. London: Sage.

Sage, G.H. 1999. 'Justice Do It! The Nike Transnational Advocacy Network: Organization, Collective Actions, and Outcomes.' *Sociology of Sport Journal* 16(3): 206–35.

Said, E.W. 1978. *Orientalism.* New York: Pantheon Books.

Scherer, J., and S.J. Jackson. 2010. *Globalization, Sport and Corporate Nationalism: The New Cultural Economy of the New Zealand All Blacks.* Oxford: Peter Lang.

Silk, M., and D.L. Andrews. 2001. 'Beyond a Boundary?: Sport, Transnational Advertising, and the Reimagining of National Culture.' *Journal of Sport and Social Issues* 25(2): 180–201.

Takada, H., M. Mizuno, and L. Bith-Hong. 2012. 'Analysis of the Relationship between Advertisers and Advertising Agencies in the Global Market.' In *Handbook of Research on International Advertising*, edited by S. Okazaki, 497–518. Cheltenham: Edward Elgar Publishing.

Tomlinson, J. 1991. *Cultural Imperialism: A Critical Introduction.* London: Pinter Publishers.

Tomlinson, J. 1999. *Globalization and Culture.* Chicago, IL: University of Chicago Press.

Varisco, D.M. 2007. *Reading Orientalism: Said and the Unsaid.* Seattle: University of Washington Press.

Whitley, R. 1999. *Divergent Capitalism: The Social Structuring and Change of Business Systems.* New York: Oxford University Press.

Yoshioka, H. 1995. 'Samurai and Self-Colonization in Japan.' In *The Decolonization of Imagination: Culture, Knowledge and Power*, edited by J. Nederveen Pieterse and B.C. Parekh, 99–112. London: Zed Books.

Conclusion

Roland Robertson and Didem Buhari-Gulmez

The opening chapter by Roland Robertson raises the principal issues that have been discussed in this volume. He is particularly concerned with the question of global culture and global consciousness, at the same time stressing the problems involved in emphasizing connectivity as the primary characteristic of globalization, a characteristic which is very common in the vast majority of discussions of globalization; although the latter has been increasingly tempered in recent years by the concept of glocalization. Indeed, connectivity—or what some commentators even call hyperconnectivity—severely neglects the significance of ideational and symbolic factors, particularly in view of the fact that planet earth has over many centuries become increasingly relativized. He discusses the latter in reference to the comparatively new idea of the cosmic society. In fact, what he calls the cosmic turn is regarded as transcending the global turn and other 'turns' in social science. He concludes his chapter by a series of short discussions that highlight the problem of the relationship between connectivity and culture. These include the Internet and the world wide net; virality; new media and cybercultures; global and extraterrestrial imaginaries; and migration, diasporas and multiple consciousnesses.

The chapter that follows by Manfred Steger and Paul James offers an alternative new definition of globalization that puts an emphasis upon 'relation' instead of connectivity and that captures both objective and subjective relations. This means that globalization is regarded as 'the extension and intensification of social relations across world-space and world-time.' In this chapter Steger and James convincingly attempt to produce what they call 'engaged theory.' Their contribution emphasizes that there are different forms of consciousness—such as the consciousness of sensory experience, practical consciousness, reflective consciousness and reflexive consciousness. They suggest that there is a need for the rethinking of connectivity within the context of four different levels of social *meaning*: ideas, ideologies, imaginaries, and ontologies.

The chapter by Barrie Axford attempts to define key concepts such as globality, global consciousness, communicative connectivity and mediatization, that are needed in order to study the potential and actual effects of digital connection and affect global consciousness and emerging globalities (such as world citizenship). Axford investigates the constitution of three digital worlds in different analytical and empirical domains through specific examples: global 'microstructures' (such as connectivity and consciousness in financial trading and terrorist networks); the logic of connective action (social networking sites); and networked individualism (a global society beyond the territorial state).

The chapter that follows deals with the cultural consequences of globalization. Robert Holton provides a framework based on the trichotomy of homogenization, polarization, and hybridization; before exploring alternative ways of thinking about globalization as a cultural process, as is involved in Robertson's thesis of glocalization. Holton argues that glocal complexity implies the paradoxical co-existence of different trends that are about control and dominance, such as homogenization and polarization, with glocalization processes bringing these together in terms of standardized themes of diversity.

The two chapters that follow are significantly influenced by the work of John Meyer, although each deals with different aspects of his work. In the chapter by George Thomas a critical review of the literature on international norm diffusion, and global disjuncture, difference, and functional differentiation, is provided. He maintains that norms are embedded within institutionalized cultural structures and reflected in the discourse concerning states, international government and non-government organizations. Thomas emphasizes the major sites of contention and domestication in global-local dynamics while at the same time accounting for the general conditions of global diffusion. This means that global cultural models are first, abstract and theorized; second, reified through scientific authority; and, third, regarded as markers of civilization. These are spread through emerging discursive sites in which identity, action, policy and discourse, are received, framed, and contested.

The main focus of Gili Drori's contribution is on the global expansion of scientized education. She argues that the latter has profoundly transformed the nature of contemporary society by altering modes of thinking and consciousness, organization, social engagement and connectivity, in general, as well as the understanding of citizenship and personhood in particular. As a global institution that increasingly claims a significant level of cultural authority, scientized education shapes the functioning of economic and political processes at regional, international and global realms.

Jose Casanova's chapter explores the contribution of the Jesuits to the formation of a world society in terms of carrying the wider culture of universal Christian humanism and constructing Jesuit colleges as models of educational institution. It treats Jesuits as pioneers of globalization in the sense that they acted as an NGO of global missionaries and global educators. Therefore, studying their visions of the world and their uneasy encounters with European hegemony and other rival (Christian, Protestant, and secular) movements can shed light on the emerging global structures associated with the decline of Western hegemony.

In the chapter that follows Richard Giulianotti interrogates the ways in which processes of glocalization influence the sports culture, identities and solidarities worldwide in terms of the dual cross-cultural dynamic of homogenization (of sport *forms*) and heterogenization (of sport *contents*). Giulianotti emphasizes that sports culture is not only shaped by the duality of glocality and relativization but it also plays an important role in contributing to processes of globalization. It is worth noting that much of Giulianotti's writing on glocalization has been co-authored with Roland Robertson, Giulianotti frequently taking the lead in this respect.

Peggy Levitt's intervention dwells on the relationship between migratory flows and the transformation in migrating culture in the global context. She specifically raises the question as to how in the contemporary world the movement of people contributes to and transforms the movement of culture. She pays particular attention to what she calls sites of encounter and processes of vernacularization. This she does in order to move beyond simplistic accounts that neglect the multiple and unequal transnational networks and assemblages, and to assist in the explanation of the constitution and transformation of culture in motion.

The remaining three chapters of this volume attend to three specific regions of the world -- ones that have been and still are of crucial importance to the world as a whole.

Wang Ning investigates, in terms of globalization and glocalization theory, China, a vast country that is now commonly perceived to be the fastest growing and, potentially, perhaps, the most influential and powerful in the contemporary world. In so doing he contests the thesis that China has been a passive receiver of a singular modernity imposed by or acquired from the West. Rather, his study of Chinese literary culture emphasizes the rise of relatively autonomous alternative and diverse ways of understanding and practicing global culture, while maintaining China's 'unique' characteristics. In so doing he pays particular attention to the problems associated with translation and the unavailability of many translated Chinese classics in the West.

In his chapter on Americanization Frank Lechner argues that global consciousness is by no means always driven by connectivity. Indeed, it has frequently preceded, framed and transcended the latter. He characterizes the shifting European imagination and discourse about 'America' as being inferior to 'America' as model, mirage, or menace. In fact, he shows how such external imaginaries and discourse have contributed to shaping the trajectory of America as a global actor as well as 'Americanization' as a global process.

Koji Kobayashi's chapter, focusing upon the case of Japan, offers a critique of the latter as a passive recipient of global capitalism and Western culture. Through a comparison between Western (Nike) and Japanese (ASICS) sports brands, he emphasizes the pioneering role of Japan in enacting *glocal* strategies in the cultural-economic sector, which has inspired Western corporations and, at the same time, has led to a process of 'self-Orientalization' (or self-stereotyping).

Many chapters agree on the fact that globalization is not to be identified with Westernization, nor is to be characterized as involving a single hegemonic process. As has been said, much of the discussion of glocalization runs strongly against the grain of the idea of globalization equaling Americanization, or even homogenization. Globalization studies—indeed global studies generally—urgently need to consider the complexity of the relationship between sameness and difference *in an increasingly relativized and relativizing world*. In addition, even though this book has not dwelt much upon this, the increasingly prominent issue of what some have called the cosmic society is the next major step that we must take with respect to the advancement of global studies. We hope that the essays assembled for this volume will have enhanced our understanding of some of the most salient issues in the contemporary exploration of the terrestrial and extraterrestrial conditions under which we now live.

Index

Africa, 9, 29, 43, 61, 63, 109–10, 149, 151
Americanization, 7, 58–9, 69, 129, 165, 179, 180, 182–3, 187–9, 213
Appadurai, Arjun, 6, 30, 57, 59, 65, 81, 130, 187
authoritarian, 62, 63, 95
autonomy, 6, 23–4, 27, 101, 103, 183, 200, 202–4, 207
  autonomous, 76, 103, 117, 202, 213

Barber, Benjamin, 61–3, 127
Beck, Ulrich, 24, 32, 43, 56–7, 101, 103, 129, 187–8
Bourdieu, Pierre, 30–31, 77

capitalism, 27–8, 55–9, 61–2, 64, 109, 117, 162, 184–6, 188–9, 194, 213
  capitalist, 28, 37, 55–6, 58–61, 75, 82, 111, 114, 118–19, 153, 180, 184–6, 193, 196, 204
Castells, Manuel, 21, 23, 42, 56, 58, 61, 63, 67
Christianity, 29, 112, 115–16, 121, 123, 179
China, 2, 3, 8, 68, 111–12, 115–16, 119–21, 147, 150, 161–76, 193, 200, 204–5, 213
  Chinese, 65, 115, 118, 120, 150, 161–76, 206, 213
citizenship, 14, 60, 82, 93, 98–102, 132, 211–12
city, 27, 29–32, 35, 36, 95, 120, 138, 143, 153, 154; *see also* urban, urbanization
civilizations, 63–4, 85, 88, 110, 115–16, 120, 182, 212
  civilizational, 58, 61, 63–5, 82, 112, 120–21
  intercivilizational, 122
class, 50, 61, 86, 114, 149, 163, 171, 185–6
  class conflict, 61, 185
    working class, 185–6

Columbus, Christopher, 112, 181–2
colonial, 109–12, 114–15, 117–18, 120, 131, 151, 165, 168, 204
  post-colonial, 8, 57, 59, 67, 131, 151, 153, 167
communication, 6, 10–12, 14, 21–4, 27, 32, 35, 41–2, 45–50, 55, 58, 60–62, 66, 68, 99, 152, 167, 169, 170, 173, 180, 197–201
community, 12, 25, 29, 31–2, 43, 45, 50–51, 60, 62, 86, 101–3, 120, 148, 151–2, 165, 179, 184, 201
conflict, 10, 21, 44, 61, 63–4, 66–7, 114, 139, 147, 185
Confucian, 63–4, 115, 204
connectivity, 1, 2, 5–6, 8, 10–12, 21–37, 41–7, 50–51, 55, 60, 75, 93, 109, 118, 127, 132, 134–6, 179–80, 182–3, 188–9, 195, 207, 211–13
  hyperconnectivity, 211
  interconnectivity, 30, 36, 195
consciousness, 2, 5–8, 10–14, 21, 23–4, 26, 30, 36, 41–51, 57, 75, 80, 88, 93–4, 96, 109, 118, 127, 136, 143, 179–85, 188–9, 193, 195, 211–13
conservatism, 26, 188
  neoconservatism, 32
corporations, 55, 57, 59, 61, 78, 80, 99, 102, 128, 134, 139, 193–4, 196–8, 201, 205, 213
  TNCs, 193–7, 200–201, 203, 205–6
cosmopolitanism, 42, 65, 103, 136–7, 139, 149, 153, 161, 182
  cosmopolitan, 55, 60–62, 65, 67, 69, 103, 116, 118, 143, 153
creolization, 65, 133, 137, 139
culture, 1, 2, 5–7, 9–14, 27, 44–6, 48, 55–60, 64–6, 75, 78–81, 84–5, 88, 98, 102, 110, 113–16, 120–21, 127–39, 143–5, 147–8, 150, 152–5, 161,

163–70, 172, 174–6, 180, 182, 186–7, 189, 193–5, 197–207, 211–13
global culture, 1, 2, 5–6, 9–11, 13–15, 55, 58–9, 62–6, 68–9, 75–6, 81, 86, 88, 96, 103, 110, 129, 139, 143–4, 146–7, 153–4, 164–7, 169, 172, 175, 187, 194–5, 197, 205–6, 211–13
cyber-power, 10

dance, 15, 139, 149, 151
democracy, 29, 60, 62–3, 98, 102, 162, 181
democratic, 24, 60–62, 77, 98, 149, 162, 165, 182–3, 185
diaspora, 13, 22, 43, 65, 67, 86, 134, 139, 211
diasporic, 65, 134, 139, 148, 151, 164–5, 169
diffusion, 75–6, 78–80, 82–6, 88, 93, 95, 129, 148, 200, 202–3, 212
digital, 21, 30, 41–3, 45, 47, 49, 58, 134, 211
Durkheim, Emil, 5, 6, 132

economy, 31, 34, 48, 56–7, 62, 150, 161–3, 167, 169, 204
cultural economy, 48, 193–5, 197, 205, 206
knowledge economy, 94, 102
Enlightenment, 8, 94, 101, 116, 118, 199
erotic, 11–12, 59, 62; *see also* sexuality, sexual
ethnic, 14, 63, 132–4, 151, 194
ethnicity, 50–51, 65, 144
Eurocentric, 8, 115, 116, 171
European, 7–8, 13, 65, 87, 110–12, 117, 120, 129, 153, 166, 171, 179–82, 185, 187, 202–3, 205–6, 212–13

Foucault, Michel, 77–8

gender, 10, 50, 86, 113, 147
women, 11, 146–7, 150, 152
global, 1–2, 5–15, 21–3, 25–6, 28–36, 41–51, 55–69, 75–6, 78–88, 93–6, 98–104, 109–22, 127–39, 143–8, 150, 152–4, 161–3, 165–8, 170, 175, 179–89, 193–207, 211–14

globalization, 2, 5–7, 9, 11, 21–4, 26, 28–30, 32–7, 41–2, 45, 55–9, 61–2, 64–8, 75, 80, 82, 88, 94, 101–3, 109–15, 117–21, 127–8, 130, 133, 136, 139, 143, 147, 152–3, 161–70, 172, 175–6, 179–80, 187, 189, 193–5, 197, 200, 202, 206–7, 211–13
glocalization, 2, 5, 8–9, 15, 55, 59, 64–9, 101–2, 115, 127–9, 131–3, 137–9, 147, 152, 161, 167, 175–6, 193–7, 200–202, 206, 211–13
von Goethe, Johan Wolfgang, 171, 173

habitus, 30–31, 115, 120
Harvey, David, 37, 193
hegemony, 66, 100, 102, 110, 120, 122, 150, 188, 203, 206, 212
hegemonic, 3, 114, 121, 165, 175, 188, 195, 213
heterogenization, 11, 127–30, 212
history, 6–8, 13, 30, 33, 35, 59, 77, 109, 112, 121, 131, 135, 145, 154, 167, 171–2, 176, 180, 184, 186, 200
historical, 2, 6–8, 13, 31, 33, 62, 69, 82, 110, 114, 116–17, 120–21, 132, 134, 145, 163, 183–4, 189, 200–201, 205
world-historical, 7, 163, 183–4
homogenization, 11, 55, 57, 58–62, 66–9, 127–9, 193, 196, 197, 207, 212, 213
human rights, 60, 63, 84–5, 87, 100, 103, 146–7, 151–2, 162
Huntington, Samuel, 61–4, 127
hybridization, 55, 57–8, 64–8, 133, 147, 152, 200, 212

ideology, 13, 28, 56, 165, 201, 203
ideological, 24–6, 28–31, 33, 34, 49, 173, 180, 186
individuals, 6, 21, 31, 36, 41–6, 49–50, 55, 67–8, 75, 78–9, 81–4, 95, 100, 114, 119–20, 122, 128, 130–32, 136–7, 144–5, 148, 188, 193–4
individualism, 43, 46, 50–51, 76–7, 82–3, 86, 88, 153, 204, 212
INGOs, 75, 83–4, 86, 96
integration, 5, 27, 30, 35–6, 41, 150

Internet, 10–13, 24, 42–3, 46–8, 50–51, 57–61, 170, 211
Islam, 9, 58, 63, 87, 112
  Islamic, 10, 29, 60–64, 86

Japanese, 66, 193–207, 213
Jesuit, 2, 109–22, 212

legitimacy, 26, 45, 96, 100, 102, 120
liberalism, 24, 26, 56
  neoliberalism, 29, 32, 63–4
literature, 9, 13, 22, 32, 45, 56, 75, 127, 129, 139, 161, 164–8, 170–76, 183, 188, 198, 212
  Chinese literature, 161, 164–7, 171–6
local, 11, 14, 23, 32, 34–5, 37, 43, 48, 51, 55, 59–60, 65–8, 75, 79, 82–3, 86–7, 102, 115–17, 121–2, 128–31, 133, 137, 139, 145–6, 148–9, 151–4, 161, 175, 188, 193–7, 199–203, 206–7, 212
  locality, 28, 31, 34, 36–7, 152
  localism, 55, 59
Luhmann, Niklas, 45, 80

McDonalds, 58, 62
  McDonaldization, 56, 190, 196
  McWorld, 62–3
market, 2, 28–9, 31, 35, 43, 47–8, 56–7, 59, 62, 64, 82, 86, 102, 127, 135–7, 146, 149, 151, 163, 169, 173, 194, 196–7, 199, 203, 205–6
  marketing, 21, 57, 59, 66–7, 128–9, 136, 172, 194, 197–9, 201, 203, 205, 207
  marketers, 197–9, 203, 205–6
Marx, Karl, 24, 185, 186
  Marxism, 32, 57, 147, 164, 185
Mead, George H., 131, 189
media, 11, 42, 44, 46–51, 55, 58, 60–61, 81, 86, 133–5, 137, 139, 149–50, 153, 162, 172, 211
  social media, 10–11, 21–4, 49, 51, 58, 61, 75, 127, 134, 136–7
  mediatization, 42, 44, 46, 48, 134–5, 211
Meyer, John W., 45, 59, 77–8, 82–3, 85–6, 93–103, 113, 130, 212

Middle East, 9, 29, 43, 61, 63–4, 110
migration, 2, 13, 133–4, 139, 155, 211
  emigration, 168, 170
  immigration, 64–5, 183
modernity, 33, 36, 56, 64–5, 80, 94, 96, 114, 120–21, 161, 163–6, 176, 193, 213
  modernization, 33, 58, 120–21, 165, 201
multiculturalism, 13, 153–4
music, 15, 62, 65–6, 118, 133–4, 139, 143, 150

nation, 8–10, 29–32, 35–6, 56–8, 64–8, 78–9, 82–3, 85–7, 99, 101–2, 109, 112, 114, 117, 119, 130–33, 136, 139, 144, 148, 150–51, 153–5, 161–2, 168, 170–71, 179, 182, 184, 187, 193, 204
  transnational, 6, 50, 67, 80–81, 86, 97, 103, 113, 116–18, 121, 127, 130–38, 144–5, 150–51, 153–4, 185, 193, 195, 198, 201–2, 207, 213
  international, 6, 8, 10, 15, 32, 57, 60, 75–9, 82–7, 101–2, 111, 119, 121, 127, 129–33, 136–8, 146, 152–3, 162, 165, 168, 171, 179–80, 183, 193, 196–9, 212
network, 6, 21, 23, 28, 35–6, 47, 49, 113, 135, 150–51
  networks, 29, 34, 43, 47–50, 56–8, 61, 63, 75, 77, 80–81, 86, 144, 147–8, 150–51, 154–5, 195, 211, 213
NGOs, 49, 77, 83, 109, 121, 147, 211
Nobel prize, 164, 172, 174, 183
norms, 45, 58, 60, 75–9, 82–8, 143, 145, 148, 212
  normative, 13, 24, 26, 31, 44, 59, 69, 75, 95, 97, 113, 138, 146, 189

olympic, 63, 127, 130, 132
orientalism, 13, 116, 162, 172–3, 203–4

polarization, 55, 57–8, 61–9, 194, 212
political, 2, 23–5, 29–30, 32, 34–7, 41, 43, 48, 50, 55–64, 66–8, 76, 82, 86, 95, 98–9, 102, 111–12, 117, 119–20, 139, 144, 148, 150, 155, 161,

163, 165, 170, 180, 183, 186, 202, 204–5, 212
power, 3, 10, 24, 26, 28, 31, 56–9, 61–3, 66, 68, 77, 81, 84, 99, 111, 118, 120, 133, 145–8, 152–4, 168–9, 179–80, 182–5, 187–8, 193, 203–4; *see also* cyber-power; soft power
protests, 2, 49, 56–8, 61, 66, 83

race, 10, 50, 65–6, 149, 151, 182, 187
 human race, 67, 120, 179, 184
 racist, 60, 65, 116, 181, 187
rationalism, 75–8, 80–81, 83, 85–8, 195
 rational, 47, 62, 76–8, 80–84, 96, 103, 119, 121, 189, 196
 rationalization, 2, 78, 80, 83, 87, 93, 96–9, 101–3
regions, 2, 9, 58, 65, 96, 112, 130, 135–6, 146, 165, 213
 regional, 14, 100, 132–3, 145, 148, 212
relativization, 8, 14, 67, 128, 131–3, 138–9, 212
religion, 1, 2, 10, 29, 63, 78, 80–81, 87, 112, 115–16, 121, 179
Robertson, Roland, 2, 3, 5–6, 9–10, 13, 15, 23, 42, 55, 57, 59, 65–9, 75, 78, 100, 109, 114, 120, 127–9, 135–6, 175–6, 179, 187–8, 193–4, 200–202, 204, 211–13
Roosevelt, Theodore, 182–4

Said, Edward, 13, 57, 61–2, 129, 203
science, 1, 7, 9, 37, 77, 79–80, 85, 93–6, 98–102, 113, 166, 169, 204, 211
 scientization, 2, 93, 95–9, 103
secular, 42, 58, 86, 111, 117–18, 184, 204, 212
sexuality, 10, 12, 139, 152, 181
 sexual, 11–12, 149
Shakespeare, William, 13, 171, 173
society, 6, 31–2, 35, 37, 41, 43–4, 46, 50, 56, 62, 67, 78, 80, 83, 86, 88, 93–4, 96–8, 101–4, 109–11, 113, 121, 139, 162–3, 169–70, 174, 193, 195, 201, 204, 211–12, 214
sociological, 1, 47, 56, 64, 81, 100, 127–8, 154, 193

soft power, 10
space, 1, 6–7, 12–14, 23, 25–8, 30, 33–7, 41–2, 44–5, 48, 51, 67, 68, 84, 135–6, 144–6, 150–52, 164, 183, 211
sport, 2, 14, 69, 127–39, 148, 150, 179–80, 194, 198, 202–3, 206, 212–13
standardization, 100, 194, 196–7, 201
Stead, W., 59, 179–82, 187

Taylor, Charles, 31, 122,
terror, 11, 43, 58, 61, 64
 terrorist, 47–8, 62, 211
de Tocqueville, Alexis, 181
trade, 2, 55–7, 97, 120, 129, 149–50, 185, 193
 traders, 47–8, 110, 150
tribalism, 34, 37, 62
 neo-tribalism, 136

United Nations, 67, 85, 87, 143, 146
urban, 31–3, 35–7, 133, 153–4, 163, 205
 urbanization, 2, 32–3, 204

vernacularization, 148, 152, 213

war, 1, 8, 10, 14, 58, 61–4, 182–3, 188, 196, 201
 World War II, 13, 86, 94, 102, 196
 cold war, 6, 23, 186
Western, 7, 8, 29, 59, 61–2, 64–5, 78, 83, 93, 100, 103, 110, 118, 120–22, 146, 162–6, 168, 171–5, 193–8, 201–7, 212–13
Westernization, 59, 64, 115, 121, 129, 161, 165, 167, 172, 195, 204, 213
Wittgenstein, Ludwig, 24
world polity, 2, 45, 60, 75, 82–3, 101, 113, 143
world society, 45, 96–7, 103–4, 113–14, 117, 119–20, 189, 212
world system, 43, 55–6, 60, 67, 110–11, 117, 120–22
world wide web, 21, 24, 46, 60, 205

Žižek, Slavoj, 43, 46